Prayer
In The Shadow of
DEATH

*BASED ON a TRUE story names and places
have not been changed – none fiction*

By

Robert Vidal

Ezekiel 18: **21** "But if a wicked man turns from all his sins which he has committed, keeps all My statutes, and does what is lawful and right, he shall surely live; he shall not die. **22** None of the transgressions which he has committed shall be remembered against him; because of the righteousness which he has done, he shall live. **23** Do I have any pleasure at all that the wicked should die?" says the Lord GOD, "*and* not that he should turn from his ways and live?

Romans 5: 8 But God demonstrates His own love toward us, in that while we were still sinners, Christ died for us. 9 Much more then, having now been justified by His blood, we shall be saved from wrath through Him.

Scripture taken from the New King James Version. Copyright © 1982 by Thomas Nelson, Inc. Used by permission. All rights reserved.

National Library of Canada Cataloguing in Publication Data

A cataloguing record for this book that includes the U.S. Library of Congress Classification number, the Library of Congress Call number and the Dewey Decimal cataloguing code is available from the National Library of Canada. The complete cataloguing record can be obtained from the National Library's online database at: www.nlc-bnc.ca/amicus/ index-e. html

ISBN 1-41203307-1 New ISBN-13: 978-0615579511 ISBN-10: 0615579515

Published by Gifted in Christ Enterprises 364 Monroe Ave Kenilworth NJ 07033

gifted@giftedinchrist.com

robertfvidal@hotmail.com

Acknowledgments

Above all, I would like to thank my Eternal Heavenly Father YAHWEH through His Son Jesus Christ for his Mercy and Forgiveness, and the United States of America for being a "Nation under God, Indivisible, with Liberty and Justice for All." God bless America!

To my praying Christian mother Georgina Vidal, sister Hilda Vidal, brother John Vidal (NYPD), daughter Erica Vidal, son Robert Vidal, Jr, and my beautiful 7 year old Gianna Vidal. A special thanks to all my family members and all the saints that prayed for me.

I would also like to extend my thanks to United States District Judge the Honorable Mary Anne Trump-Barry, Kevin McCarthy, FBI Special Agent Steve Thornton, Joseph Ferrante, Esq., Raymond Beam, Jr., Esq., Robert Goodman, Esq., Kathy Waldor, Esq., Candido Rodriguez, Jr., Esq. (the best Puerto Rican lawyer in the New Jersey area), David Wolffe, Mike Garcia, Emilio Enriquez, EPD Juan Guzman, Jr., Frank Giantomazi, Esq., Gary Goodman Esq., Cranford NJ - for his help in a time of need. To my ex-fiancé Monica Mendoza for her help editing the book, and my (computer) genius cousin Jorge Maestre, George Kostas, To my cousin, the Dentist, Ralph Santana who purchased and gave me my first barber clippers back in September 1997.

To my other cousin Ed Calixto who got me my first job as a barber when I was living in a Federal halfway house in Newark, NJ. That opportunity in Elizabeth, NJ along with God's blessings led me to owning six successful barbershops.

Thanks to my brother John again because he gave me my first pair of jeans, sneakers, belt and sweat shirt. Also, thanks to all my friends and family for all their help, prayers, and support. FINALLY, I would like to dedicate this book to ALL those who pray to our Heavenly Father in Jesus

Christ's name for the lost. To my loving Christian mother who hated the criminal lifestyle that I was involved with, but loved me like a lost son and never stopped PRAYING for me. God's mercy spared my life from violent enemies and Death Row, then hell fire. To my father Roberto Vidal, Sr., who passed away while I was in prison, and to whom I made a PROMISE that I would never return to drugs, crime, and guns. PLEASE SAY NO TO DRUGS!

2 Corinthians 5:[17] Therefore, if anyone *is* in Christ, *he is* a new creation; old things have passed away; behold all things have become new. [18] Now all things *are* of God, who has reconciled us to Himself through Jesus Christ, and has given us the ministry of reconciliation, [19] that is, that God was in Christ reconciling the world to Himself, not imputing their trespasses to them, and has committed to us the word of reconciliation. [20] Now then, we are ambassadors for Christ, as though God were pleading through us: we implore *you* on Christ's behalf, be reconciled to God. [21] For He made Him who knew no sin *to be* sin for us, that we might become the righteousness of God in Him.

Fourteen years have passed since I have been out of prison after serving eight years of special Parole with the US federal Parole Board. The Spirit of God in Christ has kept me growing strong in the power of the Lord through constant prayer, fellowship and reading God's word. Spreading the gospel of SALVATION in Jesus Christ, at work to my employees and customers, visiting prisons, halfway houses, homes, hospitals. God has helped me keep my PROMISE to give back to our youth and society, as I also promised to the Federal USDJ the Honorable Mary Anne Trump-Barry before she sentence me. To God be the glory through His Son Jesus Christ.

On December 16, 1998 "Yahweh "YHWH God opened doors for me to appear on a Spanish television talk show called Cristina, were I asked my Christian mother to "forgive me mother! "Perdoname madresita" This show was viewed by Latin America & South America. I was told it was viewed by 50 million people. See Youtube.com/Robert Vidal "To God be the Glory"

2 Peter 3:1 Beloved, I now write to you this second epistle (in *both of* which I stir up your pure minds by way of reminder), ² that you may be mindful of the words which were spoken before by the holy prophets, and of the commandment of us,[a] the apostles of the Lord and Savior, ³ knowing this first: that scoffers will come in the last days, walking according to their own lusts, ⁴ and saying, "Where is the promise of His coming? For since the fathers fell asleep, all things continue as *they were* from the beginning of creation." ⁵ For this they willfully forget: that by the word of God the heavens were of old, and the earth standing out of water and in the water, ⁶ by which the world *that* then existed perished, being flooded with water. ⁷ But the heavens and the earth *which* are now preserved by the same word, are reserved for fire until the day of judgment and perdition of ungodly men. ⁸ But, beloved, do not forget this one thing, that with the Lord one day *is* as a thousand years, and a thousand years as one day. ⁹ The Lord is not slack concerning *His* promise, as some count slackness, but is longsuffering toward us, not willing that any should perish but that all should come to repentance.

It is the author sincerest intent NOT to glorify the criminal lifestyle, violence, adultery, greed, murders and sins mentioned in this true story. It is my new God given heart's desire to share how sincere REPENTANCE of all my sins in Jesus Christ made me a bless man to bless others. I have been forgiven of my rebellion against God and my godly parent's childhood education. Again I Thank God for the great grace and mercy he had through Jesus Christ in answering my Christian mother's fervent prayers to protect me from evil and save me. May her example of FAITH and trust in God's WORD to answer her prayers; encourage you to believe all things are possible with God. Luke 1:³⁷ For with God nothing will be impossible."

Luke 18: The Parable of the Persistent Widow

¹ Then He spoke a parable to them, that men always ought to pray and not lose heart, ² saying: "There was in a certain city a judge who

did not fear God nor regard man. [3] Now there was a widow in that city; and she came to him, saying, 'Get justice for me from my adversary.'[4] And he would not for a while; but afterward he said within himself, 'Though I do not fear God nor regard man, [5] yet because this widow troubles me I will avenge her, lest by her continual coming she weary me.'" [6] Then the Lord said, "Hear what the unjust judge said. [7] And shall God not avenge His own elect who cry out day and night to Him, though He bears long with them? [8] I tell you that He will avenge them speedily. Nevertheless, when the Son of Man comes, will He really find faith on the earth?"

Mark 16: [15] And He said to them, "Go into all the world and preach the gospel to every creature. [16] He who believes and is baptized will be saved; but he who does not believe will be condemned. [17] And these signs will follow those who believe: In My name they will cast out demons; they will speak with new tongues; [18] they will take up serpents; and if they drink anything deadly, it will by no means hurt them; they will lay hands on the sick, and they will recover."

Introduction

I am not the first to be grateful to have been in prison. And, unfortunately, I will not be the last. Prison is a horrible place. But it can also be a cleansing place, a place to purify the body and soul. Thank God, that is what it was for me.

I arrived at the FCI El Reno Penitentiary in Oklahoma and found myself living amongst a population drawn from every race, culture, and ethnic background. I was living with gang bangers, bank robbers, members of organized crime, extortionists, murderers, and terrorists. In short, I found myself living amongst men I understood. These were, sadly, my people.

Upon my arrival, a number of inmates from the state of New Jersey, inmates who had been getting the *Star Ledger,* addressed me by the name used in that newspaper.

"Hey, Prince of Darkness!" they called out to me.

"Yo, Mad Dog Killer!"

I did not respond. I kept my eyes straight ahead. "F—You," I thought to myself. I did not respond, but others wanted to know about this new inmate, this "Prince of Darkness." Word quickly got around that I was not a man to mess with. In the world of federal prison, that was a reputation worth having.

After being medically cleared, I was assigned to the food services section. Getting fresh milk ready for the 1,800 inmates was a far cry from the things I was used to doing. Getting up at four in the morning—the time I was usually going to bed—was hard to get used to. But I didn't complain. I was a survivor and I meant to survive my twelve years in prison.

Television programs, books, or movies that romanticize prison are lies. Prison is horrible. It is evil. There is nothing to compare to the sound of those bars closing on you and the feeling that seeps into you after lights-out. There is nothing to protect you from the muffled sound of men—murderers and federal criminals—sobbing into their flannel blankets.

Eighteen hundred men jammed together into five stories of concrete and steel. A seething, angry, explosive place. A place of dangers, real and imagined, were stabbings and murders were sadly part of the prison fabric. I had no choice but to adapt. There was no survival but by adapting.

Not long after arriving, I was walking on the second tier hallway when I heard noises in one of the cells. I forced myself not to look. "Keep your eyes straight ahead. Nothing's your business until someone makes it your business." Eyes that wandered were invitations for trouble.

"What you looking' at?"

"Nothing'."

I had to keep my eyes straight ahead but, at the same time, I had to sense, I had to know what was happening all around me. Anything could happen at any time. Someone could jump out and jam you with a shank (A prison made knife) for having done something you didn't even remember you did. It didn't take much to trigger a fight in a high-security prison.

So, when I heard those noises, I kept my eyes straight ahead. But, from the corner of my eyes, I saw what was happening. I saw everything and more than I wanted to see. Another homosexual attack. I kept walking. "Keep your eyes straight ahead. It isn't your business until someone makes it your business."

In prison, you always know where you are, and where you're not. After the last meal of the day, when the afternoon gave way to night's darkness, I would walk the prison yard. That was when it hit me the hardest. That was when I could see the city lights of Oklahoma City coming on, out past the fifteen-foot fence and the forty-foot-high gun towers where the Bureau of Prisons guards were on watch twenty-four hours a day, seven days a week. They were always ready with their M16, shotguns and 9mm hand guns. You get to close to the wire you get a warning shot.

In the twilight, I felt a longing that was physical! The city was so close but it might as well have been a thousand miles away. At that point, I was completely immersed in prison life. I'd been inside for four years. I had another ten years before I was eligible for parole.

Ten years! It might just as well have been a lifetime. Early on, I learned not to think about my friends and family. It was too painful. I had to close my heart to all that or else I could not have made it through a single night, let along fourteen years worth of nights.

It took me a while, but in the long hours of loneliness, I began to focus on Bible verses. I memorized God's promises about strength and peace. Isaiah 26 [3] You will keep *him* in perfect peace, *Whose* mind *is* stayed *on You,* Because he trusts in You. [4] Trust in the LORD forever, For in YAH, the LORD, *is* everlasting strength. Once I was able to draw on faith to absorb the Word of God; I was able to rise above the pain. My faith allowed me to stand apart from the conduct and behavior that drew so many of the other prisoners. Gambling. Drugs. Gang activity. hiding a weapon, frequent fighting. I learned to take care of my soul and my body. I found myself using my free time to stretch and to master self-defense skills. Martial arts were forbidden to practice or teach in prison so I, like the other prisoners, had to hide the fact that I was training with two other inmates who were instructors back in society.

The hardest thing to deal with when in prison is the long hours of...nothing. Boredom and fear eat at your mind during those long hours. Thoughts feed on themselves. Your mind wanders to all the things you've done and all the things done to you. You imagine yourself walking the streets again. Being free. And you see people walking free when you're not. It eats at you.

But you can also learn to be thankful. I learned to be thankful to my God, Yahweh, for answering my mother's prayers. Before I came to prison, I used to tell her that she shouldn't worry about me. One day in 1985 I went with my bodyguard Tarzan to visit her at her apartment in Elizabeth NJ, and she spotted my bulletproof vest. She became very nervous and crying and hands shaking."Felipe tu vida esta en peligro "Phillip your life is in danger" Mami no llores por favor! Mom please don't worry and don't cry"

"I wear a bulletproof vest," I told her.

She didn't care about that. "The bulletproof vest won't save you. Only God can save you.""Solo Dios Felipe te puede salvar;"Yeah, right, Mom," I'd say. "Stop crying, huh?"

She always called me by my middle name"Felipe". I was named after her Christian father Felipe Rojas Mulet of Spaniard and French descent, from my father's side I had Spaniard, Italian and Jewish.

She cried a lot when she saw me or talked with me. And she prayed constantly for me. She was always praying for me. Her prayers were the only things that saved me; I know that NOW. The Feds who arrested me were amazed that I'd lived as long as I had.

"You have more contracts out on you than a car dealership," one of them joked as he ducked my head and stuffed me into the car. "F—-you," I whispered under my breath.

"Don't worry about that now," he said, laughing at me. "You'll have plenty of time for that in prison."

Man. How had I ever let myself fall this far? I had been an altar boy when I was at the St. Casimir Grammar Catholic School in the Ironbound section downneck Newark NJ. How the streets that I'd traveled from that honest youth had been twisted and tortured and lost in darkness!

Of all the things I had done or had been expected to do, nothing had taken me so low as when El Padrino, the Cuban Kingpin, Oreste's supplier wanted me to be the hit man on a contract he'd put out on "Oreste."

"Yeah, I got you covered, El Padrino," I promised.

But day after day, Oreste managed to remain alive and El Padrino was losing his patience. "Vidal, what are you waiting for?" he would ask me. "Kill the fat f—already."

My reputation in the neighborhood was solid. I was known to be a violent and fearless fighter and a successful drug dealer. I was both feared and respected. I went where I wanted to go and did what I wanted to do. So what the hell was holding me back from taking care of Oreste?

I wrestled with the contract. Should I have someone else take care of it or should I take care of it myself? I didn't really care. I didn't want to do it so much, but my ego kept intruding on my decision-making. If I handed it to someone else, would that make me seem weak?

"Dammed, I'll do it," I snapped to myself. "The hell with it."

Once I made that decision for certain, I only had to decide on the exact time and place. I chose a winter night in January 1986. It was bitter cold, the kind of cold that ate through your gloves and your jacket, getting into your bones so you shivered from the inside out. I'd been watching Oreste for a couple of weeks. I knew his habits and I knew where to find him.

Besides, he and I had been partners for a while. When El Padrino chose me to take out Oreste, he'd chosen well. Oreste would never suspect me of being the one to kill him. That would be a betrayal.

The only problem was, where there was no honor, there could be no betrayal.

Criminals sometimes talk about honor on the street, but that talk is just bullshit. There is no honor out there. It's a jungle that answers to just one law—the law of strength and power. He who has the power has the control. And that can change from week to week. Even from hour to hour.

I wasn't betraying anyone. At least, that's what I told myself when I entered the Steamers Bar in Newark.

"Hey, Vidal!" he called to me when I came in.

I nodded in his direction. Oreste was easy to spot, what with his fat belly and pasty white face. The guy was barely five foot eight inches and He weighed over 260 pounds. He was almost fifty years old and the way he huffed and puffed when he walked along, he was sure to be dead on his own soon enough. But El Padrino wasn't interested in waiting for Oreste's fatness to do him in. He wanted something a little more immediate.

"Vidal, come have a drink with me," he called over. "I haven't seen you in a while."

It was true. He hadn't seen me for a while. But I'd seen him. I'd been watching him every day. I walked over and took the stool next to him. I shook his fat hand. It was sweaty and soft.

"What're you drinking?" he insisted.

I shrugged and told him. He gestured to the bartender and, a moment later, a glass was placed on the bar in front of me.

"What the f——, eh?" he said, raising his glass in a toast.

"What the f——."

For the next hour or so, the liquor flowed. Drink after drink. Oreste had been drinking before I got there and by the time we were ready to leave, he was good and drunk. Me, I drank with him, but I wasn't drunk. The whole time I was drinking and laughing with him I hadn't forgotten that I had a job to do. I was going to murder him.

"Oreste, you're a drunken pig," I told him. "Come on, I'll take you home."

"Come on, Vidal! One more!" he insisted.

"No way. Let's go."

We argued about it but in a drunken, good-natured way. I didn't want to piss him off. That would only make my job messier. Things were going pretty good so far. Oreste was drunk and I was going to get him into my car. From the bar, I could drive him anywhere I wanted.

We were driving along a dark, lonely road when Oreste reached over and patted my shoulder, pulling me out of my thoughts, which were centered on how I was going to kill him.

"What do you want?" I asked him.

"Pull over," he said.

For a second, I thought the tables were being turned and he was going to try and kill me. "No."

"I have to pee," he complained. "Come on."

I groaned but now the groan was playacting. "Dammed, Oreste, you're being a pain in the ass. You know that?" He laughed as I pulled over to the side of the road. He dragged himself out of the car and waddled more than walked to the trees beyond the shoulder of the road.

"Now," I told myself. "Do it now!" How easy it would have been to put two in the back of his head. There was no one around. Nothing but trees and abandoned factories. Pop. Pop. Then it's over. "What the hell are you waiting for?" I asked myself. My heart was pounding in my chest. I could hear Padrino's voice in my head. "Just shoot him already!" But something was stopping me. I couldn't bring myself to do it.

I argued with myself. I'd killed before. Why not again? Padrino wanted Oreste dead. Just do it.

The glasses of scotch on the rocks I'd drunk at the bar hadn't done much to calm my nerves. My heart was racing and my stomach was knotted tight. My mouth was dry and my vision seemed blurred.

"He's right there!" I told myself as I looked at that fat fool Oreste, struggling to get his zipper down so he could pee. He must have spent four minutes just trying to open his zipper. Then he had to fish into his pants to get his penis out so he could pee.

"Do it!" I reached behind my back and slipped my new Smith & Wesson 459 9mm with a thirteen-bullet clip from the leather holster. I felt the hard metal of the gun's grip. Pop. Pop. Padrino would be happy and the pressure would be off me.

But I couldn't do it. I just couldn't make myself kill again. I let the gun slip back into the holster. "Come on, man!" I laughed at him. "Let me take you home already."

"A second. Give me a second," he said as he shook his penis and then stuffed it back in his pants.

So I took Oreste home and watched him go into his house. I sat in my car for a while, just thinking. Padrino had ordered me to kill Oreste but I hadn't done it. I wasn't exactly sure why I'd turned away from the order. Not then. Now I understand that I was beginning to realize that my conscience had been touched by a power greater than me or any other man.

Thou shall not kill. I heard those words echoing in my head and, for the first time in my life, they seemed to have real meaning. Thou shall not kill.

"Damn," I thought to myself. "This is weird."

I had never felt like that before. It wasn't as if I heard a voice so much as I felt a voice. I didn't spend a lot of time considering the sensation, though. I had a more pressing concern. What I was going to tell Padrino?

A couple of days later, I went along with Tarzan to see Padrino, that skinny, white Cuban who seemed to have less conscience than I did.

"What the f—- do you mean telling me that Oreste is still alive? Didn't I tell you to off that F—-er?"

"Yeah, you told me, Padrino," I said.

"What's the F—-ng problem?"

"There's no problem," I told him. "But you have to understand. I'm like Burger King in this town—very popular with the Newark Police Department. They're dragging my ass into jail for things I don't do. If I don't choose my moment right—" I felt into deep thoughts thinking of Detective Tommy Gilsen from the Essex County Prosecutors warning "The Feds are watching your whole crew Robert"

"Yeah, yeah," Padrino said, interrupting me. He was annoyed and impatient but he knew I was right. Every time there was a beating or a shooting, the cops brought me in for questioning. They figured that even if I hadn't been a party to the incident, I was sure to know someone who was. "Look, what I'm telling you is that this has to be done. And soon. Look, Vidal, this fat man's got to be dead. He's smoking cocaine and flashing lots of money and coke—my cocaine—in hotel rooms all over the city. He's got several girls messing with him for the coke. Damn, all this brings heat on him. Sooner or later, it's going to be trouble for us. You got that, Vidal?"

"Yeah, I got that," I told him.

"That fat s—t is going to be trouble for me if I don't get him killed." All I know about what happened after that was that I had nothing to do with it. On that count, my conscience is very clear.

It was a good thing I didn't kill Oreste. Almost every guy that was running with me then, ended up cooperating with the FBI. They told them everything—from the amounts of cocaine we were moving to the guns we had available to us. They listed every murder and attempted murder we'd been party to. It was the police that got Oreste, not me. He was busted picking up one hundred kilos of cocaine from Colombia in one of the New York airports. Trying to save his own ass, he turned over for the Feds. The DEA, FBI and US Customs had him wear a microphone. He ended up setting up Manolo Vigoa in Ave P, downneck Newark NJ, with a shipping container containing- -705 kilos of cocaine—over twenty-five million dollars worth. The Feds cancelled our retirement plan and gave us all instead federal inmate prison uniforms and ID numbers with lengthy prison sentences. Manolo received a (40) year sentence and I received a total of (33) years between Federal and State sentences, with (10) years of special Parole. Thank God if we would have gotten arrested a year later we would not have Parole eligibility; but we had to do 85% of our sentence. This went into effect on November, 1, 1987.

I was blessed USAA Michael Gilberti and Edward Belinkas these Federal Prosecutors fervently petition the USDJ the Honorable Mary Ann Trump- Barry for a life sentence with NO PAROLE under title 18/21 the Drug Kingpin 848 conviction, plus another additional 46 years for the other counts that I was convicted at trial. Thank God my mother did not STOP praying for me.

Drug criminals represent eighty percent of our prison population—the largest prison population in the world. But prison can't solve the problem. Prison cannot turn a man's life around. Only God can do that. Prison can give a man the time to think and reflect and, in turn, prompt him to give God the opportunity to come into his life. But we are all responsible for where we are.

My dear father was found dead in his sleep by my cousin Ralph Amado on August 1, 1990. I took his death as hard as he had taken my incarceration. Drugs and crime had put me in prison. Alcohol had taken his life.

Two days earlier I had talked to him from the prison phone system, I told him that I was changed. "God has changed me," I swore to him. "When I get out of here, With God's strength I'm going to stay drug free and be successful." He sounded doubtful but I told him it was true. And I promised him that if he and my mother got back together, when I came out of prison I would buy them a house for them to live.

My father is dead, but I kept my promise for the sake of my loving, praying mother. God had come to me and saved me. I was going to be all right.

In the Raybrook NY Federal Correctional Institute, I was working as the head cleaning man of Mohawk Unit and attending the Bureau of Prisons' vocational school, studying to become a "Barber/Hairstylist." As with everything I did after I let God into my life, I dedicated myself to doing the best I could do. Within a year, I was a famous barber among the 1,200-man prison population. Men would line up to have me cut their hair.

My life in prison was very active. I had two jobs. In addition, I was a volunteer on Suicide Watch and very involved in church activities and sharing the gospel to staff and inmates. This book is my account of my life. I have tried to be honest. I have tried to give credit where it belongs and accept blame where I deserve it. But to understand what I have done, it is important to understand the things that brought me to prison to begin with and the opportunity prison gave to me.

It is only by knowing all these things that you can appreciate how I felt on that day when I was cutting hair in the prison barbershop and I was called to my housing unit. I finished cutting the hair and then I went as instructed.

"Is there anything wrong?" I asked.

"Nothing's wrong," my case manager said. "In fact, things are very right. You've been approved to go to a halfway house as long as you maintain your good behavior. You'll be transferred on September 16th."

I was speechless with joy. I had spent twelve years in prison and now there were only thirty days to go. I could see the "light at the end of the tunnel." I was still ecstatic when I returned to my cell.

"I'm getting out. I'm getting out." I turned and looked at myself in the mirror above my small, metal sink. The person looking out at me wasn't the same person who had entered prison all those years before. I wasn't a twenty-six-year-old kid anymore. I was thirty-eight.

My hair was salt and pepper. I was divorced. And 1 was ready to return to the streets free of drugs, with hope and the love of God in my heart and $400.00 I had saved in the (12) years I worked in prison jobs making ..11 cents an hour.

John 8:[36] Therefore if the Son makes you free, you shall be free indeed.

Chapter One

It wasn't supposed to play out the way that it did. All I wanted was to find a career that I could be proud of and to take care of my family. In that way, I wasn't any different than anyone else. A good job. Friends. Family. My family came to America from Cuba in 1969, seeking the gifts that America holds out for everyone—freedom and the opportunity to pursue prosperity and happiness. At different times, I wanted to be a professional baseball player, or a kick boxer, or even a state trooper.

By the end of my senior year of high school, reality was setting in. No one was knocking down my door to sign me up for the majors. So, I pursued the opportunity that I'd been considering for awhile: the United States Navy.

"This is what you want to do?" my mother asked when I told her about my decision.

I could see the moisture welling up in her eyes. I could hear the emotion in her voice. "Mama...," I began. But then I stopped. This was a big decision. I had always been a "tough" kid, the kind of kid that others thought wasn't scared of anything. But the fact of the matter was that I was scared to be away from the family I loved so dearly. But I didn't see any other choice. "Mama, it's the best thing," I told her. "They'll train me. I'll be able to go to college...." I was reciting things straight from the recruitment posters I'd been reading for the past two years.

My mother nodded her head. She understood. A deeply religious woman, she accepted a great many things that were difficult for her, knowing that somehow, someway, they fit into God's plan in ways she could not see. She told me to be careful.

I went to the Federal Building in Newark, New Jersey. There, I confronted the maze of people and paper that confronted any new recruit. I

sat down and took the required test. I felt more pressure to pass that test than any I'd ever taken in school. I wasn't just relieved when I passed. I was ecstatic. I signed up under the delayed entry program. Upon completing all the paperwork, I was told to "surrender myself" on September 13, 1977.

After the initial excitement of my plans began to wear off, I realized that I would have to find something to do between my exam date and the date when I surrendered myself to the navy and began boot camp. I felt obligated to contribute to my family's financial well-being. So, I managed to find a job at a nearby service station. There, for between $80-90 a week, I pumped gas, fixed flats, and did a little mechanical work on cars that came in. My cousins, Fred and Ralph Amado, owned the station, so they were willing to give me the hours to work. From my paycheck, I gave $30 a week towards my mother's bills. I felt the burden of my contribution.

My brother, John, the "angel" of the family, the one my mother loved best, was seeking an athletic scholarship that would allow him to attend college. There was a time when I might have gotten such a scholarship myself. My baseball skills were good enough. But I wasn't doing as well as I should have in classes and I hung out with some guys that weren't focused.

In the end, I squandered my athletic potential. John didn't. That was one of the reasons my mother loved him best. He never gave her any trouble at all, while I was the one to keep her up nights, praying and saying the rosary.

My sister was also working at the time. She was a cashier in the local Pantry Pride Supermarket where she worked so many long hours that her legs ached when she came home.

"You're working too hard," I would tell her as she massaged the cramped muscles in her calves.

She'd just shrug. "I don't have a choice," she'd say. And she didn't. She was trying to help out with the rent money while at the same time trying to save enough money to buy a car.

Maybe things would have been different if my father, Roberto, had been still living at home. But he and my mother had recently separated after years of fighting. All men have demons that they fight. My father's was alcohol, and it sapped him of his strength and ability to be the husband and father he wanted to be. My father's alcoholism made him less of the man God intended him to be. My mother, always devout, understood

that. There was no reason for her to have been hurt by his drinking. After all, that was his real curse. He did not chase after women. But the alcohol gutted him. He would disappear from home for weeks at a time. He would spend his entire paycheck on drinks.

"It made him mean, too," my mother told me years later, reminding me of things that I had tried hard to forget and push out of my childhood memories.

A man isn't an alcoholic unless he is trying to numb demons that he doesn't believe he has the strength to fight head-on. But alcohol doesn't defeat a man's demons. It only numbs him and lets the demons play with his mind in other ways. Too often, they make him mean and violent. There were times when, drunk and defeated, my father beat my mother, when he was unable to contain the sense of defeat that lapped at him except by lashing out at the very person who loved him most in the world.

"I knew it wasn't him that was hitting me," she told me, her voice sad and far away. "It was something that was hurting him so much that he thought he had to hurt me to beat it. It was an evil thing inside him." Then she sighed. "I saw and heard of it too much in too many men."

It was true. How many men, tormented by inner demons that they cannot name, try to dull the confusion and pain they cause, and drink? But the drink only lowers their own self-control and they do things that they would likely not do if they were not dulled by drink.

I can still hear echoes of furniture falling and my mother's voice asking him not to hurt her. Sometimes, just before I fall asleep, I can still hear the sound of his fist on her defenseless flesh. But then, I sometimes confuse that sound with the sound of my own fist beating a man. And, just as I slip into sleep, I ask God to forgive me for doing violence to others so I could mask the sound of violence being done to those I love.

Whatever hurt my father inflicted on my mother—physical, emotional, or spiritual—she was careful not to show it to us, her children. She did not make excuses for our father, but she did not demonize him either. As a result, despite my awareness of his troubles, I always held him up as my personal hero. I suffered, too, from his neglect and his absence, hurt from his distance. But I always loved and respected him.

My mother made sure that I always knew my father was my father, even when he wasn't at home. Because of my mother, I always worried about my father when he was away. I hoped he had enough to eat and that he was all right.

At home, my mother took on the role of both mother and father. She was disciplinarian and nurturer. I don't know how she managed to do it, but she made sure that we went to school. We went to the doctor and the dentist regularly.

She was only too aware of the dangers the streets could pose to her children. She was very strict and limited what we could do and where we could go when we returned home from school.

"No." That was the answer we received from our mother if we asked to leave our second floor apartment after school. We heard that answer so consistently and so determinedly that we learned not to even ask. We were virtual prisoners in our small, three-room apartment. A bedroom. A kitchen. A bathroom and a small balcony. That was the geography of our school years.

It was no different when my father was home. Five of us crammed into these small quarters. How we chafed at the walls that seemed to close in month by month and year by year.

"I don't care," my mother would say if we complained. "There's nothing I want you doing out there," she said, referring to the world outside our apartment. "All that is out there is trouble."

There wasn't much for us to do in the apartment. We didn't exactly have tons of toys. Toys were not easy to get in Cuba. We were allowed one toy each at Christmas. It wasn't that my mother and father didn't want to be generous, but the scarcity of toys in the country meant that toys were expensive and not easy to get. Few families could manage to get many toys for their children. What was more, too many toys were considered contrary to the goals of Castro's Cuba, where we were all to be equal in brotherhood and socialism.

As difficult as it was to stay inside and live in such close quarters, I was not unhappy at all. I was a good boy. I maintained high marks in school and showed an artistic talent that my teachers remarked about.

Despite the promises of Castro's Cuba, everyone was rationed only a small amount of agricultural products each month. Fresh milk, in particular, was very difficult to find, so my mother would take condensed milk and mix it with sugar and water. The concoction was sweet to the taste and reasonably good for us. However, even that was not easy to obtain. My mother was only able to get that extra condensed milk for us because she possessed an old sewing machine and had a wonderful ability to sew.

She would make wedding dresses, shirts and pants—clothes that she would then trade for the condensed milk.

In a society where there is little money, bartering is the most efficient method of acquiring good and services. So my mother traded on her skills as a teacher seamstress to provide for her children. Her efforts were vital but hardly enough. I remember times when she was not sitting down with us at the dinner table just to make sure we ate. At eleven years of age, the combination of severe asthma and the lack of sound nutrition conspired against me. I was only fifty-two pounds.

I was a wisp of a boy, but I had heart and spirit. My mother made sure of that. She had raised us all the "old-fashioned" way—to respect others, to be polite and considerate, and to show obedience to God.

These qualities served me well as a boy, and they helped make our transition into American society successful. However, like so many others, my good school habits as a young boy did not carry through to my young teenage years. Me, the altar boy at the St. Casimir Grammar School in the Ironbound section of Newark.. I had squandered my skills so that my greatest hope for a profession and for taking care of my family when I came out of high school was to join the US Navy.

Chapter Two

I finally began basic training in Orlando, Florida, on September 14, 1977. The journey down from New Jersey had given me a lot of time to think, but I hadn't focused on anything more than uncertainty. At the beginning of the journey, I was both nervous and excited. But then I dozed off, and when I woke up, I was a bit disoriented. It was like waking up from a nap and thinking everything was a bit strange. I just wanted to go home.

"What the hell was I thinking?" I wondered.

There wasn't anything I wanted more than to be able to simply "undo" my decision to sign up. I wanted to go home. I felt a powerful longing, a longing that tightened the muscles in my stomach. I didn't want to be a soldier. I just wanted to live the life I'd always lived. But I knew that was impossible. That was what convinced me to enlist to begin with. Whether I liked it or not, I was leaving high school and I was going to have to do something. I had to make money. And I had to figure out a way to better myself in the world.

College didn't seem like an option. Sitting in classrooms wasn't for me. I was smart enough, and a quick learner, but I wasn't a student. I'd squandered whatever artistic talent I had. I was like a lot of young men in the late 1970s. The military seemed the best option. Vietnam was over. The draft was ended. The all-volunteer military had to con-vince more and more people to join up, so they promised all sorts of incentives. Money for college. Training. Seeing the world. Hell, they'd tell you just about anything to get you to sign your name at the bot-tom of a recruitment contract.

I was still dreaming of all the stuff I would learn and the exotic places I'd visit as I traveled down to Florida. My first dose of reality came when

I arrived at the recruit training center. Along with hundreds and hundreds of other guys just like me, I went through the process. One line after another. We were given uniforms. Assigned areas. Put in units.

"Shit, this sucks," the kid in front of me said when we found our-selves in another line, being shuttled to another place.

"You got that right," I told him, feeling a little tired on my feet, too.

When we were finally placed in our unit numbers, I went to my assigned area. There, as I stood before my training officer, my uniform still folded and pressed in my arms, I felt his withering glare.

"Vidal?" he asked, looking down at the piece of paper on his desk and then back up at me.

"Yeah."

"Yeah?"

I nodded.

"Vidal, I'm going to tell you this once and only once. When you talk to me, you say 'sir.' Got it?"

"Yeah," I said. "Sir," I added quickly.

My training officer shook his head in disgust. "Try it again, Vidal."

"Yes, sir," I said, my voice a bit reedy. I already hated this guy's guts.

He stood up and came around from his side of his gunmetal desk so that he was standing directly in front of me. He was maybe four or five inches taller than me and built like a rock. He brought his face right up to mine so that our noses were almost touching. He came so close that when he talked, I could feel the heat of his breath on my face.

"Vidal, you bought the farm when you signed up to come here. You understand that? Bought the whole f—- farm."

I looked at him funny. I wasn't sure what he was getting at.

"See, you're nothing here unless I tell you you're something. A bug crawling along the floor has more humanity than you do, unless I say so. I'm your everything here. I'm your mother and your father. I'm your worst flicking nightmare. If I tell you to jump, you say how high. If I tell you to clean the latrine with your toothbrush, you scrub away and then brush your teeth when you're finished. You will do as I say and be glad to do it. You understand me?"

I was quiet.

He leaned closer. "You understand me?" he barked at me. "Yes, sir," I said in a voice barely louder than a whisper.

"What? I couldn't F—-ing hear you!"

"Yes, sir," I said sharply. I felt hate for that man flowering in my heart.

I was not alone. My unit was made up of eighty-four recruits, ages seventeen to twenty-three. When we arrived in Orlando, we didn't have very much in common. In no time, we shared a hatred for our training officer.

"Okay, you dumb shits," he said, addressing the whole unit. "By the time I'm finished with you, you'll be more than the pitiful gathering of shitbags you are now. You'll be F—-ing soldiers."

"F—- you," I was thinking to myself. I wasn't the only one.

On that first day, we received our clothing, toothpaste, soap, and some very clear instructions. "Wake-up is 4:30!" our training officer announced.

There were some groans.

He frowned. "What the hell was that?" he demanded. "What the hell did you candy-asses think? You were coming to a F—-ing resort?" He laughed a short, cruel laugh. "4:30. And I don't put up with pussy groans from my men. Got that? You've got fifteen minutes to shower, shit, and shave. Then you have to get your bunks made properly—and don't worry, I'll show you how to have your bunks made up properly. Listen Children, I'm going to want your bunks made up so tight that you can bounce a dime off them. "You report to chow hall at 5:00 sharp."

He eyed us up and down for a minute, practically daring one of us to challenge him. No one made a sound.

"6:00 we'll start with orientation. That's when you'll really start to understand what it means to be a sailor in the United States Navy."

However tough and difficult the officer made basic training sound those first couple of days, it turned out to be ten times worse. Every day, the bugle sounded at 4:30. Within three days, we were a fairly practiced unit. We didn't like it, but we got up and did what we had to do.

I thought we were all dealing with the routine pretty well until I got up one night to take a piss. When I got to the latrine, I found another recruit, a tall, lanky guy name Gus, crouched alongside one of the toilets, shivering.

"Hey, Gus, what's the matter, man? You sick?"

He looked up at me and his eyes were wide with some kind of weird terror. "I can't take this shit anymore, man," he said.

I shrugged. "Ah, come on, man. I mean, it sucks, but it'll be over soon."

He shook his head. "Naw. It'll never be over. It'll only get worse."

"You're just tired, man. Get back to bed."

"I can't sleep."

"You want me to get a medic?"

He shook his head. "No, I don't want them to know anything," he said. Then he turned his eyes toward me and I shivered looking into their emptiness. "They'll only try to kill me."

I took a step toward him and he shrank away from me. "Hey, you feel okay?"

"Yeah, I'm good," he said.

I wasn't convinced. After my piss, I went and got a medic. They took Gus to the infirmary. They kept him there for a while. He didn't have a fever or anything, but something was very wrong with him. Basic training had prompted something to snap inside him. He remained in the hospital for a while. He was discharged back to the unit.

Two days later, they found him bleeding in the latrine. He'd cut his wrists with a razor blade. They managed to save his life but he was gone from the unit.

Gus wasn't the only one to snap in basic. The military isn't real restrictive about the people it lets sign up. Like I said, our unit was made up of kids like me, mostly seventeen or eighteen years old. We'd never been away from home in our lives and no matter how tough we were on our home turf, we were scared shitless in basic. We missed home. We missed our families and friends.

Basic training either toughened you up or broke you. The day started with a ten-mile run-hike through hilly terrain. Then there were calisthenics and all sorts of hand-driven physical exercises. The physical shit was nothing compared to the psychological stuff they pulled on us. It was like they wanted to break us down until we were quivering little nothings who were willing to do whatever they said. Most of us could take the constant bombardment. Some of us couldn't.

After ten weeks, the original eighty-four recruits in the unit had been reduced to sixty-three graduates of basic training. Some recruits were discharged for medical reasons. A lot of others for the same reason Gus was—the basic took hold of something weak and bent it and twisted it until it snapped.

Basic was the hardest thing I'd done in my life to that point. I would have told you were crazy if you had told me that I would do what I was told, no more, no less. No questions asked. But I did. When my training officer said, "Jump," I said, "How high?"

It wasn't easy. I wasn't a person to take orders blindly. I was homesick. I hated the routine. I hated the boredom. I hated the work. I wanted to see my mother and my father. I didn't want to listen to the muffled sound of men crying as they fell asleep anymore.

But day by day, I became more disciplined. I became stronger. I'd always been a good athlete and the intensive training only heightened my natural abilities. I passed the various tests and exams we had to take. My average was pretty good. At the end of ten weeks, I was a sailor.

From Florida, I was sent to Oakland, California, for duty aboard the USS *Mars*. The *Mars* was a supply ship. My assignment was as a machinist in the engine room. It was only later that I learned that, upon our arrival, the *Mars* was to go on a "west pack," a voyage to the

Atlantic on a training mission that would serve to demonstrate our readiness to fight in a war situation.

For our launch, I was assigned to the main deck. We moved from Oakland and the San Francisco Bay. We moved through the cold, choppy waters under the Golden Gate Bridge and 1 looked up at one of the most beautiful things I'd ever seen in my life. I breathed in deeply the cool, salted air as I braced myself against the railing. I felt a surge of pride. I was a sailor. That positive feeling didn't last long.

"Vidal, to the engine room."

Some fifteen or twenty miles out to sea, I began to feel a queasiness in my stomach. I felt dizzy. I could feel a headache coining on. I was lightheaded and felt like I could collapse at any second.

"Dammit," I snapped to myself. "Suck it up."

I couldn't believe this was happening to me. I'd gone through basic. I was as strong as a bull. I was ready to face whatever came my way. And less than two hours out of port, I was feeling like 1 was going to die.

I tried to concentrate on what was happening around me. As an apprentice in the engine room, I had to learn all my tasks. I listened as closely as I could, but the words were fuzzy and hard to understand.

"Vidal? Hey, Vidal, you okay?"

I tried to answer but my words felt like they were spoken through a wad of cotton candy. I stepped forward. Or was it backwards? Or sideways? I had the sense of the deck being above me and hands reaching toward me. I tumbled through an open hatch and fell into the boiler room, where I hit pretty hard. The next thing I knew, I was in a helicopter heading toward San Diego.

"What the hell happened?" I asked. Or I thought I asked. I was still fuzzy. Things were spinning around and I couldn't focus. The noise was deafening. I tried to prop myself up but I ended up falling backwards again, losing consciousness.

The next time I awoke, I was in the Balboa Naval Hospital in San Diego. I was in a bed in a room when a naval doctor, a captain, came in. He glanced down at the chart and then at me in the bed. "Robert Vidal?"

"Yes, sir," I said and my words sounded normal.

"How're you feeling?"

"Weak, sir."

He nodded. Then he glanced at the chart again. "Looks like you felt a lot worse than weak."

I shrugged. "I never felt like that before, sir."

He grunted softly and wrote something down. He listened to my lungs and heart, took my pulse. He looked into my eyes and ears and mouth.

"I'm going to send you for some tests," he said. "X-rays. An EKG" He wrote something down and then looked up at me. "I doubt we'll see anything, though."

"Then what happened?" I asked. "Was I just sea sick?"

"We'll have to look into it further. Let's get these tests out of the way and then we'll go from there, okay?"

When the tests came back negative, I was discharged from the hospital and turned over for psychiatric examination. The psychiatrist was a thin, bald man with a tight voice.

"You think I'm crazy?" I asked.

He didn't look up at me. "I don't know," he said.

I took a battery of tests. There were a lot of written tests with questions about whether I ever wet my bed and if I heard voices speaking to me. Then there were other tests where I had to put things together and answer simple questions.

"Tell me about growing up," the psychiatrist said after he'd evaluated the results of the tests. "Do you get along with your mother and your father?"

I was as honest as I could be.

"Did you get in fights at school?"

I shrugged. "Sometimes. Who didn't get into fights at school?" "What were the fights about?"

"The usual bullshit," I said. "Nothing special."

He asked me a lot of questions about whether I had trouble sleeping. If I had fears, anxieties, that sort of thing. I answered all his questions the best way I could.

"Tell me again exactly how you felt on the ship," he said.

I described all of my symptoms, from the feeling of pride I had when saw the Golden Gate Bridge, to the sudden dizziness and fuzziness, to how I got angry with myself for getting dizzy.

"How've you been eating lately?" he asked.

"Well, the food at basic sucked, sir," I told him.

"But did you eat it?"

"Not so much the last couple of weeks. I felt like I was coming down with a bug or something."

"Did you go to the infirmary?"

"One day. I didn't have a fever so they sent me back to the unit." He nodded and made a note in the chart.

"I couldn't stand up straight," I volunteered, referring to my experience on the ship.

"How did you feel about shipping out to the Atlantic?" he asked. "It was messed up," I said.

"What were you expecting to happen when you got to California?"

"I don't know. More of the same as basic, only on the ship," I told him.

After our interview, the psychiatrist looked at me and said, "I think what happened was that you had a panic attack," he said. "There's nothing wrong with you. Nothing at all. I'm recommending that you return to duty on your ship."

It took a second for his words to sink in. I don't know what I was expecting but it wasn't that. I glared at the psychiatrist. He wasn't even paying attention to me. He was writing something on my report.

"You F—-ing idiot!" 1 shouted. "I'm not going back to that ship!"

With that, I became violent. I stood up from the chair and grabbed it by the back and threw it across the room where it slammed against the wall. Then I grabbed his desk and upended it, sending all his papers flying. I couldn't believe that this asshole was thinking of sending me back to that ship. I'd almost died when I fell into the boiler room and now all they wanted to do was send me back like nothing happened? I didn't think so!

Chapter Two

The navy clearly didn't give a shit if I lived or died. But I did! I wasn't going to let them send me off somewhere to die! I stood in front of the psychiatrist, who was sitting at his chair but no longer had a desk between us. My fists were clenching and unclenching. "There's no way I'm going back to that ship!" I screamed at him. "You got that? So you can just change whatever the F—- you've been writing," I shouted, swatting the papers from his hands. "You don't think I'm crazy? Bullshit! I'll show you what crazy is!"

Apparently, I'd gotten his attention. He stood up. "Just hang on a second," he told me in a voice that was supposed to calm me but had the exact opposite effect on me. It enraged me even more than I was already enraged.

"Just stay right there," he said, moving quickly from the office and into the hallway.

I wasn't letting him get off that easy. I moved like a cat after him, following him into the hallway. "You want to know what crazy is?" I screamed after him. "I'll show you flicking crazy!"

As I chased after the psychiatrist, I could hear the nurses calling for help. I was midstride when five male nurses appeared with a straightjacket and, with amazing efficiency, ended my chase. They held me down for a time until they decided I had calmed down enough to continue my evaluation. They weren't shy about using their elbows in getting me under control either.

Once I was forced into a straightjacket and brought back to the psychiatrist's office, the psychiatrist eyed me solemnly. "Are we ready to continue now?"

I spit on the floor.

He frowned. "Look, I understand that there's more going on here than I appreciated a while ago. And I'm willing to reevaluate you with further testing. But," he added, and his voice was stem and his eyes were narrowed, "if you get violent with me again, I'll have you locked up for a good long while."

I worked hard on breathing slowly and getting control of my emotions. Although I had a healthy temper, I couldn't remember blowing up like that before. "Sorry," I said softly.

"Good. Now, are you ready to have those restraints eased?"

I nodded my head. The doctor motioned to the orderly who had remained to assist if any assistance was required. The orderly raised his eyebrows in surprise. It seemed to him that the doctor was taking a terrible risk in letting me free of the restraints. But the doctor just nodded his head, indicating that he felt he knew what he was doing.

"It's all right," he said to the orderly.

The orderly shrugged and began unbuckling the buckles on the straightjacket. He did it cautiously, not yet convinced that I wouldn't become violent again.

"You want him in wrist restraints?" the orderly asked.

"No, I think we're all right."

The orderly shook his head but understood that there was nothing else for him to do. He left the room but didn't close the door all the way behind him.

"Now," the psychiatrist said when I was free of the restraints. "Let's talk a little more about what's going on here. Why don't you describe the way you've been feeling to me?"

Slowly, I described how I hadn't been sleeping well for the past two or three weeks. I told him about having nightmares when I had been able to sleep.

"Let's talk about your accident on ship," he said, prompting me to describe exactly how I'd felt before I lost consciousness.

"At first, I thought it was sea sickness, you know?" I began. "But then it became more familiar. Sometimes it's happened before, where I start to feel light-headed and I think I'm going to pass out. I never passed out before, though. But this time, being on the ship and stuff..." I stopped for a second, remembering vividly the sensation I experienced on the ship, how I felt like I was losing my mind.

"How have you been eating?"

We both knew that we'd been over this before but that it was something he had to ask. I shrugged. "Not as well as I'd like. I don't really like the food...."

He smiled. He knew I'd cleaned up my answer since the last time I'd answered his question about my appetite. But the fact of the

16

matter was, my appetite was gone. Sure, military food sucked, but that hadn't stopped me from eating it when I first arrived at basic. No one liked military food. But you ate it because you were so hungry you'd eat anything.

Basic was so tough physically that I was burning more calories than I'd ever burned before. I was famished when I first arrived. More than once, I'd asked for additional helpings. But all that started to change midway through basic. We started doing more ordnances and more practice with live ammunition. And we were also doing a lot of training in hand-to-hand combat. There was always something about seeing the eyes of someone I was going to kill that unnerved me. That always stayed with me, even after the military.

"I started thinking about what would happen if the ship was going down," I told the psychiatrist. Then I shuddered. Once a watery grave was a real possibility instead of a faraway idea, it gave me the willies and woke me up in a cold sweat at night. I was a city boy, born and bred. What the hell was I doing on the water?

After the continuation of my evaluation, the psychiatrist decided that rather than send me back to the ship, he was going to admit me to a medical hold facility for further evaluation.

Although I was pleased I wasn't going back to the ship, I was troubled by the fact that I didn't know my fate. "How long am I going to be there?" I asked him.

He shrugged. "We won't know until we do some more evaluations," he said simply.

I could feel my muscles tense. That crazy angry feeling was taking form somewhere at the base of my spine. He could clearly see that my personality was changing before his eyes and he called for the orderlies, who must have been waiting outside the door, they came in so fast.

"We're going to be admitting this sailor," he said simply.

"No!" I shouted. "I just want to go home!"

I was fighting and kicking, but this time the orderlies were prepared and subdued me right away. I had surprised them with my violent behavior the first time I'd blown up. I would never have that element of surprise again.

Every day I was in that cold, sterile facility, my frustration grew. I paced my room, gnawing at the skin of my knuckles, feeling myself going crazy. All I wanted to do was to get out. Couldn't they see I didn't belong in the military? It was a mistake. I had to get home.

My frustration and anxiety wasn't helped by a message I'd received from home. In a letter, my mother described the problems she was having at home. My father had gotten even more violent. He was drinking more and more. She didn't know what was going to happen.

Using the letter as proof that I had to do something, I went to the psychiatrist and requested a fourteen day leave to go home and see if I could help my mother.

The psychiatrist eyed me suspiciously. "You know what will happen if you don't come back, don't you?"

I nodded.

"Tell me in your own words."

"I'll be arrested and put in jail. I'll be AWOL. A deserter. I could spend a long time in jail."

"You sound pretty much in control to me. I'm going to approve your leave request. But, sailor..."

"Yes, sir?"

"You need to come back. You need help. We can help you here. Do you understand?"

"Yes, sir."

The paperwork went quickly, and the following morning, I was headed back to the Ironbound section of Newark, to where my family was living. Ironbound is an isolated part of what is otherwise a cold and crime-infested city. Populated almost exclusively by immigrants, mostly Portuguese people, Ironbound seemed like an island of sanity in a crazy, mean city.

Unlike most of Newark, the residents of Ironbound kept its streets immaculate. Shops were clean. There was no graffiti on the walls. Litter was picked up and leaves were raked up. People took care of their yards and their cars. It was a comfortable, secure place to live.

Chapter Two

Walking through Ironbound, you could walk along streets filled with friendly people who were happy to smile at you and say hello. The street corners were gathering places where people stopped to talk and joke. The shops were bustling. There were tables outside diners and restaurants, so people sat in the sun and drank coffee and had lunch or dinner. There were social clubs where people played cards, or darts, or dominoes. Ironbound was a place where people knew you.

So, when I suddenly reappeared on its streets, dressed in my naval dress uniform, I was immediately greeted by many of my neighbors.

"Bobby!"

"Hey, look who's here!"

More than one woman came up close and whispered to me how good I looked in my uniform. I just soaked up their warmth and their pride. It seemed like I had been gone from there for years and now it felt so good to be back.

"How about a picture, Bobby?"

I must have posed with about fifteen people, all wanting to have a picture with me in my naval dress uniform. They wanted pictures with me next to them, or standing in front of their stores, or having a cup of coffee at their restaurant.

It made me feel good that I had earned their respect. It also made me feel bad that I was struggling so much to stay in the navy. I realized that I would have to return to my naval career if I was going to maintain their good wishes and respect. The last thing I wanted to do was to let them down.

After all the well-wishing, I started to head toward my mother's house. On the way, an old friend of my mother's started walking next to me.

"Hello, Elena," I said, leaning down and giving her a kiss on the cheek.

"Hello, Bobby," she said, beaming at me. But there was a warning in her eyes and it made the smile on my lips disappear.

"What's the matter?"

"Your mother's being having a very hard time with your father," she said. "He's been hitting her again," she added, in a voice that dropped to such a low whisper that I almost couldn't hear it. She shook her head sadly. She was not a neighbor who enjoyed gossip. She was a good friend of my mother's and the difficulty my mother was having pained her almost as much as it did my mother. "If only he could stop drinking," she said absently. "It's the drinking that does him in. When he isn't drinking, he isn't a bad man, but when he drinks..." She left her thought and trailed off.

"I know," I said softly.

"She'll be so grateful to see you," she said to me before parting company with me midway down the block. "Does she know you're coming home?"

I shook my head.

Elena's eyes filled with tears. "You don't know what this will mean to her," she said. Then she touched my elbow. "Your father's behavior is embarrassing her so much she can hardly look her sisters in the eye."

My mother had nine sisters, each and every one of them married. Each one of them had a nice home, with a husband who held down a steady job and supported his family. Not my mother. She had to have the husband who drank too much and beat her up.

Everything that Elena was telling me weighed heavily on me. Her words brought back all the emotional pain that I had endured through the years I was growing up. Why couldn't my father be like my uncles?

Elena was right; my mother was thrilled to see me. When I first walked in the door, she just stared at me like she couldn't believe it was really me. She started to talk and then she blinked, unable to form a single word.

"Hi, Mama," I said, smiling.

"You came home," she said finally, still stunned by my presence.

A few minutes later, she was telling me everything that had been happening since I'd left for basic training. I heard not only her words but the emotion under her voice. Clearly, the situation at home had become unbearable. The problem was...what could I really do about it? While I was home, my father would not lay a hand on my mother. That much I could guarantee. But what would happen after I left?

While I was home, my father managed not to drink himself into a violent frenzy. He and I talked. He had lots of questions about the navy and my training. It was nice to talk to him. But I knew that it was only a mask I was seeing. He hadn't changed. Having me home for a few days was not going to change a lifetime of drinking or his treatment of my mother.

So, while I was home, I was caught up in the crosscurrent of so many emotions. It seemed I was thrust back into the emotional role I'd been playing since I was a small boy, caught between my parents and their battles. I loved both of them and wanted nothing more than to be able to change the lives they were living. But I didn't know how. The same feeling of helplessness that plagued me as a young boy came back—only now I was a man and fighting that same feeling was terrible.

In addition, I now had the added burden of my difficulties in the navy. All these things were churning inside me and making me feel as anxious and panicky at home as they had in the navy. I clearly needed some kind of distraction.

So, I did what I had always done when I was younger. I went out. I saw old friends. I went dancing and out for drinks. The second or third night I was home, I met a very pretty girl named Anita. She seemed to enjoy the dancing and the fun. When I was with her, my mind was completely away from my troubles. I felt young and free. And happy.

The night I met her, I walked outside the club with her and, in the moonlight, I looked into her eyes. "You know, you're very pretty," I told her.

She smiled a smile that just about melted my heart. "That's nice of you to say," she said.

"I really want to see you again," I told her when the night was coming to an end.

She shrugged. "I'd like that," she said.

We started seeing each other all the time. I couldn't seem to get enough of her. When I was with her, all my troubles seemed to disappear. I felt alive again. It was a great feeling. I felt like I was really falling for her.

So, when I received my orders to return to a ship, I knew I wasn't ready. I hadn't done much to change what was going on at home, and I sure hadn't changed anything about what was going on inside me. What I had done was fallen for a very pretty girl. All I knew is that Anita made me feel good and that I liked feeling good.

I didn't tell anyone about my orders. Instead, I just stayed on at home. I promised myself it would only be for a day. Then two days. Then three. Then a week.

After eleven days, I was contacted again. I'd been AWOL and the navy frowned on sailors who were AWOL. My time at home was over. I had to go back. It was hard to say good-bye again to my mother. It was harder to say good-bye to Anita. She said she would write to me but I didn't think it would happen. I had been a distraction for her just like she'd been a distraction for me. I kissed her good-bye.

My assignment was to the USS *Flang* stationed in Portland, Oregon. Oregon might just as well have been in the Far East as far as I was concerned. I was a Jersey boy. I didn't know much about the Pacific Northwest. I only knew about California because of Hollywood and the Golden Gate Bridge. I guess I hadn't paid very close attention when we were studying United States geography in school.

When I'd been in basic in Orlando, it was a rugged environment but mostly a dusty camp. Although it was different than Jersey, it somehow wasn't all that different. Oregon was big time different. I was used to concrete and neon. Oregon was all green and trees. When I got there, it was like stepping out into a dream. Everything was so lush. The trees were all so colorful. Everyone's lawn was thick green.

"Man," I said, letting out a low whistle, "this is beautiful."

And it was. Oakland had been like Newark—urban, ugly, and rough. But Portland was a slice of small-town America I'd never experienced before. I really thought it was beautiful.

"This is all right," I thought to myself as I traveled to the port and to the USS *Flang*. Arriving on ship, I reported directly to the officer of the day.

"Vidal, sir," I said.

He checked my name against the manifest.

"Sir?"

"Yes, sailor?"

"I can't adjust to the ship, sir."

"What's that, sailor?"

"I get terribly sea sick," I told him but he wasn't interested in hearing what I had to say.

"According to the paperwork, you were supposed to report eleven days ago, sailor."

"I just couldn't...." I started to explain.

But he wasn't interested in explanations any more than he'd been interested in my seasickness. "You'll be fined $175 and given extra duty for two months," he told me. "In addition, you will be restricted to the ship for a period of thirty days."

"What?"

He looked at me with the look of an officer who did not like to have his orders challenged in any way, shape, or form.

"Sir," I said my voice softer.

"That's better, sailor."

"But, sir...," I said, continuing my protest.

"But nothing, sailor. You're in the navy now. Act like it."

Restriction to the ship did not seem like the best medicine for someone who suffered seasickness. And the fine would make it very difficult for me to assist my family financially—one of the main reasons that I signed up to begin with.

I wanted to argue with the officer but I knew that it would do no good. I didn't really have much of an argument to begin with. After all, I was the cause of my problems. No one made me stay AWOL for eleven days. That was all my doing.

"Damn," I thought to myself. "Why do you always cause yourself such problems?"

I didn't have an answer for myself. The question itself haunted me. It seemed to me that I had always been the cause of my own problems—mine and just about everyone else's as well.

"Why can't I ever do the right thing?" I demanded of myself. But no answer came. I was lost *in* my emotional horror. I felt like a black cape had been dropped over me. I had gone home when I was completely unhinged emotionally because I was needed to try and solve some of the terrible dynamics in my family. However, far from solving those problems, I'd only made my own problems worse. Wasn't I ever going to be able to make things better?

In an instant, I told myself that the answer was "no." I would never make things better. Things weren't going to get better, either. My life was doomed to this constant defeat. I walked off the ship, believing that I would be leaving the ship for the last time. I wasn't leaving the ship and the navy—I was leaving everything. I couldn't bear the weight of my problems anymore. I might have been dressed sharp in my navy uniform, but inside I was a mess. The black cape that had descended on me seemed to stick at me like a damp, plastic bag. It pressed against my face and nose, making it nearly impossible to breathe.

I tugged at my collar, loosening it. I was feeling like my throat was closing in on me. I could feel sweat forming between my shoulder blades. I started walking faster and faster. It took all my energy not to break into a sprint. I just had to get away. But I had no clear idea where I was going. I was hurrying through the downtown area, with its clean shops and brick walkways.

Suddenly, I realized that I had a destination, that I'd had a destination from the moment I'd left the ship. Without consciously realizing it, I was walking toward the Portland Broadway Bridge.

As it loomed before me, I felt terribly tired, more tired than I'd ever felt before in my life. Not physically tired. Emotionally tired. I didn't think I could take another moment of dealing with my worries. I couldn't stand the feeling of blackness clinging to me, suffocating me. I was beaten and I only wanted to end the suffering.

"Get over it, Bobby. You can't win. Jump. End it all." I couldn't silence the voices in my head. They were whispering to me. They were yelling at me. I heard my mother's voice telling me that it was all right. Then I heard her friend's voice. "Do it, Bobby. It will make your mother happy. She's been so embarrassed."

I turned around, thinking Elena was right next to me. Her voice was so real. But she wasn't there. Still, her message remained with me. It wasn't my father who embarrassed my mother. It was me. I was the problem. I was the cause of all the problems in my family and in my life. Me. No one else.

"End the suffering." The voices were moving me closer to the bridge. The bridge was my escape. My salvation. There I would finally put an end to the sadness that weighed down so heavily on me.

I was oblivious to most everything around me. I didn't see the cars or other people. I didn't feel the sun on my face or the breeze brushing against my skin. I just marched forward, certain in my goal. But as I approached the bridge, 1 suddenly noticed what looked like a big bundle of old clothes on the sidewalk. I unconsciously started to steer clear of the bundle just because it was in my way. But then a hand reached up from the bundle and gestured that 1 come closer.

"What the f...?" I walked closer and I saw that the bundle of clothes was actually an old man, homeless and bundled up in rags.

"Young man," he said, his blue eyes twinkling up at me and his hand outstretched in my direction, "Please, could you spare a dollar to give an old man who's been down on his luck?"

I didn't answer him. Instead, I stuffed my hand into my pocket and pulled out all the money I had. What did I care? I wasn't going to need any money where I was going.

"What's this?" the old man said, jerking his hand back. He thought I was taunting him, teasing him with the money, and that I would only take it away if he reached for it. He was a pitiful creature who had been abused many times by those who had feigned to offer him help.

"Take it," I told him.

He smiled a toothless smile at me. "I can't," he said.

"Why not? You need it and I won't be needing it anymore."

"Everyone needs money, young man," he said as he studied me with his eyes.

"The only people who need money are those who are going to be around to spend it," I told him.

He narrowed his eyes. "And what does that have to do with you?"
"See that bridge?" I said, nodding in the direction of the bridge loom-
ing out behind him.

He propped himself up and craned his head around. Then he
looked back at me. "Yes, I see it."

"I'm going to jump off it. That's what I'm going to do. And then I
won't need any money. So you should take it." I let the money go so it
fell to the sidewalk in front of him. Then I started to walk again.

He gathered up the money and then gathered himself up, all
one hundred pounds of him, and got up from the sidewalk. "Wait a
minute, young man," he called after me as he continued to gather his
blankets and rags.

I didn't answer. Truth was, I barely heard him. My eyes were focused
on a point halfway along the bridge. That was the point I was heading
to. That was the point I planned on jumping from.

The old man hurried his steps until he'd caught up to me. He
grabbed my arm. "Wait," he said. But I shook him off like he was nothing more than a fly.

"No," he said in a voice barely above a whisper as he struggled to
catch up with me again.

My eyes remained focused on that point halfway on the bridge. I
could see it clearly. Too clearly. It was like it was magnified. I could see
every rivet in the metal. Everything.

"Stop," the old man said, running around so he was in front of me.
He leaned his full one hundred pounds against me, but I just pushed
him away. He staggered back and I just kept walking forward.

I had made up my mind. This was it. The end. I couldn't bear the
sorrow any more and no hundred-pound toothless homeless man
was going to convince me to change my mind. In a strange way, I
was oblivious to everything but completely aware of everything, too.
I didn't know what time it was, but I was aware of the passage of time.
It seemed to slow, but I knew that it was only another three or four
minutes until I reached the middle of the bridge, the very spot I had
been aiming toward from the moment I'd first left the old man bundled on the sidewalk.

I rested my hands on the railing. I could feel the cool metal against my palms but the sensation seemed to come from far, far away. I looked out toward the distant shoreline. The trees were so green and full. The flowing water was so beautiful. It all seemed so right.

I looked down. I estimated it to be a two-hundred-foot drop. I drew a full breath. Two hundred feet and then everything would finally stop hurting. I felt a strange sense of satisfaction. I was glad that no one could hurt me anymore.

Once again, I looked up at the distant shoreline. So beautiful. Just so beautiful. Then I quickly climbed over the rail. I looked once more at the water swirling two hundred feet below me. Then I closed my eyes and took a step forward.

Suddenly, a rough tug on my belt pulled me back toward to bridge. My eyes opened at the same time that a hand reached out and grabbed my jacket. I was confused. I didn't struggle but I didn't assist either as I was pulled back up over the railing of the bridge.

"What's going on?" I stammered. I couldn't figure out what was happening. Or why it was happening. "Hey, cut it out...."

Moving quickly, the police officer turned me around and pushed me against the railing. He yanked my hands back behind my back and put handcuffs on me.

"You can't arrest me!" I shouted.

"Take it easy, pal. I ain't arresting you. I'm saving you."

"Let me go," I begged him. "Let me do what I came here to do. It'll be better for all of us."

He shook his head. "I can't do that, pal. Come on. That's never the way. Just take it easy."

For the first time, I began to resist, but my resistance was weak at best. I had been hollowed out by my desire to kill myself. I could not muster the energy to put up a good fight. Besides, my hands were handcuffed behind me and the officer who had pulled me from the bridge was half a foot taller than me and outweighed me by fifty pounds. I was no match for him. Not right then.

He led me to his police cruiser, which was parked alongside the road, halfway along the bridge.

"How did you know?" I blurted out as he ducked my head and put me into the back seat.

He jerked his head back toward the sidewalk. "You can thank your friend there," he said as he buckled me in at my waist and my feet.

I looked up and out of the car. There, smiling his wide, toothless smile was the old man. He gave me a little wave.

The officer backed out of the car and closed the door. The whole time I kept my eyes on the old man. He watched me, too. I could see in his eyes and expression a look of pity. How could someone who had fallen so far in life have pity on me? Unless he understood that I had fallen even further.

I was not taken to jail. I was taken to a hospital and transferred immediately to the mental ward. I was not the first one to be brought to that place from the bridge. Sadly, I would not be the last.

The police officer half-dragged, half-led me to the reception area where the nurse took care of the paperwork. As I stood there, answering some of the questions, I looked around the ward. It was crawling with people who were clearly disturbed. They were crawling, scratching, screaming, crying, whirling...you name it.

During the week I was there, I saw people with mild craziness and people in the full flower of lunacy. Those people could have howled at the moon. There were three people there who were convinced they were Napoleon Bonaparte. During that week, I was evaluated, spoken to, medicated, and evaluated again. Then I was transferred to a medical holding facility, the Seattle Washington Naval Hospital.

While I was there, I received an honorable discharge on June 5, 1978. I was out of the navy and I was alive. I had the old man at the foot of the bridge to thank for everything...but I was far from out of the woods and it would be a long time before I would feel grateful toward him.

Chapter Three

I returned home to my mother's house where I was welcomed with open arms by my mother, sister, and brother. For the first few days, I was just glad to be home and far, far away from the hospital in Washington. I did not explain my presence at home again to my mother. In fact, after the first week, when she asked me when I was going to be going back to the navy, I told her that I was waiting for shore duty.

"Shore duty?"

"I got very sea sick every time I went on the ship," I explained to her. She smiled and shook her head. She wasn't the first person who was amused that a sailor would get sea sick.

My mother did not press the issue of my return to the navy very hard. And, after being home for a while, I knew I couldn't just sit in my mother's living room, so I went out looking for employment. I was raised in a family in which we all took responsibility for contributing to the family's finances. That was the primary reason I had entered the military. That hadn't changed with my discharge.

I went to job interviews, filled out applications, and waited. Day after day, nothing happened.

"You can't just sit around the house all day," my sister told me.

"I've been out looking,"I told her, snapping because I was frustrated I hadn't been able to find work. "You know I've been out looking."

"Well, you just got to look harder," she told me. "You can't expect us all to support you. You're a grown man now."

"Hey, if you know of anything, tell me. I'll go get the job," I replied angrily to her.

I had started to collect unemployment checks, which helped a little but not much. Meanwhile, my sister kept her eyes and ears open for any potential job opening that I could fill. Finally, a friend of hers told her about an opening in Hyaat Roller Bearing, a General Motors subsidiary in Clark, New Jersey. The pay was $8.00 an hour. No way to get rich, but a damned sight better than sitting on my ass in my mother's house doing nothing at all.

I started out as a laborer, draining oil and mopping oil spills from machines that made the outside diameter to the roller-bearing assembly. I started out working the night shift—the graveyard shift. This was a tough shift for me. I was a day person. I slept when it was dark out and came to life when the sun came up. But I didn't have any choice this time.

"Just shut up and do the work," my sister said when I complained about the hours.

"Don't worry, I will," I told her. Complaining was one thing. It wasn't going to get in the way of my working. Not this time. I worked hard and diligently. I did what I was told and I did it well. As a result, I was promoted to forklift driver on the second shift—from three o'clock in the afternoon until eleven o'clock at night.

Now this was more like it! I loved this shift. I got off work early enough to still go out and I didn't have to report the next day until late enough that I was able to sleep. I liked driving the forklifts and doing the work. All in all, things seemed to be going just fine.

But then I was laid off during a period of cut backs at General Motors. I was disappointed, but I will say one thing for GM. They had provided their workers with some good benefits, one of which was to receive 95% of their pay during lay-offs. At the time, I had been making $290 a week take home. When I was laid off, I was bringing home $240 a week.

Not bad for someone twenty-one years old and still in search of a career. Still, it isn't a good thing to have too much time on your hands. I was still convinced that the military was my best option for training and preparation for a career.

So, during the time I was laid off, I joined the National Guard, army division. One thing to remember is that during all this time, although I was twenty-one years old, although I had been working, although I had signed up with the National Guard, I still lived in my mother's home and she was, as she had always been, very strict. Even now, when I was a man, she set a strict curfew for me.

"One o'clock?" I asked her when she stood at the door, her arms crossed across her chest. "But, Mama..."

She shook her head. "Nothing good comes of a man staying out to all hours. If you live in my house, you come home by one."

It didn't matter if I was at a disco or a private dance. My curfew was set and I had to adhere to it. I loved my mother and understood where she was coming from. She had been raised a very strict Catholic and had lived her entire life committed to the teachings of the Church. We were raised as Catholics and we were expected to live like good Catholics. Even as an adult, we went to Sunday Mass with our mother.

Anita, the girl I had fallen for before reporting to ship in Oregon, was also from a very strict, religious family. When we went on dates, we had to go with her brother as a chaperone. Most of the time I didn't mind so much. He was a decent guy and understood that Anita and I wanted to be together. But he took his role as chaperone seriously.

Anita's parents weren't going to let us go anyplace alone, and Anita's brother was there to make sure their wishes were covered. Still, I loved being with Anita. She was beautiful and fun and I felt happy with her. At the time, I was still laid off from General Motors but I was receiving my weekly check and I purchased a brand new Thunderbird to drive around. I loved seeing Anita, but I had no illusions about how far I could go with her. She was a virgin and she was going to remain a virgin until her wedding night. So, if I was going to enjoy any sex, I was going to have to go to clubs and meet other women.

One night while on my "woman hunt," my brother and I went to a disco not far from our mother's house. Out on the dance floor, I first noticed a very pretty girl with light green eyes who seemed to have a whole pack of young men trying to get in her good graces. She danced with a few of them but just laughed them off when they tried for a second dance.

"Look at her," I said to my brother.

"Pretty," he agreed.

"Maybe I'll dance with her," I told him.

"Go ahead," he laughed. He knew I was going to no matter what he said.

A minute later, I was moving across the dance floor toward this beautiful young thing. "How're you doing?" I asked when I got close to her.

She shrugged. She was used to being spoken to by strange young men and she handled the situation easily.

"Dance?"

She shrugged again and then nodded, following me to the middle of the dance floor. Once out there, we moved easily together. I liked dancing with her and she seemed to like dancing with me. We started a second dance and, as we moved together, I asked her name.

"Zeizel," she said.

"Sounds exotic," I replied.

She laughed and continued to dance. I rested my hand on her hip and moved close to her so our pelvises were moving in unison. Just then, an older Cuban man made his way across the dance floor. I saw him from the corner of my eye and thought to myself that he looked out of place the way he was walking.

Zeizel saw him as well, but she turned away, shaking her hair and continuing to dance.

I focused on her, her beautiful eyes and her body and how she was moving along with me. Then I felt a hand on my shoulder. I turned my head and saw the older Cuban man.

"I'm dancing with Zeizel," he announced to me.

I smiled at him. This kind of bullshit happened all the time in discos so I didn't give the man much thought. "Not this dance, pal," I told him. "This dance, she's dancing with me."

"I'm dancing with her," he repeated, only this time he shoved me to the side.

This did not work for me at all. Although he was an older guy and a little bigger than me, I became immediately enraged. While I had been a smooth dancer with Zeizel, I was suddenly a lion. I wheeled around and began to swing at him, connecting several hard blows to his face. His nose and lips were split and he was bleeding heavily.

"Asshole," I started to say but the word was choked out of me when I felt myself being yanked into a hard headlock from behind. I could feel the guy's muscles and sense the size of his arms as he squeezed my neck tighter and tighter.

I raised my arm and then hit him in his midsection with my elbow. At the same time, I kicked him just below the knee. The combined pain of the two blows caused him to loosen his grip. I pushed away and then turned around and, without so much as looking at him, kicked him hard in the groin. That caused him to cry out in agony. I swung my leg across his face and then swung at him with my fist. He dropped to the dance floor like a sack of potatoes.

It was only when he hit the floor that I realized how big he was. He .was easily over six feet tall and weighed more than two hundred and fifty pounds.

"Bastard," I muttered.

Just then, I felt a hard punch to my right eye and a second one behind my ear. A second later, I was down on the floor with another bouncer on top of me. He might have weighed about two-fifty but he felt like he weighed a F—-ing ton. The first bouncer, the guy who had put me in a head lock, got up and began hitting and kicking me in the face. I could feel the blood pouring out of me. I could hear screaming and shouting all around me. I knew my brother and my friends were trying to help me but they were being held back by the club's numerous bouncers.

Meanwhile, Zeizel couldn't believe what dancing with her had cost me. When I finally looked up and spotted her, I could see that she felt terrible. I was bloodied and held between two big bouncers. These guys half-carried me, half-threw me out of the club.

I was a bloody mess. My clothes were torn and I hurt all over. That was some F—-ing beating. Those guys knew what they were doing. The worst part was I knew exactly what had happened. I had been used by Zeizel to make someone jealous. I couldn't believe I'd fallen for it. What a fool!

"Hey, you."

I looked up at the door of the club.

"Here. You'll probably need this."

The guy threw me a towel to wipe my face. "Thanks," I groaned. I began to wipe my face, but the cuts and bruises were too heavy. I wasn't going to be able to just wipe them away and stop the bleeding.

"Hey, you all right, Bobby?"

I looked up at my brother. "Yeah," I told him.

"We tried to kick their asses," he said.

I nodded. "I know."

He and my other friends had gotten involved but they couldn't do much. That was just the way it was when the bouncers got involved in a club. You were outnumbered and outmanned. But I wasn't worried. I knew I would get even some time. No, I had bigger worries just then. Namely, my mother.

I knew that she would be furious when she saw me. She never liked me going to discos and clubs. To her they were "dens of iniquity." Coming home bruised and bloody would only convince her that she was right.

As soon as she saw me, a cloud came over her expression. She proclaimed, "See what happens at those clubs! Nothing but trouble." She was terribly upset that night and refused to allow me to go to any more disco clubs for a while.

I could go along with that—for a while. What I couldn't do was not see Zeizel. She'd gotten under my skin somehow. Her eyes, something. So, three weeks later, after the swelling went down and my cuts healed, and after my eyes were no longer blackened, I went out looking for her. I found her in the store where she was working.

"Hey, how are you?" I asked, coming up to her.

Her eyes widened in recognition. "How are you?" she asked. "I couldn't believe what happened at the dance."

I shrugged. "I was having too good a time to let that old buzzard cut in on me like that."

She laughed. "I was having a good time, too."

"So, how about dinner?"

"Okay."

I met her family when I went to pick her up. They were nice people—a mixture of Cuban, Jewish, and Spanish. Like most families in my neighborhood, they wanted to know everything about me before letting Zeizel go out with me. They wanted to know my history, my family's history, where I worked, what I did, what I wanted to do, what my parents did for a living.

No one ever went out with just one person; they always went out with that person and that person's family. That was just the way the culture worked where I lived.

Even after they agreed to allow Zeizel to go out with me, Zeizel wasn't allowed to go out with me alone. Her sister acted as our chaperone, staying with us and making sure we didn't do anything wrong.

Over the next few weeks, Zeizel and I started to see a lot of each other. We really started to like each other. Her sister gave us more and more "space" to be alone, even under her watchful presence.

Zeizel's parents could see that I was becoming more and more serious about their daughter, so their conversations with me became more serious.

"Are you going to be going back to work at General Motors?" they wanted to know. Ultimately, everything came down to having a job and a source of income. Love and romance was fine and good, but no family was comfortable with their daughter getting into a situation where she couldn't be properly taken care of.

"Sure," I told them. And that was my intention. For Zeizel, I would have worked for GM my whole life.

We'd been going out about a month when I took Zeizel and her sister to my mother's house on Lafayette Street in Newark to meet my mother. My mother was pleased to meet such a nice and pretty young lady. But she was shocked when we told her that we planned to get married.

She pulled me to the side. "Son, you can't get married yet!"

"Why not?" I asked her.

"You have to have a steady job first. You can't have a wife without a steady job!"

A lifetime with my father, who could not maintain a steady job, had taught my mother just how difficult life could be without income to take care of the needs of a house and a family. Then she turned her attention to both Zeizel and me.

"Do you have any idea how serious this is?" she asked. Then she proceeded to lecture us on marriage. In doing so, she would touch on many of the things that would stay with me for the rest of my life. So much of what she said was based on her own experience, but a lot of what she said was based on what she had seen in her sisters' marriages, marriages that she considered to be successful. When she had finally finished telling us everything she wanted to tell us about marriage and successful relationships between men and women, she smiled a quick smile.

"Well, I guess I've filled you with enough of my thoughts for now. Would you like to stay for dinner?"

"Sorry about that," I said to Zeizel after we'd eaten and we'd left my mother's house.

She smiled. "Don't apologize. She was right," she added. "Don't you think she was right?"

I shrugged. "I guess so," I admitted. I love my mother, but like most sons, I pretty much allowed what she was saying to go in one ear and out the other. That would prove to be to my discredit for a long time.

"So," she said, taking my arm, "What should we do now?"

I turned and looked at her. Her smile was so arresting I couldn't help but smile back. "How about dancing?"

Zeizel and I would go out to restaurants and discos together all the time. And, because there were only so many different places we could go, a lot of the time I would bump into friends of mine from the neighborhood and from school. These old friends were out cruising for women, just like I had always done. They couldn't believe that I wasn't doing that anymore. They couldn't believe that I had found the girl I wanted to stick with.

"Vidal, you're crazy, man," they'd say to me when they shook my hand and greeted me when we were out at night. "Married? Come on, look around."

I would look around a crowded dance floor or a filled restaurant and bar. "Yeah, I'm looking."

"Don't you see them? All the beautiful women just begging you to dance with them?"

"I just see a lot of people."

"Ah, Vidal, you're bustin' me up, man. Why pay for the cow when you can have the milk for free?"

"F—- you, man," I said good-naturedly.

"I'm serious. These girls are practically begging to put out...."

"Give it up," I told them. "You're just jealous that I'm not out running with you guys anymore, that I have a girl I'm happy with."

Up until then, our banter had been good-natured, joking. But suddenly, my comment had turned the conversation serious.

"Yeah, Vidal, that's right," one of the guys said, his face bearing an angry expression. "You don't come around anymore."

"Maybe you don't want any part of us anymore."

"But it ain't that easy, Vidal," another said ominously.

"Remember us, Vidal? We're your friends. The Pacific Street Boys. We're the ones you want to be hanging with."

These were guys I had known for years. The Pacific Street Boys was a small gang of about twenty of us. Neighborhood friends. Mostly we just hung out together and had a good time. We'd pile into vans together and smoke some weed, drink ourselves drunk, and then head out to the discos for a good time. Lots of times we'd end up in a fight but we always covered each other. We watched each other's backs, and the fight was usually the way we preferred to end the night.

"Hey, Vidal, you remember that time we took on those fifteen bouncers at the Fountain Casino?"

I couldn't help but smile. Sure, I remembered.

"We did some F—-ing damage that night, didn't we?"

"Yeah, we did," I admitted.

"Their mamas didn't recognize their F—-in' faces when they got home!" one of the guys said, smiling widely.

I looked around at the faces of the guys surrounding me. Emilio, Santi, High One, Carlos, and Tony, along with the others. There had been ten of us that night at the Fountain Casino. Ten of us locals against fifteen of those big ole bouncers. We kicked their asses....

I was a good fighter. I'd always wanted to be a professional karate kick boxer, so I was in excellent fighting shape. I trained regularly with two black belts in the neighborhood, getting ready to be the best fighter 1 could be.

"Yeah, I remember all that, guys."

"Just don't forget us," they said. And they meant it.

Friends like I had in the neighborhood weren't just friends. We were brothers. We all came up against the same hardships, the same bullshit. We knew each other's families. We knew the secrets that people tried to hide from others. We didn't talk about that shit. We just knew it. They all knew about my father. I knew about their families. We didn't have to talk about it. We knew. We watched out for each other. We took care of each other.

Zeizel didn't like me getting together with my old friends. "You're not the same Bobby I know when you're with them," she said. "I'm the same guy you've always known," I told her.

But she shook her head and looked at me with a worried expression on her face. I guess I could understand her worry. After all, I'd told her about some of the things I'd done with my boys. I told her how we'd get together and get high and go out cruising for women.

"I don't want to lose you," she said, holding my hand tight. "You're not going to lose me," I promised her.

I liked that she was a little jealous of me and what I was doing. It was good to keep a woman a little jealous—not too much, though!

Meanwhile, I was trying to get all the pieces of my life back together and in balance. I wanted to stay tight with my friends. I had my love for Zeizel. I was free from the navy. And I was starting back at work.

I went to work in another General Motors plant; this one was the Linden Assembly Plant. It was the beginning of 1981. Now that I was working, Zeizel and I made plans to be married on February 28th of that year.

"You're sure you want to do this?" my mother asked me.

"Yes."

She looked to Zeizel, who looked at me and then back to my mother. "Yes."

"No marriage can really last without Jesus," she said firmly. With that, she took the two of us to the Evangelical church where she had found spiritual healing in the Lord Jesus Christ.

Although she had been raised a devout Catholic, during her life she had sought greater comfort than the Church afforded her. When my father was mistreating her, she found solace at the Evangelical church and there was reborn to salvation in Jesus Christ. She found real healing at that church. Her high blood pressure and heart condition were responding to the healing power of prayer.

During this time, I was aware of my mother's spirituality, but it wasn't something that I had participated in. When I was younger, my mother took us all to Mass and we attended church regularly. But that was the Catholic Church. I was not at all ready for what we experienced when we went with my mother to the Evangelical church. I couldn't explain why, but I was nervous about going to the church.

"What's the matter?" Zeizel asked. "You're acting strange." "I don't know. These people are strange."

"They're just Christians. You're a Christian."

"I'm a Catholic. My family's Catholic," I said. "I know the Mass. I don't know what's going on at that church."

"Well, your mother wants us to go with her so we should go."

In spite of her good intentions, Zeizel was nervous, too. Growing up in the Church, we knew exactly what was expected of us and it didn't seem like much. I had seen the change in my mother from when she had let Christ into her heart, and in some ways I just didn't know what to think.

When we got to the church, it was already packed. People were in the pews, in the aisles, they were singing. During the service, a man suddenly stood up and started crying out in strange sounds.

"Amen, brother! Amen!"

"That's the Lord speaking!"

Zeizel grabbed my hand. "What's going on?"

I shrugged my shoulders. "I don't know," I admitted.

Unlike the very solemn rituals of the Catholic Church, this service was like a free-for-all. The minister was leading the service while people stood up and cried out in strange tongues. Others danced in the aisles, moved by the Spirit of the Lord.

"The Spirit is here tonight," my mother said with a smile on her face. Her eyes were alight with joy, and it filled me with a strange emotion, seeing my mother so moved and happy.

"I don't like it here," Zeizel leaned over and whispered to me. "It'll be over soon," I promised her.

The minister led the service with a sharp, emotional voice. He read passages from the Gospel of John and the Book of Revelations. "Do you believe the Lord Jesus Christ is here with us tonight?" he shouted to the congregation.

"The Lord is here!"

"Amen!"

A man tumbled from the pew and writhed around on the floor. "Heal us, Lord!"

"Jesus loves us all!" the minister cried out. "But we must allow His love into our hearts! We must open our hearts to Him!"

He railed on about sin and how it is sin that keeps our bodies infirm and our minds troubled. "It is sin that roils the waters of the soul!"

As the service came to a conclusion, the minister invited anyone who wanted Jesus in his or her life "to come forward to the altar and to receive the blessings of our Lord and Savior!"

At first, only three or four people started to go forward.

"Amen, brothers and sisters. Be free from the shackles of sin! Free your hearts and your souls!"

More and more people went forward.

"Repeat after me," the minister cried out to the growing throng. "Tell the Lord, 'I am a sinner!' Tell the Lord you want Jesus Christ to be your personal Lord and Savior! Invite Him into your hearts now! Don't wait another second. Free yourself from your sins!"

People streamed past us, bumping us as they surged toward the altar.

"Tell me the truth!" the minister cried out. "Jesus Christ died on the cross for the sins of the world. Jesus Christ, the Son of God, died for your sins! Invite Him into your heart now!"

Zeizel and I stood in place, frightened by the scene that was being played out all around us. We didn't know what to make of it. The emotion. The heat. The voices. The crying. It was overwhelming. Zeizel was clutching my arm. Her eyes were wide in a kind of fear.

"Come, you two," my mother said, pulling us forward. "Come forward to the altar with me."

We resisted at first but soon found ourselves carried along with my mother until we were at the foot of the altar, where the minister stood. "This is my son," my mother called to the minister.

He looked at me with his piercing eyes. "Do you want peace in your life, son?" he asked me.

I just looked at him, unable to answer.

"Do you want to give your problems over to the Lord?"

I couldn't speak.

"None of us can rise above sin. We are all sinners. Only through Jesus Christ can we be saved! Repeat after me, 'I am a sinner! I want Jesus Christ to be my personal Lord and Savior! I want Him in my heart now!'"

At first, I still couldn't speak. My mother nudged me. "Go on, son. Let Jesus save you."

I repeated the words as best I could. The minister touched my forehead. The next I knew, I was on the ground. I had been thrust there by the power of the Holy Spirit. I could feel the ground beneath me but my eyes were clenched shut and I felt like I was swimming but I couldn't get to the surface. I was swimming and swimming. I was holding my breath. I needed fresh air. I needed it so bad. And then, just like that, I broke the surface and I could breathe. I opened my eyes. I felt completely different than I had only a few minutes before. It was as if a valve had been opened and all the pressure that had been building up inside my head had been released.

I felt that some tightness between my shoulders was suddenly gone. I felt almost weightless now that I was not held down by the weights I had been struggling with for so long. I had never felt like that before.

I couldn't find words to describe the emotions moving through me, or the gratitude I felt in having the pain lifted from me. But what had happened to me? Why had I fallen to the ground from the minister's gentle touch? And why had I passed out? I had no idea how long I was on the floor. Had I been like those others I had seen earlier in the service, writhing on the floor, crying out in tongues?

And why hadn't Zeizel passed out? Like me, she had received Jesus Christ as her Lord and Savior, yet she had not felt the same physical sensation that I had. I did not understand, but as I would come to realize, there was a great deal that I did not understand and that I still had to learn. As Paul said, you cannot feed a child more than he is able to eat.

Spiritually, I still saw through the eyes of a baby. It would be a long time before I began to see through the eyes of a man. Still, I felt an immediate growth in spiritual knowledge. Some things were given to me whole.

I understood speaking in tongues and the presence of the Holy Spirit. I felt as if I knew exactly how the Apostles felt at Pentecost when they first received the Holy Spirit. What had felt strange to me only a week before now felt to me to be the most natural thing in the world. I had been looking through glass. Now I was trying to look "face to face."

My friends in the Pacific Street Boys didn't exactly embrace my newfound spirituality. To them, it was even more difficult to understand than me getting married.

"Man, Vidal, now you're a Holy Roller?"

"What's happened to you?"

I just smiled. "The greatest thing in the world's happened to me. You guys got to experience what I've experienced. Come to the church with me. Then you'll see what I'm talking about."

But getting those guys to come with me to church was harder than getting them to hang out with me in a disco when I was with Zeizel. They weren't ready yet to have their lives changed. They weren't ready to be saved.

Chapter Four

As we planned, Zeizel and I got married on February 28th, 1981. We were married in St. Joseph's Church in Union City. My brother was my best man. Zeizel's sister was her maid of honor.

We had a small wedding. There were seventy-five guests at our reception. We could have invited a thousand people, but we were both children of poor parents. Zeizel's father had recently been laid off from the Ford Motor Company in Mawa, New Jersey, so there wasn't a lot of money to spend on a party. Still, we both loved the reception. We enjoyed fine Italian and Spanish food. There was an open bar.

All through the reception, Zeizel kept squeezing my hand and looking at me with those beautiful eyes. We were both anxious for the reception to be over. We wanted to go to our apartment on Davis Avenue in Harrison to celebrate our wedding in the special way that newlyweds do. We had been getting the apartment ready for weeks before the wedding. I had taken money I had been saving from my job at General Motors to buy furniture. I didn't want to live in our first apartment together with milk cartons and makeshift furniture. I wanted our first apartment to be perfect from the beginning.

Although I had savings to buy furniture, we didn't have money to go away on a honeymoon, which was fine. Zeizel and I planned on enjoying our honeymoon in our own apartment in our peaceful little town of Harrison.

After the reception, we drove to our apartment and parked our car on a side street away from our apartment. I didn't want our friends or family figuring out that we were home and bothering us. Of course, my cousins and friends drove around and spotted the car. From that moment on, they devoted themselves to tormenting us. They rang our doorbell and honked the horn of the cars. We just stayed under the blankets of our bed, making love and laughing at the commotion they were causing.

The first few months, we were as happy as happy could be. I was working and that was the most important thing. It was the message I'd gotten from my mother and from my life experience—a good husband holds down a job and supports his wife and family.

But then, after a few months, I was laid off from the GM Linden Assembly Plant. I waited on the unemployment checks but they didn't quite make up for the $400 I had been bringing home every week.

"What are we going to do?" Zeizel asked.

I didn't know what to say. I felt an anger and frustration welling up inside me. I didn't want to be powerless to do the things I knew I had to do to be a good husband.

"We'll be okay. The unemployment checks will come in and then I'll find something."

But the checks weren't enough. Zeizel started working as a secretary in New York to help pay the bills. I decided that I had to have some kind of training to fall back on. I couldn't keep working in GM plants and getting laid off. So I went to learn auto mechanics at Middlesex County College.

I'll give GM credit. One of the benefits they offered their workers was to pay for such training while they were laid off. So GM paid for my school. I was also receiving $220 a week.

Those checks took about four weeks to get to us so, in the afternoon and evening after class, I would work at a local service station doing oil changes, tune ups, and brakes. Zeizel and I probably could have gotten by on the $220 a week and her salary but we had to start saving some real money.

In the early fall, she hadn't been feeling well and I was worried she was coming down with the flu. She had to miss a couple of days of work. One morning, she went to the doctor. That evening, when I got home, she was sitting in the bedroom.

"Hey, how're you feeling?" I asked, coming into the room and kissing her.

"The same," she said. But she was smiling.

"So if you feel sick, how come you're smiling?"

Her smile turned into a grin.

"What?"

"We're going to have a baby!"

"What?"

She nodded her head. "The doctor told me. He said I was pregnant."

I couldn't believe it. We hugged and kissed. We were both so happy.

Everyone was happy for us. Even though we had moved to Harrison, we stayed close to our family and friends. I was close to Zeizel's parents, which made things easier for them and for Zeizel. They missed their daughter and were always glad to see her. We visited them often. Other family members came to visit us. My female cousins would bring their husbands. My male cousins would bring their wives. We always had fun when we were together. I was a joke teller and was called the "life of the party."

Zeizel loved to organize meals for everyone. Everyone brought a dish and we put together huge potlucks. When we weren't eating, we were just hanging around, enjoying each other's company. Despite the financial difficulties, our life seemed to be going well. I didn't know anyone who wasn't struggling financially. After all, I come from very simple roots. No one had real money. But we were family. We were happy.

I had been buying the tools that I needed to be an auto mechanic. As anyone who ever worked on a car knows, these tools cost a lot of money. A mechanic's tools can easily add up to thousands of dollars. And at every service station, each mechanic owns his own tools.

I'd been keeping my tools with me in the trunk of my Thunderbird. That way, they were right there when I went to work on cars from school. At this time, I started working as a security guard for California Plant Protection.

I was working the full-time graveyard shift—from midnight to eight in the morning—as a security guard and then going straight to the local Exxon station where I was an auto mechanic's apprentice. I went from work to work. Sometimes I was dog tired, but I was glad to be doing what I was doing. I was making money and learning a trade at the same time.

One morning, when I came out from my job as a security guard, I went to get in my car but my car wasn't where I parked it.

"What the...?" I scratched my head. I'd been working so much lately that I wondered if I'd forgotten where I'd parked my own car. I retraced my steps, thinking hard about where I'd parked. But the fact was, I parked in exactly the same place I always parked. And the damned car was gone!

"Shit!" I sat down on the curbside and put my head in my hands. Not only had I lost my car, I'd also lost my mechanic's tools and equipment that I'd been keeping in the trunk. In one piece of bad luck, I'd lost my car and the income from my side jobs. Without tools, the difficult hours just made working at the service station impossible.

I picked up a cheap 1970 Dodge Coronet to get back and forth to work. That little car seemed to symbolize everything that was going wrong in my life. Something was always going wrong with that car. Little things. A mirror would get broken. A window wouldn't work. The radio would die.

It was the same in my life. Things were looking bleak. I was feeling more and more pressure to make money right when my ability to make money had been stolen from me. The bills were mounting and my wife was showing more every day.

"Look, I'll keep working longer than I thought," she said, rubbing my neck and trying to make me feel better.

"No," I said. "No way. I'm not letting you go into New York every day anymore."

At six months, I thought it was too dangerous for her to be traveling in and out of New York City every day. She was tired from the commute and from working. I didn't want her to get sick or for our baby to be sick.

In March of 1982 I got a job driving a truck and making deliveries for a medical warehouse. I was still working the night shift as a security guard. I was constantly exhausted. I felt beat up and unable to take control of my life. Even though I had some income, which allowed me to pay the bills, the responsibilities of my life were overwhelming me. I was working like a dog. I had a baby on the way. I was barely getting by hand to mouth.

"This is no F—-ing way to live," I thought to myself as I made the lonely rounds as a night guard. I felt trapped. I couldn't stand it anymore. Get up. Drive a truck. Come home. Go to work as a security guard. Come home at dawn. Sleep an hour. Go back to work. It was crazy. Zeizel and I hardly glanced at one another except to feel the pressure of each other's needs. I thought I was losing my mind. I was sure I was going to crack soon.

Before I knew it, I was going out to bars. I just had to have a little break away from the apartment and away from work. I needed a place to blow of a little steam and to feel that my worries couldn't touch me. In a bar, nursing a drink, I was safe.

"Hey, look who's here!"

"Bobby, how you doing?"

One of the best parts of going to bars was that I was running into my old friends. It seemed that that world had been lost to me but seeing them again and being around them made me feel young again. Of course, they were doing more than just drinking. They were smoking a lot of weed, too.

"Man, Bobby, it's great to see you again!"

They were genuinely glad to see me. They crowded around me and gave me hugs. It felt great. After I had joined the church, I had completely broken from them. Not to mention the fact that being a married man made it difficult to go hang out with the guys like I'd been able to when I was single.

"Give my man Bobby another drink!"

Well, being with my guys again called for a celebration. One drink led to another and before I knew it, I was feeling no pain. I completely blew off my security job.

"So, what's the deal with the Holy Rollers?" Emilio asked. "Yeah," Tony wanted to know. "You still down at the church?"

I shrugged my shoulders. "It's not paying the bills, that's for sure," I told them.

When I left the bar, I made my way home only to find Zeizel more than a little upset.

"What's the matter with you?" she demanded, yelling at me. "What do you mean, what's the matter with me?"

"You don't report to work. I'm worried sick. And then you show up here stinking of alcohol."

"Ah, come on, I just had a few drinks with my old friends, that's all. No big deal," I told her.

"No big deal? Those losers don't pay the bills! And now you're fired from your job!" She started to cry.

"Don't start crying now," I said. "Don't worry. I'll start looking for a new job tomorrow. I promise."

She looked at me. "Really?"

"I said I promised, didn't I?" I promised, but even as I spoke the words, I knew I was in way over my head.

The next day, I started to look for a job in the Ironbound section of Newark. As I drove along the street outside the Costa Brava Bar, I couldn't help but notice a beautiful, triple-white, brand spanking new Cadillac Seville parked at the curb. I let out a low whistle. That was one beautiful car. It was beautiful compared to any other car, but compared to the piece of crap I was driving, it was incredible.

I had seen the Cadillac parked there before and I had always admired it. But today, as I dejectedly cruised through the neighborhood trying to figure out what I was going to do for a job, I admired it even more. Somebody was doing something right to be driving that car.

Not only was it a beautiful car, it was kept up and polished every day. The white was as white as driven snow and the shine on the car was shinier than a mirror. My mouth was going dry as I looked at the Cadillac.

I eased my Dodge along the curb behind the Cadillac and I took a closer look at its polished chrome rims and its big, expensive tires. I got out of my car and leaned toward the windows, peering in at its all-white leather interior. I leaned back up and let out a sigh. It even had a moon roof.

It was perfect. I would have done anything to drive that car.

"Man, oh man," I muttered as I stepped up onto the curb and walked across the sidewalk to the Costa Brava Bar. Whatever else I had to do, I had to have a quick beer just to straighten my head.

"Hey, Bobby," Leiva, the owner of the bar said, coming over to serve me a drink.

"How're you?" I asked, nodding as he came over. I looked around the bar. I spotted a guy wearing a double-breasted white suit. He had so many thick gold chains around his neck that it was amazing he could keep his head straight. Even in the dim bar, his fingers sparkled with the rings he wore on just about every finger on his hand. The sparkle of the diamonds he was wearing just about knocked me off my bar stool. They guy looked like a million bucks, which I figured he probably had to piss away.

"What'll it be?" Leiva asked.

"A Bud," I said. When he brought it over, I asked him if he knew anybody who was hiring. "I need a job bad, Leiva."

He shrugged and shook his head. "I don't know of any jobs," he told me. Then he pointed to the guy in the white suit. "You might want to talk to that guy, Vidal. He owns a body shop and a car dealership and a few other businesses."

I glanced up at the "million-dollar man" again. Then I looked at Leiva. "Ask him if he needs anyone, would you?"

"Sure."

I didn't expect so much as an answer but when Leiva came back to where I was sitting, he said that the man had ordered a drink for me. "That's Ruben Perrone," he said in a quiet voice. Then he leaned closer. "He's a very respected and powerful man, Vidal. Don't F—- with him."

I nodded and then looked over toward Mr. Perrone, who was motioning for me to join him where he was sitting. I took my glass and slid off the bar stool and headed over toward him.

"Have a seat," he said, nodding toward the chair at the table. "Thanks."

"I hear you're looking for work."

I let out a low whistle. "I'll do anything. My wife's gonna have a baby any day and I don't have the money to pay the doctor, let alone the rest of my bills." I went on to tell him that my car had been stolen, along with my tools. All in all, it became clear that I was in really bad shape.

Perrone listened until I was finished. "I know of your family," he said after I quieted down. "Your cousins own the Exxon station around the corner."

"Yeah, that's them," I said.

"You have a driver's license then?"

I nodded.

"I'll give you a job starting tomorrow then," he said.

I couldn't believe my good fortune. I thought I'd be driving a truck for him so I volunteered that I had a trucker's license but he waved me away. "Don't worry about that," he said. I hardly heard him. It was all I could do not to become hypnotized by his chains and rings. Hell, the gold watch on his wrist had to weigh ten pounds! I just couldn't believe that this man was offering me a job! I was on cloud nine!

Just then, the bar door opened and in walked a man I had come to know as Rene. Rene was wearing a Panama hat and as much gold as Mr. Perrone. He stopped near the doorway and looked around. Spotting Mr. Perrone, he began walking in our direction. I knew of Rene's reputation as a marimbero—a drug smuggler. He was the right-hand man of El Gallo—the Rooster. El Gallo controlled the heroin, cocaine, and weed smuggling operations in that area of the city.

I had first met Rene in high school. Even then, he had driven a fancy Corvette and was known as the local cocaine dealer.

"Hey," Rene said to me, shaking my hand. "Haven't seen you in a while."

He and I exchanged small talk. When Leiva came over, Rene ordered drinks for the entire bar. Then he turned to Mr. Perrone. I watched as the two men greeted each other warmly, hugging one another and kissing each other's cheek.

"So, what are you doing around here? Causing trouble?" Perrone asked Rene with a smile on his lips.

"Same thing I'm always doing around here—looking for women. Women, lots of them, and money."

I didn't think that I should be listening to the conversation between the two men so I discreetly moved away. As I drank the Scotch I ordered, I did overhear Rene telling Mr. Perrone that I was a good kid. "And a fighter," Rene said. "He's a boxer. I know him from the neighborhood. Kid comes from a good family."

The noise of the bar drowned out anything else I might have overheard, but I knew that the things Rene was telling Mr. Perrone were important if Perrone was going to trust me.

I moved closer to the table where they were talking. They both looked at me. "I have to get going," I said. "I have to take my wife grocery shopping and then to the doctor."

"It was good meeting you," Ruben Perrone told me. "You come back here at one o'clock and meet me," he said. "We'll talk then."

I knew that they were both watching me as I left the bar and that they could see me getting into my old Dodge. Getting into that car after being in the presence of those two high rollers only made me feel even smaller and less significant. But I waved off my feelings of unimportance. Starting the next day, I was going to be on my way!

I drove home with daydreams of an easier life and nicer things filling my imagination—daydreams that crowded out any doubts that I had about the kind of life I might be leading with my new "friends" and associates.

By the time I arrived home, I was filled with excitement. I bounded up the three flights of stairs to our apartment and called to Zeizel as soon as I came in the door.

"You found a job?" she asked excitedly as she kissed me.

"Better than that," I told her. "Come and sit down," I said, taking her hand and leading her to the kitchen table. There, as her eyes got moist with excitement, I told her everything that had happened that afternoon. She was so happy she didn't know what to say.

"The timing is perfect," I told her. "I'll be making real money before the baby comes."

"You'd better hurry," she joked, pressing her hands against her swollen belly. "The baby's been kicking all day. I feel like I'm going to have this child any second."

We were both excited and happy with the good things that were going to come our way. After a minute, Zeizel frowned.

"What's the matter?" I asked.

"Well, I do have some bad news," she confessed.

I narrowed my eyes. "What's the matter? What's gone wrong?" I could feel an explosive anger taking form in my gut. I couldn't bear any more bad news. I felt so beaten down; I just wanted a chance to make things better.

"The landlord told me we have to move out."

"What? Why?"

"Because we didn't pay our rent," she said.

"Bullshit!" I screamed, jumping up from the table and starting to pace. "We paid..."

"Honey..."

I was so angry I took my fist and put it through the bathroom door. Zeizel came over and grabbed my arm. "No, it's my fault," she said. "I'm sorry, I'm sorry."

"What are you talking about?"

Zeizel told me that she had never paid the rent. She had taken the money that we'd put aside for the rent and used it to pay the phone, gas, and electric bills. "I didn't tell you because I didn't want you to be upset," she told me.

I slumped down into a chair. "What are we going to do now?" I wondered.

She came over and put her arms around me. "I took care of everything," she said.

Once again, Zeizel had done just that. She had arranged for us to move to a nearby town, North Bergen. "We'll live in the basement of my mother's house," she said. She kissed the top of my head. "Everything's going to be fine, you'll see."

Slowly, I came back down to earth. Zeizel had taken care of everything. I was relieved that we would not be without a place to live but I felt an emptiness in the pit of my stomach. All the situation proved to me was that I couldn't do a damned thing right. I needed my wife to bail me out, to "protect" me from the fact that she'd been juggling the bills. She was the one to sort out where we would live. I just felt hopeless.

The next day, I returned to the Costa Brava. I got there a few minutes early. And I waited. One o'clock came and went. Then two o'clock. Two-thirty. Three. I waited eight long hours, during which I spent my last twelve dollars on drinks.

"Where the F—- is he?" I kept asking myself, all the while feeling that my great opportunity had slipped through my fingers. I was so upset that I couldn't even call Zeizel to tell her the bad news.

When Leiva came over to where I was sitting, I looked up at him. "Does Perrone always leave his appointments waiting like this?"

Leiva shrugged. "He's an important man, Bobby. If he isn't here, it's because something important came up. Be patient. If he said he'd meet with you, he'll meet with you."

I just couldn't believe that this golden opportunity was going to be lost to me. I had placed so much hope in this working out.

When I finally left that evening, I told Leiva to tell Perrone that I'd waited as long as I could. Then I walked out, feeling completely deflated. I didn't even feel like a failure. How could I feel like a failure? A failure fails at something. I hadn't even gotten a chance to fail.

As I drove through the dark streets, I thought about how my whole life had fallen apart since I'd left the Evangelist church. There, for a time, things had all been working out. But now?

I told Zeizel what happened when I got home. She was very under-standing and forgiving. Which only added to my feelings of being a failure. Why was I feeling so dejected and defeated and she was able to still believe things would work out?

"Something must have come up. Or there was a misunderstand-ing," she said. "I'm sure he didn't miss your appointment on purpose."

Maybe not. I couldn't say. I tossed and turned, unable to sleep soundly that night. My dreams from the night before haunted me. It was

as if my dreams were this close and then they had been snatched away from me, leaving me feeling empty and beaten.

The next day, I went back to the Costa Brava. This time, I wasn't leaving anything to chance. When I saw Perrone, I was going to tell him what I thought about him not showing the day before. I dressed to impress. I wore my light brown, double-breasted suit. I might not have been able to wear all the gold that Perrone wore, but I was going to look sharp. I was going to do the best I could. He might have had power and money but that didn't give him the right to string me along.

As I pulled up to the bar, I saw the Cadillac parked at the curb out-side. Well, at least he was there.

"Damn," I said to myself, looking at the car, "it is a gorgeous car." Just seeing that car changed all my courage into awe. How could I stand up to a guy who could drive that car? Who the hell did I think I was? I drew a deep breath and tried to steel my jelly legs. Then I walked into the bar. I looked around. There was Perrone with this knockout girl in his arms. And if I thought I was dressed to kill, well, I was just fooling myself. Perrone was dressed to kill big time.

"Hey, Vidal!" he called over when he saw me. "Come on over here." When I hesitated, he called again. "Come on. Have a drink with me."

When I came over, the first thing he said was that he was sorry about the day before. He turned and looked at the incredible-looking girl in his arms and said, "But if you'd been with a pretty girl like this, would you have left to make the appointment?"

My anger flared up inside me. "Yeah, I would have," I told him. But I wasn't sure I meant it. She was more than pretty. She was a perfect package. Her jeans were painted on and she had a body that just didn't quit. Perrone's good taste ran to women as well.

Perrone smiled. Then, without saying another word, lie reached into his pocket and fished out his car keys. "Well, Vidal, you're going to be my driver from today on."

I just stared at him.

"Take them," he laughed, dropping the keys into my palm. "I'll pay you a thousand dollars a week."

I still hadn't said anything.

"What? That's not enough?" he joked. Then he reached into his pocket and pulled out a wad of bills. One after the other, he counted out ten hundred-dollar bills. Then he put them in my right hand along with the keys.

I couldn't believe it. I thought he was joking with me. But the next thing I know, he gave the girl a kiss good-bye. "Okay, Vidal, let's get out of here. You drive."

I followed him out of the bar. I was still stunned and couldn't believe this was happening. I had a thousand dollars and the keys to the most beautiful car in the world in my hand.

He got into the passenger side. I slid in behind the wheel. I adjusted the mirrors and the seat—mostly just to take a minute to catch my breath and slow down my heart. Then I turned the key in the ignition. It came on like a lover's kiss. When I pulled away from the curb and started down the road, I felt like I was riding on air.

"This is the F—-ing life," I thought to myself.

When we came to the first intersection, he told me to make a left. "Vidal, take me to the Casa Rosada Bar, on Wilson Avenue."

"Yes, sir," I said.

He smiled as I drove to the bar. I pulled up to the bar. He told me to wait; he'd only be a minute.

"This is great," I was thinking to myself while he was inside. "Zeizel's going to lose her mind when she sees this money."

I'd been waiting about twenty minutes when Perrone came out of the bar with two Hispanic guys. One of them handed him a suitcase. Perrone shook both of their hands and then slid back into the car.

"Drive to Tichenor Street, by South Street. I'll tell you where to stop."

As we drove along, Perrone pushed the locks on the suitcase and opened the top. I glanced over and my eyes just about popped out of my head.

"My God," I said, "I've never seen that much money before." "Listen, Vidal," Perrone said, "this is normal, so get used to it." I swallowed, determined to maintain my cool.

"You know I'm involved in a lot of businesses—my car dealership, the body shop, some grocery stores...." He paused. "A little book making on the side."

"Book making? That's illegal," I said, realizing that my greatest doubts and worries were being realized. I was being drawn into illegal activities.

Perrone didn't seem overly concerned with my observation. "Listen, Vidal," he said seriously, "you don't get paid a thousand dollars a week doing anything else, do you?" he asked.

I felt my face flush.

"So, do something for life, and life will do something for you. That's the way it works, Vidal."

"Yes, sir."

"And don't call me 'sir,' it makes me nervous," he said. "Call me by my name."

In no time, I felt comfortable calling Mr. Perrone by his first name. As we drove, I spoke to him. "Ruben, you're right. And I have to thank you for this thousand dollars. I...my family really needs the money. I'll work for you, Ruben. I'll do what you ask me to do. And I won't make any comments or ask any questions."

Even if I still had doubts, it was too late now. I'd taken the step. Off the cliff or not, I'd thrown in with Ruben Perrone. And I didn't even know if I had doubts. I'd tried to make things work out by being honest. But nothing had gone my way. Not the military. Not working two jobs. Nothing. All that happened was that I felt like more of a failure and I couldn't even pay my bills.

I wanted a better life. I needed a better life. I didn't doubt that 1 had embarked on a dangerous path, but I didn't care. I didn't see any other way to get what I wanted. For many years after taking that first, eventful step, I never looked back.

Chapter Five

Ruben told me where to stop—at a body shop. "Wait here," he told me. He got out of the car with the suitcase. Ten minutes later, he was back, without the suitcase. As he slid into the passenger seat, he smiled at me.

"Vidal, you look good in this car. Like you belong in it. I promise you, you do your job and you'll end up with an even nicer one." Ruben was playing me perfectly. For him, it was like taking candy from a baby. And I was the baby.

That first day, I saw more of life than I'd ever seen before. I learned more that day than I'd learned in all the years I was in school or any of the time I'd been working since. I also came to envision the goals that I would pursue for a long time after that.

Some time along the way, I noticed that Ruben carried a gun. When he saw me looking, he patted it and then smiled at me. "Vidal, that's my American Express card—I never leave home without it." Then his voice grew serious. "When you're lugging around a suitcase filled with two hundred thousand dollars cash, you'd better carry a gun, too."

By midnight, we had made all the stops Ruben needed to make that day. "Let's head on home, Vidal. I'm done."

He told me to meet him again the next day at one o'clock. "In the meantime, I'm going to get you a beeper so I can reach you whenever I need you."

I gave him my phone number and told him he could call me anytime. "I mean that, Ruben. Day or night."

"I appreciate that, Vidal. I really do."

When I got home after leaving Ruben, Zeizel was up and waiting for me. Everything was packed up in boxes and ready to go to her mother's.

"Shit," I thought to myself. I had just left a fantasy world to return to all the problems of my life. I didn't want to face moving but we had no choice.

"Look, baby," I told Zeizel as I took out my first week's pay to show her.

"Oh my God!" she said, instantly excited at the sight of the thousand dollars. "What did you have to do, rob a bank?"

I shook my head and described my job as a chauffeur for Ruben. "I'm finally going to be able to take care of you," I told her. "We're not going to have to worry ever again."

Whatever else I might have felt, it was good to believe that I was promising something I could deliver. The previous couple of months had been stressful. I was ready for life to start sending things my way.

Even though our early morning move the next day was hard work, I knew that we were at the beginning of better times. And any time I felt a nagging doubt enter my mind—that what I was doing was wrong—I just pushed it out of my mind with that picture of a suitcase filled with money and all the things I'd be able to buy for Zeizel with that kind of money.

One thing I couldn't quite shake, though, was the sense that I would never be what Zeizel wanted or needed. I didn't understand the conflict that was raging inside me. I had finally started out on a new, good life. I couldn't figure why I wasn't completely thrilled. I'd been missing out on life before this. Now was my time.

The next day, I met Ruben and continued my job as his chauffeur. I drove him around New York City, Queens, and Brooklyn. As we stopped off at the various places he identified, it became clear that he was friendly with powerful people everywhere we went.

The more time I spent with him, the more important I felt, too. Sitting behind the wheel of the Cadillac made me feel powerful. It made me feel rich. And I liked that feeling. I liked not having to worry about money. After my first few weeks with Ruben, I'd paid up all my bills and had saved over two thousand dollars. I almost couldn't remember what it was like to have to worry about money.

Still, I had nagging concerns. By the end of my first month with Ruben, I became fully aware of his involvement with drugs. My first real awareness came when I overheard a woman ask him for "a lift." He reached into his pocket and pulled out a small bag filled with white powder, which I knew was cocaine.

He wasn't just dealing either. He was using. I realized that when we were in a bar in Manhattan. He'd been drinking a lot and it seemed that his energy would begin to flag. But then he'd get up and go into the men's room, only to return a couple of minutes later with plenty of energy, full of life. He'd talk loudly and call attention to himself.

"Maybe we should get going," I said to him, noticing the way a number of people at the bar were watching him. "It's getting late...."

He shrugged. He kissed the girl he was with good-bye and then we headed out to one of his apartments on Wilder St & North Broad St in Elizabeth, New Jersey. That was the first time I'd been to his apartment and I was impressed with his furniture. The carpet was white and about two inches thick. Everything about his life just cried out "Success!" The luxury of it just about knocked me off my feet.

He motioned for me to follow him. I went after him into his bedroom and to the closet where he kept racks of beautiful clothing. Damn. Suit after suit, each more beautiful than the one before it. He stepped into the closet and then slid an icebox out.

"Vidal, you're going to make some real money with me," he said. "You're a nice guy and I trust you." With that, I bent down toward the icebox. "So now I'm going to let you in on my secret."

He opened the icebox. Inside, I counted eight packages, each shaped like a football. They were each wrapped in plastic and tape.

He took out one of the packages and brought it into the kitchen and placed it on the glass table. He took out a knife from his pocket and sliced a line through the tape and the plastic. As the plastic split open, white rocks of powder came tumbling out. They covered the tabletop and glistened in the light.

I just stood there staring as Ruben took out a credit card and began to chop up the rocks until they were broken down into a fine powder. Then he used the credit card to form two thin lines of the powder. He took out a wad of bills and slipped one away from the rest. After he returned the rest of the bills to his wallet, he rolled the bill into a tight straw. I knew that the powder was cocaine. I had heard a lot about it. I'd seen how it seemed to energize people. Ruben leaned toward the lines of cocaine and snorted them up into his nose through the tightly rolled bill. Immediately, his eyes came to life.

I can't deny that I was curious, but more than that, I understood that this was a kind of initiation for me. If I did not do as Ruben did, he would not trust me any more. If that were to happen, then everything I'd come to love about my new life would end. I couldn't bear the thought of that.

I took the rolled-up hundred-dollar bill. No one else was there. No one was looking. Everything about the life Ruben had opened up to me was perfect. I loved the feeling of having money in my pocket. I loved the feel of the Cadillac gliding under my control. I liked the respect shown me whenever I went anywhere with Ruben. I didn't want it to ever end.

I snorted the line of powder he laid out for me. As soon as the powder went flying up my nostril, I started coughing. My eyes burned and became very watery. My heart was racing so fast I was scared it was going to burst out of my chest. I felt a sense of panic begin to approach. But then, just like that, it was gone. I felt confident and really full of energy. It was as if there was nothing I couldn't do.

Before I knew it, I was chattering away a mile a minute. Ruben was laughing his head off. Just like that, Ruben had become my teacher and I had become his willing student.

"Come on," he said to me, leading me to the living room where he opened a bottle of red wine. We drank and laughed and talked and snorted coke until about three in the morning. I knew Zeizel would be worried.

I looked at my watch. "Ruben, you think it's okay if I got going...."

He waved my protest away. "Vidal, this is the best time to keep going. But leave if you must. I'll call a friend and she'll come up to keep me busy."

"Thanks, Ruben," I said. "For everything."

"Take the Seville," he told me. "I don't like you driving around in that Dodge. Come and get me tomorrow." Then, before I left, he went over to one of his drawers and took out five thousand dollars. "Here," he said, handing it to me. "Get yourself four or five suits and some shoes. Go over to Garcia Designs. Tell him I sent you. On me, my friend."

"I can't...." I tried to protest. But he insisted. I had no choice but to take the money.

"I'll see you at three tomorrow."

Something inside me told me that I shouldn't take the money. A voice was warning me to leave and not come back. But I was too high, and feeling too good, even though I knew that I had reached a crossroads and that I had to make a choice about which direction to travel in my life.

I couldn't make the right choice. I couldn't walk out on the life that Ruben made possible for me. My addiction to the prospect of a good life wouldn't loosen its grip on me. The child in me was too impressed with the "candy store" Ruben was showing me. I couldn't say no. Yes, Ruben had become my teacher. But I had become the all-too-willing student.

Chapter Six

Driving home, I suffered my first real bout of paranoia. I was jumpy and nervous. How was I going to explain my late arrival to Zeizel? I couldn't tell her the truth! I couldn't do that.

Just as I expected, Zeizel was up at three-thirty, waiting for me. "Where the hell have you been?" she demanded. She was more than a little angry and the smell of alcohol on my breath more than gave me away. "You have a lot of nerve leaving me here until the middle of the night without telling me where you are...."

"Hey, hey," I said, trying to calm her down. "Everything's okay." "No, it's not!" she screamed.

"I was with Ruben," I told her.

"Yeah, out drinking, not out working!"

"Here," I told her, bringing out the five thousand dollars and dropping the bills on the bed.

"Oh my God," she said, staring at the money. Nothing calmed her down like seeing all that money. No amount of excuses or begging for forgiveness could have done that.

"There's five thousand dollars there. Ruben wants me to get some clothes. But I'll tell you what, I'll give you a thousand dollars for you to buy what you want and I'll spend the rest on myself."

Zeizel liked having no money even less than I did and all that money was a great persuader. We both calmed down enough to get some sleep. The next day, we headed for Garcia Designs to do some serious shopping—something neither of us had ever done.

I bought four suits and three pairs of lizard-skin shoes. Zeizel bought several dresses that she was planning on fitting into after the baby was born. Looking at the dresses and remembering what she looked like before she got pregnant...she made some very good choices.

I never told Zeizel about the drugs or where Ruben made all that money. I wasn't proud of that and I didn't feel comfortable telling her—or anyone—else about it.

Not too long after that, I went to Ruben's apartment. When I arrived, I found him there with El Gallo. El Gallo was about thirty-nine years old, he had a huge black mustache and stood about five foot seven and was a solid one-seventy. He was well dressed and had plenty of jewelry on him he looked like a million bucks.

When I walked in, they were standing in the kitchen. On the table were fifteen kilos of cocaine and another two of heroin. I looked at the two of them and then at the table. Then I looked at Ruben again. This was some very serious shit. I knew it and they knew that I knew it.

"Vidal, this is my friend El Gallo," Ruben said, introducing me to El Gallo.

El Gallo extended his hand. "I've heard a lot of good things about you," he said simply.

"Nice to meet you," I said. Then I sort of faded into the background, which is what Ruben preferred I do when he was discussing business with someone. He liked that I was close by but not right on top of the discussion.

They were discussing the value of the drugs on the table as well as the relative quality of the drugs coming in from different parts of Colombia.

"The horse from Lebanon is selling for $100,000 a kilo," El Gallo said. "It's pure, heroine though."

"La Cocaina"The cocaine is going for $30,000 a kilo," Ruben observed. They were talking about sums of money that, until a few short weeks before, had been unimaginable to me.

Then Ruben brought out two briefcases filled with large bills and laid them out in front of El Gallo. I couldn't help but draw a quick breath. It was an unbelievable amount of money. I was watching the scene unfold like I was watching it in a movie or something. My heart was pounding. Part of me was as scared as I'd ever been. I knew exactly what was going down and I knew exactly what was wrong with it. But a bigger part of me looked at these two men and wanted nothing more than to be just like them. I wanted to make these kinds of deals. I wanted to be able to deal in tens of thousands of dollars like it was nothing. I wanted to walk large in the world occupied by these two men.

And, step by step, I was getting there. Ruben had already given me a .45 automatic. At first, I balked at accepting it.

"I can't carry a gun," I told him.

"You're going to have to," he said.

"But..."

"Look, Vidal, everyone knows you're with me. That makes it important that you're protected the same as me."

Reluctantly, I took the gun.

I was a member of the club now. No doubt about it. But no matter what my reservations, I was too drawn to the lifestyle, to the money, to the clothes and the cars. I wanted to live that life. And I was willing to ignore the danger and the fact that what was being done to get that money was wrong.

On April 1, 1982, Zeizel gave birth to our baby, a little girl. Erica was beautiful at seven pounds and fourteen ounces. When I gazed at this little miracle squirming around in the maternity ward, I gave thanks to God for wonderful miracles. I thanked God for the good things that He had brought to my life.

I was balancing two things in my life—the miracle of life and the desire to live a life of riches and comfort. And there were times when these two things were in conflict. Looking at my beautiful daughter,

I swore I would give her all the things that I never had as a child. That meant that I could not walk away from my new life. Yet, seeing the purity of God's miracles when I looked at Erica, I felt the desire to break with my new life and to live a pure, loving life dedicated to her and to other miracles.

But I was young and inexperienced. I wanted things more than I appreciated things. The pull of money was too great. I could not resist it. I had lived with too little for too long, hungering for a life of riches and comfort. Now that it was within my grasp, I could not turn my back on it. And I would not.

I continued to work for Ruben. Over time, my role changed. I had begun as a driver, a chauffeur. However, over time, I became something more essential to him. I became his bodyguard. I was the one who watched his back when he walked around with suitcases filled with cash or with parcels filled with drugs. I was his eyes and ears.

My .45 automatic had become my American Express card, too. I never went anywhere without it.

Protecting Ruben included shaking down the people who hadn't come up with money they owed him on drug deals. My life was a weekly routine of fighting, beatings, and threats. I became numb to the sight of people begging me not to kill them. It didn't matter to me what I did or said. I had a job to do and I did it well.

Playing this role was not difficult for me. I had never been a calm, peaceful man. I grew up in an angry, violent household. It is only now, as I've gotten older and come to understand the value of my faith and God's love, that I've become more peaceful. Then, I was full of the same anger and resentment that had filled my emotions for as long as I could remember.

I was a raging bull because it had been the only way to survive in the world where I grew up. My cocaine use only exaggerated these violent tendencies. I was oblivious to "quiet respect." I wanted the kind of respect that made strong men shake with fear when they saw me coming.

The truth about cocaine is that it can turn anyone into a bully. Me, I had a head start. I came to be like Ruben. When I was high, no one was able to stop me. No one could stop me. My responsibilities as Ruben's bodyguard only added to that sense. I had to cut a wide perimeter around him to keep him safe, and I did that as roughly as I needed to.

"Hey, Vidal, you have to calm down," Ruben once told me, even though he took pride in my willingness to jump into every fight and stand down every man. I would never turn my back on a fight or a challenge, real or perceived.

Maybe I was just trying to prove to Ruben and his crowd—and to myself—that I was good enough to walk the same streets as them, that I deserved a piece of what they had. To do that, I had to show them I was tough, that I was quick with my hands, and that I had no fear.

It didn't take long for my reputation to take hold in the bars and after-hours clubs that crowded the streets of Ruben's territory. I was not a man to be taken lightly. Vidal, they said, don't F—- with him. He's crazy.

Maybe I was becoming crazy and even willing to jump in front of a bullet for Ruben.

Chapter Seven

There was one day that I remember. It was a lazy, sunny day. It was about three in the afternoon and me and Ruben were relaxing at his usual spot in the bar, having a drink.

"It doesn't get much better than this, eh, Vidal?" he observed, looking like a man who had the world on a string.

I was just about to agree when, out of the corner of my eye, I saw three men coming over to us. I immediately tensed, ready for anything. Ruben sensed my sudden alertness and became more alert himself.

"Gentlemen," he said when the three men came over. They nodded to him and introduced themselves as Carlos, Tony, and Lazaro. They were from Havana.

"Havana, huh?" Ruben said.

"Gustavo sent us up here for his money," Carlos said, looking directly at Ruben. "So we're here for the money."

Ruben straightened up. I could see a tenseness in the muscles of his face. "Hey, no one is going to rush me...."

Carlos cut him off. "F—- you. You'd better have that money or we'll be rushing you in your coffin. You got that?"

My hand went towards my gun. So did the hands of the men with Carlos. Ruben picked up his drink and feigned like he was going to take a drink from it but then he slammed it against Carlos' face. I took that to be my cue. I swung my leg around and nailed one of the others in the balls. At the same time, I was throwing punches at the third guy.

Like that, I had knocked the two other Cubans to the floor. One of their guns slid out across the floor. I drew my own .45. "Don't move!" As I kept my eye on these two, I threw an elbow at Carlos, knocking him off balance. He stumbled and then fell to the floor as well. With all three of them on the floor, I moved over and picked up the gun. Then I took each of their guns from their pockets.

"I said don't move, mother—-ers!" I shouted at them, kicking Carlos in the leg. I continued to watch them like a hawk. Meanwhile, all around us all hell had broken loose in the bar. Chairs were flying. The barmaid was screaming.

"Kill them!" Ruben yelled. "Kill them now, Vidal!" He reached over across me and tried to grab one of the guns I'd taken from them. But I stopped him and moved him away.

"Ruben," I said, trying to calm him down. "Ruben, calm yourself." But he was out of control and he only wanted blood. "Ruben, please. No more blood today," I said firmly, like I was telling him instead of asking him. I wasn't sure how he'd react to my words. Until that moment, our roles had been clearly defined. I did what I was told and I did it well. But now I was crossing a line. I was telling him what to do—and what not to do. But I didn't see that I had a choice. Killing three guys in broad daylight in a crowded bar was more trouble than anyone needed.

"Come on, boss," I said. "It's over. Let it go."

"Yeah, sure. Yeah," Ruben said, relaxing his muscles.

The three Cubans clambered to their feet and grabbed towels. They wiped off their faces and then slunk out of the bar.

"Well, that was interesting," I joked as me and Ruben cleaned ourselves up.

Leiva straightened up the bar. When things were a little bit closer to normal, Leiva brought us over some fresh drinks.

Ruben was a little calmer. He lifted up the glass of Sambuca that Leiva had brought over and he raised it toward me. "Salud," he said. "Salud," I replied, lifting my own drink.

Then Ruben began to laugh. "Shit, you're good with those hands, Vidal," he said, shaking his head. "Thanks. Now we can celebrate." "Celebrate? Ruben, you owe those guys $300,000!"

Ruben laughed harder. "Don't worry about that, Robert. I've got the money."

We kept drinking and snorting coke until ten o'clock or so. Ruben had found us two pretty women and it wasn't long before the fight was far from my thoughts. Still, in the back of my mind I knew there would be problems. No one likes to be humiliated, and we humiliated those Cubans. They were thinking of revenge, no doubt about it. How could I have known that their vengeance would be so sweet for them...or that it would come about so soon?

At about eleven o'clock, I told Ruben that I was heading home. "A couple more drinks," he said.

I shook my head. "I have to get home to Zeizel and the baby," I told him. "Beep me if you need me or if there's any sign of trouble."

On my way home, I stopped at a quiet little bar and downed a couple of shots of Sambuca to calm myself before going home. I was thinking of the fight again and I didn't want it in my mind when I got home.

As I drove home, I kept glancing in my rear-view mirror. I had the feeling I was being followed but I couldn't be sure. "Robert, you're being paranoid," I told myself. "It's the coke."

Still, I drove home a roundabout way and made sure there was no one behind me by the time I pulled up to Zeizel's mother's house and our basement apartment. I was still on edge as I walked down the dark hallway to the entrance to the apartment. I had my hand on my .45, ready for anything. Of course, my gun wasn't going to help me against my own wife's anger.

When I walked in, Zeizel was there to give me the once over, sniffing me for perfume and checking my collar for signs of lipstick.

"Come on, Zeizel, I wasn't fooling around with anyone," I told her.

Then she saw the blood on my white suit and completely fell apart. "Robert," she cried, "I can't live like this anymore. One of these nights, you won't come home at all! I want it like it was."

"What?"

"I'd rather be poor and happy with you by my side...."

"You'd rather be poor and worrying about every bill getting paid?" I challenged her.

"Yes. You have a responsibility to me and Erica, Robert. We never see you. When you come home, you stink of liquor and good times or...or...or you have blood all over you!"

All Zeizel's complaining did was annoy me. I had made my decision. I wasn't changing my life. Her bitching only added pressure and that made coming home just one more thing that I wanted to avoid. Coming home began to be more and more like getting hung up with the ways "things used to be." And while I vaguely remembered the joy that Zeizel and I shared when we first got together, I remembered the pressure and stress of no money a lot more. I remembered what it was like to have to decide which bills to pay and which bills to hold off on. I remembered what it was like to walk out of a low-paying job and stare at the parking spot where my car used to be, knowing that along with my car I'd lost the tools that would let me do any amount of honest work. All honest work had gotten me was pressure and failure. I didn't want to be a failure anymore. I refused to be a failure anymore.

Listening to Zeizel bitching and whining made me feel like that old failure again and I had already decided to leave that life behind. That was over. I had cast my lot with Ruben. I wasn't going back. Not for anyone or anything. I had gotten into the mindset that Zeizel had nothing to complain about. After all, I was providing food, money, and material things for her and Erica. What did she have to complain about? I was more than fulfilling my duties.

"I'm a working man!" I shouted at her. "Just be grateful that I'm able to give you the things that you want."

Zeizel backed away, crying, which is what she did most times after we'd argued. She came at me all fire and anger, but she'd end up crying and feeling beaten. That didn't make me feel good but it made me feel as though I'd made my point.

But this night, as I went to shower, a dark thought clung to me. That fight at the Costa Brava was not like other fights. Those Cubans weren't like other guys I'd had to shake down or beat up. They were serious players and I couldn't shake the thought that by fighting that night, I had carelessly endangered the lives of Zeizel and Erica as well as my own.

"Lord, just keep things quiet," I prayed as the hot water of the shower sprayed down over me.

When I came out and dried off, I said I was sorry to Zeizel. "Come on, there's no reason to fight," I told her.

We watched television for a while together. Then, at about two-thirty in the morning, Zeizel sat up. "What was that?"

"Huh? What was what?"

"I heard something by the door."

I listened but I didn't hear anything. She settled down but then, a few moments later, she said she heard something again.

"It's nothing," I told her, trying to convince myself at the same time I was trying to convince her.

Just then, an empty milk container fell from the top of the garbage can that was leaning against the door leading to our kitchen. I leaped up and reached under the bed, aiming at the door.

They were there, all three of them. They had handguns with what looked like silencers on the barrels. I fired my rifle blindly, hoping to scare them more than hit them. Still, I think I hit one of them in the chest.

The shots woke up Erica. She began to cry. Beside me in our bed, my wife was shaking and crying hysterically. 1 was filled with fear as well. 1 got up and saw the men run and jump the backyard fence.

"Come on!" I shouted at Zeizel.

As she tried to gather herself and get out of bed, I ran to Erica's room. I carried her back to Zeizel and put her in her arms. "Take her upstairs," I ordered her. When Zeizel didn't move, I shouted, "Now!" Then I reached for my .357 magnum and my shotgun and headed to the door.

I saw all the lights going on in the neighboring apartments. I could hear my wife's parents hurrying to our apartment.

I knew that even if I'd scared the men off this time, they'd be back. Not only to kill me. They now knew where my family lived. We were all in danger.

"Shit," I seethed to myself. My mind was crowded with fear and overwhelming guilt—a guilt that almost brought me to my knees. How could I have done this to my family? All I'd wanted was to provide for them and let them live a life I'd never been allowed to live. But now all I'd done was put them in danger.

I'd crossed a line. I knew it. And it seemed that all the things in my life that were good and sacred, that were pure and worthy were on the other, far side of the line. As much as I wanted to, I didn't believe that there was any way to cross that line again.

The piercing sound of approaching police sirens cleared my thinking. I quickly stuffed my guns into my sofa and then ran upstairs to head them off. Upstairs, I came face to face with my father-in-law who was shaking with fear and anger.

"Someone tried to break in," I told him. "I scared them off when I shot my rifle." It was the same explanation that I gave the police. "Dispatch said there'd been a shooting," the officer told me.

"These guys came to the door and I scared them off with an old rifle I keep around to protect my family...." Before I could finish, I overheard the news come over the police radio. A body had been found on Tonnelle Avenue, not far from the apartment.

At first the location didn't register with me. I knew Tonnelle Avenue well. In fact, Tonnelle Avenue was where I'd stopped on the way home for a couple of drinks.

"What a night," one of the cops said. "First a murder, and now we're here for reports of a shooting."

The radio cackled to life again. "We have an ID on the body... Ruben Perrone of Elizabeth, New Jersey..."

I could feel the color drain from my face. My knees got wobbly. "Hey, you okay?" the officer asked, seeing my reaction to the news. "You know this guy?"

In a weak and stupid reply, I said, "Yeah, he was like my brother." Without missing a beat, the officer called for the homicide squad to come and interview me.

"No," I said, protesting. "Can't it wait until the morning? too upset right now. And I have to worry about my family." I glanced back toward my in-law's apartment. "They're still upset by the break-in."

"Okay," they said. "Tomorrow morning."

After the police left, I knew it was time to tell Zeizel more than I'd already told her. I explained how I'd been the target of the shooting and that they were sure to be back to get me. As I talked, all I could hear was my little girl's crying and my in-laws trying to calm her down so she would go back to sleep. I began to cry too, realizing that all this was just the beginning. Nothing was going to be the same anymore.

I thought to myself how good Ruben had been to me. I knew he would want me to continue his business. As much as I grieved Ruben's murder, I wasn't thinking yet of avenging his death. I was suffering from regret too much to think about that. That would come with time. And I had an immediate concern—getting myself and my family out of danger.

I was a sitting duck. I knew I was next, and that after me was my family. I had to get those guys before they got me. The police would never be able to stop them. These guys were too good for the police. They operated under the radar. Protecting myself and my family was up to me. I wasn't sure I was up to it, but I also knew I didn't have the luxury of a choice. The consequences of my choices had landed on me. I might have felt as if I was in someone else's bad dream, but I was going to have to figure out a way to fight out of it.

For the next few days, I stayed close to home. I had to recuperate from the bar fight and from the death of Ruben. But then, when I felt I was as ready as I was going to be, I headed back to Newark, to the Royal Tavern.

Before I left, I showed my wife how to load the shotgun and how to fire it. Her hands shook as she tried to put the cartridge in, but I made her do it over and over until she could do it with her eyes closed. I didn't like the idea of teaching my wife to fire a gun—or that she might have to fire it—but I didn't see that I had a choice. There was no other way. I was still burdened by Ruben's murder.

I thought I had prepared myself for whatever was to come.

Ruben's brother sought me out at the Royal. "Let me know anything you hear about Ruben's murder," he told me. "I'm here to help you, Vidal. Anything you need me to do."

I told him what happened, leaving out some of the most important facts for the time being. I had gotten good at telling only parts of the story. I'd done the same thing with the homicide detectives the morning after Ruben's murder. I told them some things, but not everything. I had to straighten things out in my own mind first. And I sure as hell hadn't done that.

As much as I wanted to avenge Ruben's murder, I was determined to survive and to protect my family. I had to keep things simple for the time being. Bringing in others and their needs wouldn't aid my decision-making or my situation. Nor would it ease my grief over the loss of my friend and mentor—or my own fear of dying.

Ruben's funeral was like a bad B-movie. It was a parade of every dealer, crook, underground member of the drug world, and low-life as they came to pay their respects.

Needless to say, everyone was dressed to kill. The men wore somber expressions. In the background, there was the constant wailing of women. That is what I remember most from that day, that constant background noise of crying. It was like a mosquito hum. Always there, a sad soundtrack for a horrible day.

El Gallo made his entrance, accompanied by a full compliment of bodyguards. He was loaded and taking no chances. "Vidal, what the hell happened?" he asked me as he approached me.

I looked him directly in the eyes and started to explain what happened. As I did, I could see that he already knew everything—he knew about the fight, about who was involved, everything. I also knew that he was asking himself a question: why hadn't I killed the three men who killed Ruben and who tried to kill me when I had the chance?

"Vidal," El Gallo said in a voice rising above a whisper, "nobody kills my best distributor and gets away with it. I will have this taken care of."

I nodded. There was nothing I could say. El Gallo turned away. When he did, I felt angry and foolish. I should have taken care of the men that threatened my family and who killed Ruben. I knew what the next step was. But I wasn't ready to start murdering people.

I drew a deep breath and then turned and approached Ruben's coffin. I knelt down and gazed at his badly swollen body. As the tears rolled down my cheeks, I swore that I would make his killers pay. "I'll cover your back, Ruben," I promised him one last time.

A week passed after the funeral and I thought that enough time had gone by to allow things to cool down. I headed over to the Costa Brava. As soon as Leiva spotted me, he came hurrying over to me. "Jesus, Vidal," he said nervously, "you don't know what's it been like here. Cops all over the place, asking questions left and right. They're asking everyone all sorts of shit about you and Ruben."

"Have they asked about the fight?"

"I don't think they know about the fight yet," he said.

"Okay, that's good, Leiva. Just calm down, okay?"

"Look, Ruben left a package downstairs. If you don't take it, I'm just gonad put it in the garbage."

I put my hands on his shoulders and tried to calm him down. "Okay, Leiva. Calm down and show me this package."

He led me downstairs to the freezer. Leiva took out a shopping bag and handed it to me. "I gotta go back upstairs," he said, leaving me with the bag. I opened it and saw two football-shaped packages. I knew exactly what they were. Cocaine. Two kilos each.

I slit one of the packages open and could see how good it was. The beautiful shine of what looked to me to be Bolivian fish scales— meaning I had a pure form, A-quality coke. On the street, this would go for $58,000 a kilo.

I put the bags back in the freezer. Back upstairs, I asked Leiva if I could keep the package with him for another few days. When he hesitated, I asked him please. "Just until I find another spot for it."

"Yeah, I guess. Okay," he said.

I just needed it there until I decided what to do with it. I wasn't prepared to go into the cocaine business. I hadn't made the necessary arrangements. Hell, I hadn't even decided if I wanted to carry on with Ruben's business. I didn't want to rush into anything as important—and dangerous—as that. However, I wasn't going to have the luxury to consider my options.

The next day, when I returned to the tavern, one of Ruben's customers approached me. "Vidal, I have to get a half a kilo for one of my customers."

I shrugged. "What's that got to do with me?" I asked.

"Come on, man. This is important. I can't F—- around with this guy....

I was silent.

"Since Ruben was killed, the market's gone dry. My customers are screaming for coke. Come on, Vidal, you can help me, can't you?"

I drummed my fingers on the table. "Come back in forty-five minutes," I told him. "And bring the $30,000. I'll see what I can do."

"Thanks, Vidal," he said, genuinely grateful.

As soon as he was gone, 1 ran to Leiva's basement and poured out half a kilo into a large Ziploc baggie. Then I took it upstairs and hid it in the men's room.

When the guy returned, we went into the men's room and I let him sample the coke. It was still in rock form—pure, uncut.

"F—-," Pete said, after breaking some of the rock down to powder, "this is great stuff. You and I will be doing business again."

Pete left me with $30,000 in cash. I gave him my beeper number. When Pete was gone, I gave Leiva $5,000 for his trouble and so he would keep a special store of liquor for me in the basement.

I went out and purchased a triple-beam scale so I could weigh the drugs with accuracy. I also went into a grocery store to purchase some baggies. The decision to become a dealer hadn't been as difficult as I'd anticipated. Of course, having $25,000 in my pocket made the decision even easier. This was a tremendous inner feeling of power.

I was in business. Vidal the Newark NJ coke dealer had arrived.

Chapter Eight

The nature of dealing starts with establishing turf, protecting that turf, and then expanding it. In a lot of ways, it wasn't any different than any other business—except that it was illegal and violent, that is. 1 quickly expanded to another local bar, the Royal.

Some people might think that the bars wouldn't want the coke traffic coming in, that it would cause trouble with the law and stuff. But that wasn't the case at all. The bars loved it when I moved in. My business brought traffic and business to the bars. Big time.

Like any other successful and growing business, I took on more and more employees. In just a few weeks, I had a full staff of runners, selling coke in small quantities on the street.

Now this was living. In two months, I had made over $150,000, enough to let me buy a four-door Fleetwood Cadillac and move my family to a condominium in Secaucus, New Jersey. Zeizel felt safe again. And she loved not worrying about money.

Suddenly, there was more than enough for everything we wanted. And when the money is flowing in, no one asks too many questions. Every successful businessman needs his look. Those Wall Street guys, they have their Brooks Brothers suits and wing-tip shoes. That look would never work for a coke dealer. I bought myself a fourteen-ounce gold medallion to make it clear to anyone with eyes to see that I'd arrived.

Not so plain to the eyes was the arsenal I picked up as well: a nine millimeter, a .357 magnum, a .45 automatic, a .380, and a .32 caliber. I had more than an image to protect. I was an important and dangerous man, and that also made me a target. In addition to my personal arsenal, I now traveled with a small troop of men whose only job in the world was to watch my back.

I frequented the after-hours clubs in Manhattan. I was living large and loving it. I rented limos to take me into the city. Living large was fine and good but I had another I reason for traveling into the city. I was looking for Gustavo and his hired guns. I wanted to find them and hold them accountable for Ruben's death. This was professional and personal.

This one club had a long history of shootings and fights. When we arrived, the armed security men at the door patted us down.

"Hey, don't F—- with him," one of my guys said.

The guys at the door were respectful but unapologetic. "No disrespect, but rules is rules."

"Let it go," I told my guys. I knew the drill. Until I was known at the club, I had to be patted down like everyone else. That wasn't a problem. I could be patient.

Inside, we found a party scene hopping. My guys kept their eyes open but they also liked a scene. This one had it all. Drinks were ten bucks. A bottle of champagne, two hundred. A gram of coke, a Ben.

Even though coke was available in the club, most of the real players brought their own ounces with them. On this count, I was no exception. The difference between me and the other players was that I was handing out my goods like candy.

I wanted my presence known and felt and I knew how to do it. A gram here. A toot there. Hundred-dollar tips for the waiters and waitresses. Rounds of drinks for the whole club. Bottle after bottle of champagne. Shit like that got you noticed.

I wanted to be noticed. I wanted it all.

I know now that I also wanted to make up for the guilt I was feeling. Oh, I didn't know it then. I didn't give myself time to think about what I was doing to my family or my friends, or even myself. This wild ride was messing everyone up. I didn't want to face up to that, not then. I just wanted the rush. I wanted the party. And the power. So I did what most people who can't handle their guilt do: I overcompensated. I made myself the center of attention and I gave away everything I had.

Ask anyone from back then about me and they'd say, "Robert? Man, he was the most generous dude going." It was true, too. Except for those who crossed me, I couldn't give away enough. I was famous for my generosity.

You know, it's funny, but there's always something that eventually F—-s you up. And that something is usually the "good" thing that you try to do. That's what happened with me and generosity. That's what eventually led to some very bad things. Not that I would have changed anything. I always knew I was lucky. I didn't deserve what I had. So, it wasn't really mine, right? I figured I might as well give it away.

It wasn't long before my generosity got me noticed and respected. I became well known among the other drug dealers who came to the after-hours clubs. I was a big shot. Security didn't pat me down anymore when I came into a club. I was allowed to carry my weapon, and so were my guys. I had my own table and when people were in trouble, they made their way to my table. Just like in the Godfather movies. They came to me for help. They would have kissed my ring if I wanted them to.

One time, Mario, a Cuban refugee who dealt weed, came to me with a problem.

"What can I do for you, Mario?" I asked him, watching him closely.

He glanced over his shoulder a couple of times, showing the typical marijuana paranoia. His eyes were wide and his black hair was slicked back. "I got a problem, Robert," he said to me.

"What's that?" I asked, laughing softly. Of course he had a problem, that's why he'd come to me.

"When I came in here, I parked just outside," lie said, snapping his fingers. "You know my car, the LTD. Anyway, I parked it in a tow-away F—-ing zone...."

I started to chuckle. "And it got towed?"

"Yeah, but that's not the problem. I had a hundred and fifty pounds of weed in the trunk."

"What?"

"Yeah. I brought it by so I could let a customer sample it. When I went outside again, the F—-ing car was being towed. What am I going to do? I need to get the car back and I don't want to get jammed up."

No doubt about it, Mario had gotten himself in a jam. But I was feeling pretty good that night so I told him not to worry. "I'll take care of it," I told him.

"Serious? Oh man, you're the best...."

I waved his gratitude away. Like I said, I was feeling pretty good, like I could do anything.

A short time later, I gestured to one of the girls who were hanging around with me that night. "Let's go," I said. We left the club. As soon as I did and the night air hit me, I came down a bit. "Robert," I said to myself, "what kind of a fool are you, anyway?" I didn't know why I'd volunteered to help Mario out. What was worse, I didn't know how I was going to be able to help him. All I knew was that, having said I'd help him, I had no choice but to do it.

Dealers and criminals have a very strict honor code. Our word is all we've got to rely on. You tell someone you're going to do something, you do it. It's not like we can turn to the police or the courts to work something out. When someone goes back on his word, the only recourse is violence.

So, with or without my high, I knew I would have to follow through and take care of Mario's problem. Somehow. I had this girl drive me to the pound where the LTD would be held.

"Shit, there it is," I said, pointing to the LTD, still attached to the tow truck. "Pull over."

The girl pulled over and I jumped out of the car, running over to the tow truck driver. As I did, I was pulling the wad of bills from my pocket and peeling a couple of hundreds off.

"Oh man, thank God I caught up with you," I said to the driver. "Yeah, what you want?"

"Look, I really need that car back or my brother-in-law's gonna kill me," I said, acting scared so he'd believe I was really in a personal jam. "Your brother-in-law?" he asked suspiciously.

"Yeah, he let me borrow the car for the night. If he finds out I got it towed, I'm dead." I kept piling it on, but I could tell it didn't really matter. I'd made an in with this guy and he was eyeing the bills in my hand. "Look, take these," I said, pushing the hundreds at him. "Keep the change."

The driver didn't see any reason to have to go through the hassle of the paperwork involved, not when he was getting two hundred cash just to let the car go. So, ten minutes later, I was behind the wheel of Mario's LTD, driving it back to the club. When I got there, I parked it—in a private lot—and then sauntered back into the club.

"Hey, Robert's back!"

I waved to the cheer that went up. Mario came up to me and practically kissed my feet. "Man that was $270,000 worth of Mexican sinsemilla"

"Don't worry about it," I said. "It was nothing."

Suddenly, bottles of champagne were being passed around the club and glasses were being raised, toasting me and my courage in risking my own arrest. I laughed and waved away the praise, but deep down it made me happy. I had risked something. And everything had worked out fine. That wouldn't always be the case.

When I left the club later, Mario was by my side. We went over to his car. He carefully looked all around, then he popped the trunk and took out ten packages of marijuana, ten pounds, and he lifted them into my car. This was value at $25,000. That was my reward for my efforts. That and a lifelong friendship with Mario.

Chapter Nine

By late summer 1982, I was spending most of my evenings and early morning hours in the Ironbound section of Newark, in a place called Down Neck. It's a quiet and peaceful town, often visited by New Yorkers who come to the excellent Spanish and Portuguese restaurants. The food was good. The prices were reasonable. And you never had to worry about a safe place to park. The Newark police patrolled the area regularly.

I regularly took members of my crew to these restaurants so we could relax and enjoy a delicious meal. In addition to the restaurants, I patronized another local place, a bar called the Royal Tavern. Mostly, it was a quiet little bar. Go-go dancers. Topless. On an average day, only a handful of people in the place. But my presence there brought lots of paying customers—high school friends, neighborhood friends, and, of course, my coke-buying customers. Add them up, and they made for a good-sized crowd.

Joe Belo owned the place. He was in his mid-thirties and he loved me being around. He was a little guy, maybe a hundred and forty-five pounds. A good guy. He just loved how the crowd seemed to follow me into his bar.

After he'd gotten to know me for a while, he came up to me and asked me if I wanted to have a meeting.

"A meeting?"

He nodded. "Yeah. I got this Colombian connection. Powerful guy. A good source. This coke is really high quality. The best. 90% Pure."

I was quiet for a minute then I nodded my head. "Okay," I said. "Let's have a meeting." I might have sounded calm but I was really very anxious to meet this connection. Joe was a quiet guy and hearing him so enthusiastic about something made me very interested. He kept talking up the quality of the coke so much that I was like a little kid waiting to go to the circus.

Finally, the day of the meeting arrived. I had my stack of hundred dollar bills ready. I arrived at the bar and waited. It was eleven in the morning and I was sitting at the bar with my regular—Sambuca and Heineken. Since I had previously made myself a bad enemy, I kept myself at the back of the bar, with my Colt .45 tucked in the back of my belt.

As I waited, I glanced around the bar, making eye contact with my guys, who were stationed in strategic spots around the bar. I wasn't taking any chances. We were all armed and ready in case the slightest thing went south. I was waiting and tense. Carlos, Joe, Ralph, and Santos were occupied with their usual interest at the bar—watching the beautiful and near-naked go-go dancers on the stage.

Junior, the deejay, had the whole place hopping with his disco selections. Man, the place was packed. Joe Belo couldn't have been happier. My customers were flooding the bar. They were buying drinks and watching the girls dance. If it were up to them, they would buy some coke from me and then leave. But, as usual, I was buying rounds for the entire bar. Then they'd buy a second drink. It was all good.

Some of my friends from high school who snorted coke came in to say hello and get their free high. "Let me give you something for that," they'd say, starting to take out their wad of bills. But I'd wave them away. I wouldn't accept their money. What was a few hundred dollars to me over the course of the evening? Pennies. I was happy to hand out the free "samples."

People were dancing. The music was blaring. The lights were flashing. It was a real scene. Suddenly, the door to the bar opened and two Spanish-looking guys headed straight for Joe Belo.

"These must be them," I thought to myself as I acted nonchalant, sipping my Sambuca. I calmly watched Joe greet them and then escort them to a table in the back of the bar. Once they were seated, they huddled together in a hushed conversation. I didn't look directly at them but I watched them. Soon, I knew all three were looking right at me. Maybe Joe had pointed me out or maybe it was just the jewelry I was wearing. I had on my diamond-head watch, diamond and gold rings, and several thick, gold necklaces. My long-sleeved silk blue shirt was opened about three buttons down from the collar so that the chains would look right against my chest. Top that off with the white, lightweight summer dress suit jacket I was wearing to cover my handgun from view and I was the picture of a '80s coke dealer.

After a few more minutes, Joe waved over at me and motioned that I should come over to join them. I nodded to him, letting him know I'd be right there. As I made my way across the bar, I paused to whisper something to a couple of my guys.

"Stay sharp for any strange faces, got it? Watch out for any cars outside where someone's just sitting and waiting." Basically, I was just telling them to be alert in case any shit was going to go down.

At the table, Joe took care of the introductions. I shook hands with Paco and Julio.

"Joe talks highly of your ability to sell large quantities to a lot of dealers," Paco said, getting right down to business. "That is why we're interested in giving you the coke."

I shrugged. "I do all right, you know."

Joe chuckled. "All right? He's the best there is."

"Yeah, okay," I said, mostly wanting to quiet Joe down. This was business. I didn't need to work on bragging rights or anything.

After that, we got down to the details of the arrangements. Then we shook hands and agreed to meet the following day.

Right on time, Paco and Julio arrived with kilo quantities of rock cocaine known as "Mother Pearl." It got its name because of its beige color, fish scale quality. Mother Pearl was about 95% pure. My customers were going to love this shit. It would sell like cold beer at a ball game in July.

At the bar, Joe and I were stacking up hundred-dollar bills like a housewife with five little kids stacks laundry. As we counted out the money, I kept my eyes open for strangers and undercover cops. I was constantly on guard for cops and informants. In just a few short months, the name Vidal had become very popular in the area. My generosity had become almost legendary. Everyone knew that if you were in a bind with your rent or behind with a bill, I would help you— if you were someone trustworthy who was all right with me. I was generous with my money and I was generous with my coke. When I did collect money for the coke, I asked fair prices and provided good quality product. These things added to my good reputation on the street.

I made my real money by selling large quantities of coke known as "eighths" or eight-balls. An eighth is 4.5 ounces of cocaine. In '82, an eight-ball was going for about eighty-five hundred dollars. After adding about five ounces of Manitol to give it a little extra heft, I was making a little more than eighteen thousand dollars a kilo.

With profits like that to be made, I wasn't the only one dealing in the area. There was plenty of competition from others who could also provide good product and wanted to make money as much as I did. There were always turf battles and violence.

One of my suppliers was a guy in Miami known as El Gallo. He was a big kingpin who ran a vast distribution network of coke, heroin, marijuana, and Quaaludes. The Azulejos Brothers served as El Gallo's chauffeurs and bodyguards and they never left his side. Their name meant "Blues Brothers" and they were very popular in the coke trade. They were part of the family.

When you were a player, you had to look the part. That meant expensive jewelry, luxury cars, and good-looking women. At the time, I owned eight cars. I also wore the most elegantly tailored suits. Things were only getting better.

After meeting Julio and Paco, I began moving their product. They were thrilled at how much I was selling for them. The two of them began spending more and more time at the Royal. It seemed that they enjoyed the pretty girls.

There is one sound that a dealer knows so well that he hears it in his sleep and that is the beep, beep, beep of his beeper. That is how people get in touch with him. That is the music that accompanies him all day. My beeper had become part of my daily life. Not an hour went by without me receiving an electronic beep.

I was at home relaxing when the familiar beep, beep, beep disturbed me. "Damn," I said, glancing at the number on the beeper display. Victor Fresolone, one of my regulars. Victor was an Italian guy. He was in his late thirties at the time and owned two companies. At six foot and 185 pounds, he was an imposing presence, what with his thick, black hair. Victor had a brother who was connected with an Italian crime family. All these things added up to Victor being a man to respect.

I went to the phone and then I dialed Victor's number.

"Hey, Vidal, what took you so long?"

"Well, Victor," I said, speaking slowly and evenly, "you see, it's like this. I don't like to rush when I'm doing two things—eating or making love. It happened that I was having a little snack when you beeped, so this better be important. What's up?"

"I just wanted to remind you that I'm coming over to the Royal with the Italian man from North Newark in about an hour. Remember, the meeting we talked about last week?"

"Oh yeah, right," I said. "Okay, okay. No problem. I'll be there. We'll talk."

"Good," he said.

When I hung up, I took a hot shower and then went to my closet wrapped in my towel. 1 opened the closet door and I stood there, transfixed like some people are transfixed before an altar. Row after row of hand-tailored, double-breasted suits greeted me. Along the floor was line after line of leather shoes and cowboy boots, Italian loafers and tie-up shoes. I had more shoes than most high-priced shoe salons along Rodeo Drive in Beverly Hills.

"Damn," I sighed to myself.

Less than a year earlier, I didn't have a suit to my name or the money to buy one. Now, I had a cookie jar filled to the top with stacks of bills, each stack containing five thousand dollars. Thousands and thousands of dollars. Only a year ago, I couldn't afford to get my car fixed. And now?

After I dressed, I took a couple thousand dollars from the cookie jar—pocket money. Then I reached into the kitchen cabinet and took out my .38 automatic pistol and double-checked the clip. I took twelve extra rounds from the ammunition box that was next to the gun in the cabinet in case of anything unexpected.

Living the life I was living, that was a reflex. Plan for the unexpected and the unrepentantly violent. Some guys buy insurance policies. My insurance was strapped to my body.

I loaded my neck with gold chains, put on a few rings and a diamond-encrusted gold watch, and then I was ready. I was snapping my fingers, getting into the mood. I walked around the room but then I suddenly stopped.

Something was wrong, really wrong.

I walked through all the rooms of the luxurious condo, looking at all the beautiful things my drug money had bought for me and my family, and I knew that something was missing.

I went back into the kitchen and looked at the cabinets. I had guns in the cabinets where there should have been nothing more than plates and glasses. I had guns hidden all around the house. Everywhere. Just in case.

I had it all. Except security. There was no security and no insurance. Just cash and danger.

The men who had killed Reuben and who had tried to kill me... they weren't going away. And even if they did, there would be others to take their place. And if it wasn't them, then it would be the police. Corrupt or honest, the police were always a danger to a dealer.

These were the things that I had to think about all the time, waking or asleep. The odds were not in my favor. I knew that. I knew that as well as I knew anything, but I couldn't turn my back on this life. The money. The power. The ability to do things and have things that were only dreams before. It makes it all seem worth it. While you're on top, you don't realize that all the money and power and things are just slow-acting poison, killing you from the inside even as the people are threatening to do the same from the outside. Few made it out alive. Fewer still made it out unscathed.

I shook my head. What was I doing? But then I glanced at my watch. I didn't have time to think too much. I had a meeting. I had to get to the Royal, my "office."

As soon as I got there, I could see that it was going to be a wild night. The place was already packed and it was only six o'clock. As I walked in, I looked over at the dancers.

One of them I hadn't seen before caught my eye. I felt my mouth go dry. My heart started to pound. I'd been with a lot of beautiful women but this five-foot-ten-inch goddess with blonde hair and beautiful brown eyes was something else. On a scale of one to ten, ten didn't come close. As soon as I saw her, I knew I wanted her. No, I needed her.

As soon as she came off the stage, I motioned her over to me. When she came over, I asked her what her name was.

"Juliana," she said.

"Well, Juliana, my name's Robert Vidal." The whole time I was staring into her beautiful eyes and I couldn't believe how incredible she looked. "You and me will be talking some more later."

She smiled. "I'd like that," she said simply.

As she walked away, I shook my head and muttered to myself over and over about what a body she had.

After she'd disappeared into the crowd and backstage, I went up to the bar and ordered drinks for everyone—not just my friends, everyone in the entire bar. I was feeling that good. Then I made my way to the back corner of the bar and stood with several of my friends.

As the minutes passed, more and more people gathered around me. I was like the candy man, ready to give out the candy to all the little children. Everyone was happy, laughing, and having a good time. I was laughing, too, but in the back of my mind, I remembered that I was there for business.

A little later, Victor walked in with a short man, about five-seven. The guy looked to be in his late forties. Along with them was another man, this one bigger. About six-two and two hundred and twenty pounds.

"Darling," I said to the barmaid. "You see those three men?"

She turned and looked. "Yeah."

"Go serve them whatever they want and put it on my tab."

The three men accepted the offer with a casual nod in my direction, acknowledging that they knew who had extended the gesture. When the drinks arrived, they raised their glasses in the air in my direction. Salud.

As they sipped their drinks, I motioned for one of my guys to take a position in the corner near the exit. After he had discretely moved over, I walked over to the table where Victor and his friends were enjoying the drinks I'd sent over.

"Robert," Victor said, extending his hand to me. "I want you to meet a couple of friends of mine." He introduced me to Sam, the older, shorter guy, and then Bobby Fosseli, the younger guy.

We ordered a fresh round of drinks and then got down to business. "Look," I said, taking control of the meeting right away. "As a rule, I don't deal with people I don't know but Victor says you guys are okay and that's good enough for me, so let's talk."

They were quiet for a second and then Sam spoke. "Well, Vidal, I'm looking for a sample today. An ounce, say. Victor says you get good stuff. So, how much for the ounce?"

I didn't have to do the calculations. I knew the price. "Street price for an ounce is $2,400. You come to me with good credentials. I'll let you have an ounce for $1,800. Almost all rock. Hardly any powder." I could see from the look in their eyes that I had made them an offer that they would find hard to say no to.

Most people who buy coke prefer to buy it in rock form. Rock form assures them of higher purity. The powdered form can be cut too easily.

"Think about it," I told them, getting up. "I'll be back in a few minutes."

Nonchalantly, I made my way toward the door. As I passed my guys, I reminded them to keep their eyes open. "Be on your toes," I told them.

Then I went into the basement of the bar to where I kept my stash. I took out a kilo of coke, carefully weighed out an ounce, bagged it, and put it in my pocket. I made sure the coast was clear and then I went back up from the basement to the bar. I knew how good the stuff was. The bag looked like it contained diamonds. They'd be impressed. I wasn't worried about that.

"Everything okay?" I asked my guys as I passed them.

"No change," they reported back.

I nodded. Things seemed to be all right. I continued to the table. As I sat down, I passed the package over to Sam.

He let out a low whistle after examining it. "Vidal, if you can guarantee this quality at these prices, I can guarantee you a steady customer." "That's good," I said, remaining noncommittal for now.

A minute later, Bobby said he had to take a leak. When he came back, I could tell from the look on his face that he'd inhaled a few blows while he was in the bathroom. He slipped back into the booth. Then he ordered me another drink.

As we waited for the drink, he leaned toward me and delivered a blockbuster. "By the way, Vidal, I have a cousin you might have heard of. Campizi."

I could feel the muscles in my neck tighten. Victor hadn't given me a clue that these guys were part of the Campizi family.

"Anyway," Bobby went on, "Sam says we'll be back. Right now we have to clean up in North Newark."

I walked to the door and watched Sam as he drove off. Sitting shotgun in his car was his German shepherd. Bobby followed close behind in his white '84 Camaro.

As they drove around the corner, I could feel the tenseness leave my muscles. Finally, business was over and I could relax a little. Immediately, Juliana's image came into my mind. "What a damn body she's got on her," I whispered to myself.

When I came back into the bar, I could see that two of the other girls were dancing. That meant that Juliana was free. Now was the time to make my move.

She was standing near the bar, comfortable in her bikini bottom overflowing with five, ten, and twenty-dollar bills. She watched me walking toward her. I could see her looking at my jewelry. I didn't come right up to her, though. I went to the bar instead and ordered a drink as well as some drinks for my friends.

I reached into my pocket and pulled out two hundred-dollar bills. Moving the bills slowly, I allowed her to watch them. Then, looking directly into her eyes, I could see them register surprise as I held them out to her.

"Don't you tease me like that," she said in one of the sweetest voices I've ever heard.

"I'm not teasing," I said.

"You're playing with me," she said.

I shook my head. "Keep the money," I told her. "I liked the way you danced."

She took the money and put it in her bikini, near her private parts. She flashed that dazzling smile at me every time she looked in the direction of the group I was standing with.

A short time later, she was up to dance again. Every eye in the place was riveted on her sinuous, sensuous movement. But she had eyes for only one person there—me.

As soon as she finished her dance, she walked through the bar, cutting through the crowd like a hot knife in soft butter. She came right to where I was sitting and took the seat next to me. She leaned over and wrapped her long arms around my neck and then she planted a lingering kiss on my cheek. "Thank you," she said again.

I had been with hundreds of women, but this one, sitting next to me in that scant little bikini, was driving me wild. She kept an arm loosely draped over my shoulder as we continued to talk. It took a few minutes, but she eventually came to the question I knew she was dying to ask. "By the way, Robert, what do you do for a living that you can wear such expensive jewelry and give me a couple hundred dollars without batting an eye? Not to mention buy drinks for the bar."

I smiled. "Well, Juliana, it's like this. I sell used cars. I'm a used car salesman. And I have my own car-cleaning business."

She hung on my every word like it came from on high. But me, I couldn't keep my eyes from roving up and down her long, pretty legs and her shapely body. I tried to be cool about it. I didn't want to be too obvious.

She kept leaning over and kissing my cheek, thanking me over and over for the generous tip. We kept drinking and talking.

"So, you got a ride back to New York?"

She smiled.

"Because if you don't, I'd be more than happy to take you."

She said she didn't have a ride and that she'd love to accept my offer.

By the end of the night, we'd become more than a little friendly with one another. I waited until she finished her last dance and then I led her into my private office where we shared several long and passionate kisses. No more pecks on the cheek for me, no matter how affectionate. We ended up at the closest Holiday Inn.

In addition to drugs and drink, sexual adventure had become a fixture in my life. Beautiful young women were always hanging around. But Juliana was something more, something special. After that night, she had become something to remember.

Crazy thing was, even after getting my socks knocked off by Juliana, when I was back at the bar the next day, I was eyeing another woman. This time, it was a young lady named Jackie. I don't know why, but I found myself attracted to her. She was very different from the other women I'd met. Very quiet. Very cute.

She was the daughter of Jimmy Fresco, a member of the very large and popular Italian family from Newark. Jackie was to become a very close friend to me in the coming years. We endured and stayed together through things that would have tare most people far apart. But at the age of nineteen, she was unaware of the dangers that lay ahead. We were both young and had little idea of what was to come.

Chapter Ten

After collecting drug money and spending time with my friends and associates, I cleared my head and turned my attention to watching my back. Caution was the watchword when it was time to return home to my lovely wife and child. I wanted there to be a clean line between work and home. No way I ever wanted to put either of them in danger again.

But it was as hard to put a physical boundary around who I was as it was to put a spiritual boundary around my soul. How could I be who I was in the clubs and think I could be a different person at home? But I tried.

Driving home, I took the back roads and truck routes, Route 1 and 9, through Jersey City on my way home to Secaucus. I avoided the New Jersey Turnpike like the plague. That stretch of road is probably the most heavily patrolled stretch of road in the world. The New Jersey State Police will pull you over for anything—driving ten miles above the limit.

One of the last things I needed was for one of them to get suspicious of my car and pull me over. Hell, I had guns and large amounts of cash in the car with me. They'd put two and two together fast enough. The state police were well known—and feared—for busting people after pulling them over for doing nothing wrong.

So I was on the back roads, three-thirty in the morning, liquor on my breath, still high as the proverbial Georgia thanks to that good coke. My eyes were on the rear-view mirror as much as they were on the road ahead, always looking. Looking, looking. I worried about being pulled over by the police, but the police were hardly my greatest enemy. Even with my home in sight, I couldn't afford to let down my guard. If anything, I tensed up. So close to home, I didn't want anything to go wrong. This was my home. My wife and kid were here asleep. Whatever else might happen, I had to keep them safe.

"Damn," I whispered to myself as I pulled up to the condominium. Zeizel had parked her car in the spot in the front of the building. That meant that I had to pull my four-door, burgundy Fleetwood into the back lot. I eased the car around the corner of the building and into the larger lot out back. I pulled slowly into an available spot and turned off the engine. Then I sighed a deep sigh.

Everything seemed to be alive and electric. My eyes were sharp, looking around the parking area. My ears seemed to hear every-thing—the creaking of the parked cars in the early morning breeze. I hated parking in the back. The tall grass in the back offered great concealment if anyone was planning an ambush.

What was that? I turned quickly. It was nothing. But my nerves were too much on edge. A cat moving through the grass had me reaching for my gun. As I locked my car, I scanned the cars parked all around me. The back parking lot was where the visitors to the condos parked, so there were always unfamiliar cars back here.

I scanned back and forth, over and over. I wasn't going to take any chances. The coke in my system had sharpened my senses. I felt I could hear the slightest sound or movement.

As I walked toward the building, I had my .38 snub nose palmed in my hand. My .380 automatic was tucked comfortably and reassur-ingly against the small of my back. My shoes crushed the gravel in the back, making a noise that would have alerted any would-be attacker.

I tried to walk even lighter on my feet. Every few steps, I stopped and listened to see if anyone was following me.

My heart was pounding by the time I made it inside my condo. I locked the door behind me and then waited for a moment, allowing my eyes to adjust to the change in lighting. Then, moving stealthily like a cat, I made my way through the house, checking every room and window. I opened every closet door and pushed back every drape.

With my fingertips, I pushed open the door to my daughter's room. I felt a rush of relief and emotion as I stepped into the room. Relief that there was no danger there, but also incredible guilt as I came over and looked down at my beautiful daughter sleeping so peacefully in her crib.

Erica was only seven months old. Sleeping there under her little blanket, she looked like an angel with her tiny hands still holding her tiny cloth bear.

"What's the matter with me?" I wondered. "What kind of a man lives a life that puts such a blessed child in danger? Not a man, an animal!" I felt so guilty then, so filled with remorse. I had provided so much for my daughter but all of it could be taken in the blink of a violent eye.

When I went into my bedroom and looked down at my wife sleeping soundly, my guilt intensified. She looked like a beautiful lost angel alone in our king-sized bed. I shook my head and turned away. What was the matter with me? Here I had a beautiful wife and daughter at home and I was out every night, dealing and partying. I was having affairs left and right, never giving a thought to my wife or her feelings. I was spending money like water out of a spigot.

I spent hours in bars and after-hours clubs. How much time had I spent with my family? With the ones I truly loved and who loved me? Out there, people liked being with me because I was the party—I had the money, the coke, the energy. In here, they loved me because of who I was. But who was I?

I went over to the mirror and stared at my reflection. I shook my head in amazement and disgust. I had enough jewelry on to feed a family for a week. I was still holding a gun in my hand. I had another in my belt. I had guns hidden all around the house. That made sense. I didn't want to be caught anywhere in my house should an enemy show up. But what in what danger did my "protection" put my family?

In the pursuit of money, power, and a good time, I had created a life that put my wife and child in constant danger. Drug dealers weren't like the Old World organized crime padrons. These guys did not respect "civilians." They'd harm my wife and daughter without so much as a second thought.

To rival dealers, my family was my Achilles' heel. They were where I was vulnerable. If they really wanted to get to me, they'd get to me through my family.

"My God," I thought, turning from the unfamiliar image looking back at me from the mirror, "what have I done?" All I'd thought about was the things I'd given them—the cars, the jewels, the clothes. I'd moved them into a magnificent home filled with new furniture. I'd given them everything money could buy. What I hadn't given them was the one thing they needed—me.

Suddenly, Zeizel stirred. I turned and looked at her just as she opened her eyes.

"Robert!"

"It's me, baby. It's me. Everything's all right."

She started to cry. "I had another dream...."

"Don't worry about it, baby. It was only a dream."

"Robert, I can't go on like this. I don't know when, or if, you're ever going to come home. I don't know if you're alive or dead. We need you, Robert. Me and Erica."

I started to say something but no words came out of my mouth. What could I say? She was right. I couldn't even find the words to give her momentary comfort. I couldn't reassure her. I never knew if I'd be coming home. I knew I had enemies out there, enemies who would be happy to kill me, and my family. But I wouldn't allow that. I wouldn't let anyone hurt my wife and baby. And if they wanted to take me out, they'd have to do it smart. They wouldn't take me out easily. I wasn't about to become a sitting duck.

"What's going to happen?" Zeizel wanted to know.

"I don't know, baby. I'll think of something."

"Promise?"

"Yeah, I promise."

She quieted down after that. But she didn't stop crying.

Chapter Eleven

I t was October 1982 now. Traveling the after-hours clubs and talking to people, I learned that Gustavo and his men liked a particular after-hours joint in lower Manhattan called Club 19. Once I knew where I could find him, I knew what I had to do.

Remember, this guy wanted to take me out. He put me and my family at risk. Just hearing his name filled me with rage. In my mind, I'd been playing out all the scenarios for taking him out that I could imagine. I was ready to make at least one of those scenarios real.

I founded up three or four of my best guys, heavyweights that I knew I could trust to do what had to be done.

"I don't know how it's going to play out," I told them. "This is Gustavo's turf. He's probably got an army around him."

"Robert, you know we're with you, man."

"Yeah, that's right. Don't worry about a thing. We got your back."

I knew that's what I would hear but it was still good to hear it. "Okay, then let's do this thing."

We were all armed to the teeth. I wore a bulletproof vest. I didn't have any illusions about what I was walking into. There was going to be a firelight that night as far as I was concerned.

We were all quiet and edgy on the drive downtown. I don't know what my guys were thinking but I was thinking revenge. I was imagining every possible situation we might encounter. If only one of us was going to leave that club that night, I swore to myself it wasn't going to be Gustavo.

When we pulled up to Club 19, there were a handful of people hanging around outside and two huge bouncers by the downstairs doors. The club itself was up on the tenth floor, where another set of doors, steel, would be waiting for us.

Me and my guys got in and went up the service elevator toward the club. It was there, at the second set of doors, that we would be patted down.

"Shit," I seethed to myself. No way I wanted to go in there unarmed. But I knew this would happen. "Just be cool," I said to my guys as we moved forward with the rest of the crowd, moving toward the security guys patting everyone down.

As we got closer, my mind was racing. What was I going to do? Should we shoot our way in? A whole cowboy scene?

Just as we were about to get to the security guys and I would have to decide, the decision was made for me. Lady Luck called out to me in the voice of Ralph, my wife's cousin.

"Cousin!" he called out to me. "Hey, cousin, how you doing?" He looked over to the security guys. "Don't worry about him, he's with me. No need to check him out."

The security guys grunted and let us go in along with my cousin. What luck! I knew that if Gustavo and his men were there, they would be armed and ready for anything. The last thing I wanted was to go into the club at a disadvantage. Ralph saved our asses.

"Robert, talk to me, man," Ralph was saying, standing close to me. "You don't seem to be the same guy I met at my cousin's wedding, man...."

I shrugged. "Come on, Ralph, we all change. You know how it is." "But you got a baby now...."

"I take good care of my family," I said. "I love them. You know that. Life's tough. Gotta make a living."

"Maybe," he agreed.

Just then, I spotted Gustavo from the corner of my eye. Whatever else Ralph was saying, I didn't hear it. Fear shot through me like an electric current. For an instant, my feet felt like they weighed a hundred pounds each. But then my anger overcame my fear. Just like that, I was light as a feather and ready for action.

I moved through the crowd and came up alongside Gustavo. As I did, I dropped my arm to my side and kept my hand close to my .357 magnum. With my other hand, I tapped him on the shoulder.

He looked like he had seen a ghost.

We were right there, eye to eye. I could feel the heat of my anger coming up from the pits of my soul. He must have felt that heat because after holding my glance for a second, he turned his eyes down. I could see that he was shaking. At least, it looked like he was shaking to me. He was surprised by my showing up, that much was certain.

That first moment was crucial—for both of us. It was terrifying, too. Don't let anyone tell you that you don't feel fear at a time like that. You feel it so much you can smell it coming off your skin.

Gustavo was the first to speak. "Vidal...how about a drink?"

At the same time, my guys came over to us and, in the process, brought some sanity and calm to a tense situation that was ready to explode.

Gustavo tried to look me in the eyes. He knew why I was there. He knew what this was about. "Vidal, do not let Ruben's death stay between us," he said. He looked nervous but lie tried to shrug his shoulders in a way that would make it seem like he was in control. "What did you expect after the fight in the bar? Come on, Vidal, you left them with scars. You took their pride. They didn't have no choice but to come back at you. And they weren't even my men, Vidal. They were sent up by my boss in Florida. He sent them up to kill you and Ruben. Dammit, man, you scarred them for life. You can't expect they didn't want revenge. They had to try to get even with you. But, Vidal, they didn't get you. You see, you left us with no choice...."

Gustavo was talking faster and faster now. He was nervous and anxious to stall my anger. At the very least, he wanted to buy some time. He knew I'd come for revenge but he was desperate to try and take the edge off whatever it was I was planning on doing. He was working hard at it, too.

I wasn't about to shoot him in cold blood in the middle of a night-club. I still had enough good sense to know that. Besides, his fear calmed me down. I knew that I was in charge of this situation. This wasn't the time. These things have to be done at the right time and this wasn't the right time.

"Vidal, Ruben cried while we were beating him," he said. His voice and his words tore at my heart. "He's the one who told us where you lived. That's how we found out. He told us he would give us all his money, everything, if only we didn't kill him." He spread out his hands. "He was begging for his life, man...."

I was only half-listening to Gustavo's words. I mean, I heard him and it made me cringe, thinking of Ruben begging like that. But my thoughts were on more immediate concerns. I knew that the timing was all wrong to take my revenge on Gustavo. I knew that much in my gut. And I'd learned to trust my gut.

"Give me your beeper number," I told him.

"Huh?"

"Your beeper number."

He gave me the number and then I left the club, putting off my revenge for a better day.

My hands were shaking when I got back to my Cadillac to drive home. As I was driving, I felt that my personalized plates, VIDAL, made me vulnerable. I kept looking in my rear-view mirror the whole way.

It was five in the morning when I got home. My wife and baby girl were still sound asleep. I watched them both sleeping for a little bit and then I quietly set myself up to sleep in the living room. I curled up on the sofa with my dear friends, my shotgun and my .357.

As I fell asleep, I heard Ruben's voice crying out for his life while he was being beaten and killed over on Tonnelle Avenue. I shook my head. For probably the first time, I realized that Ruben had been just like everyone else—scared of dying. He had spent his whole life manipulating people with cash and coke, all because he was damned scared. And I was just like him.

I opened my eyes and sat up straight. "I'm just like him," I whispered out loud. "Just like him."

In just a short time, I had become just like Ruben. Only a few weeks earlier, I'd been a nobody. Now I was a player, with all the dangers and fears that every player had. I had gone from a basement apartment where I was barely making rent to a luxury condominium, fully furnished with only the finest quality furniture. Everything was the best.

I tried to close my eyes and go to sleep, but the image of Ruben begging for his life kept getting in the way. I thought of all the things I had given my wife and baby to make our lives better, but they seemed like hollow gifts right then. Just things. What did any of it mean?

Finally, I closed my eyes and started to drift off to sleep, wondering if I would be like Ruben in that, one day, I'd have to beg for my life—or for my family. I felt a shudder go through my body as I began to fall deeper and deeper asleep, my shotgun and my .357 my only bedmates.

Chapter Twelve

You never forget your first time. The first time you get arrested, that is. I was on the edge for months...no, over the edge. I guess it was only a matter of time before either your enemies or the cops get you.

It's always hard to know which one you'd prefer. No one wants to think about getting gunned down by rivals and enemies, but by the same token, the thought of living in a cage...that's no way for a human being to live. Given a choice between the two, I'd have chosen...NEITHER. But it wasn't my choice.

I was sitting at the bar on November 2, enjoying a drink and shooting the shit with friends when my beeper went off. Damn beeper. Can't I ever be left in peace? I glanced down at the LED display to read the phone number of the caller, which was 99999. Emergency code.

My spine stiffened. My guys knew to enter five 9s only if it was a real emergency. Until now, no one had used the code. My heart started to pound. This was trouble. Real trouble.

"What's up, boss?" Ralph asked. He was like my bodyguard and already sensed that something was wrong.

I didn't answer as I slid off the stool and headed to the phone to return the call. I quickly dialed the number of the Royal Tavern. It was answered on the first ring.

"Robert!" one of my guys said. "You got to move, man. About ten undercover cops just went through the place. They're asking for you, man. Get the F—- out of Newark. Now!"

"Got it! Thanks. Call me later."

I motioned for Ralph to join me and we both walked outside. Controlled, but fast. As we walked toward where my car was parked, I filled him in on the phone call. "We got to get out of town," I told him.

"Shit," he said, throwing down his cigarette. Ralph was a pretty levelheaded guy, but he was clearly as nervous as I was. The shit was coming down and we didn't have much time to get out of the way.

We walked up to my brand-new, black and gold Buick Riviera. "Shit!"

"What's the matter, Robert?"

I looked at the car. "We can't take my car."

"Why not?"

"Look at it!" I snapped, pointing to the vanity license plates that practically screamed out in neon that it was my car.

"F—-."

"Come on," I said, turning back to the bar. As we walked, more quickly now, we discussed our dwindling options.

"We'll get someone else's car," Ralph said. He shrugged. "Nothing else we can do."

When we went back in the bar, I asked if anyone had a car we could borrow "for a few minutes." One of my coke customers immediately volunteered his. "Just one catch, Robert," he said.

"What's that?"

"You need a screwdriver to start it."

"What the F—-?"

He shrugged. "It's stolen, man. The ignition isn't on."

Now, under normal circumstances I'd probably have laughed at the absurdity of the situation. But these were not normal circumstances. The shit was hitting the fan and I didn't want to be there when it did.

"Fine," I snapped. "Let's go."

He led us to a shiny, new, black Corvette L-82 with a four-speed stick.

"What the...?" Ralph said, starting to hesitate.

"What's the matter now?" I demanded.

"I don't want to drive a stolen car, boss. That can really get me jammed up."

I narrowed my eyes at him. "Jammed up? I'll show you F——-ing jammed up if you don't get moving! We've got to get out of town now!"

I slid into the driver's seat and Ralph, still reluctant, got in on the passenger's side. I turned the screwdriver and the motor roared to life. I jammed down the clutch and put the stick in first gear. Then I popped the clutch and slammed down on the gas, shooting out of the parking lot.

I came to a red light and stopped, revving the engine for when it turned green. As I waited, I glanced over to my left. A two-door burgundy Cutlass Supreme pulled up alongside us. The driver looked over at us. Staring directly into my face, I saw the light of recognition fire up in his eyes.

"Pull over!" he shouted at me. At the same time, he raised a red light and stuck it on the roof.

"F——-!" I snapped. They were undercover cops and they had spotted me. My heart was pounding so fast I thought it would burst through my chest. The adrenaline was coursing through my body like floodwater.

Pull over my ass. I wasn't going to give up that easy. I floored the gas pedal and could smell the fumes from the rear tires as they fought to gain traction. The burning rubber sent up a cloud that momentarily blinded the driver of the Cutlass. That was the only window of opportunity I was going to get. I released the clutch and dropped the 'Vette into gear. I was a half-block ahead of them before they'd had time to recover.

I raced down Walnut Street, which was wide and had two-way traffic. I was pushing eighty miles an hour and Ralph was just about out of his F—-ing mind.

"Let me out! Let me out!"

I didn't look over at him. Ralph is a body builder and looks like nothing in the world could scare him, but he was out of his mind scared right then. "What the F—-...?"

"Let me out!" He was near hysterical.

Most of the time, 1 could put up with shit like that and just ignore it. But we were in a situation where it was contagious. The crazier he got, the crazier I got. If I was going to maintain the right frame of mind, I was going to have to get rid of him.

I glanced in the rear-view mirror. I'd put four or five blocks between me and the Cutlass.

"Okay, you big punk," I snapped. "I'll let you out around the next corner."

As soon as I got to the next corner, I slowed down and let Ralph jump from the still-moving car. He dropped to the ground and rolled under the nearest parked car.

I didn't give him another thought. I had more immediate worries. I slammed down the accelerator and picked up speed. I had to make it to the highway. As I swerved in and out of traffic, I waited for the right opportunity and then I threw my .45 out the window.

At least I was still thinking. I knew that if this little chase didn't work out, I would be a lot better off not being in possession of a firearm.

"Just get to the highway," I kept repeating to myself. That was my goal. That was my hope. On the open road, I could easily out-race the cops. The Cutlass was no match for the Corvette. They'd need a miracle to catch me.

They got their damned miracle.

Just as I was increasing speed, the car started to cough and back-fire. It was stuttering and losing speed. What the F—- was wrong? I looked at the dashboard and my eyes focused on the gas gauge. The damned needle was past empty! The F—-ing customer had given me a car with no gas in it! And, in my hurry to get away, I hadn't checked.

"Shit!" Now what was I going to do? Thinking fast, I realized that I was only a short ways from Manny's body shop, Classic Auto Body. He was my friend and I knew that if I could get there undetected, I could make my escape.

I pulled over not far from the body shop. I looked up and down the street. No sign of a cop anywhere. There was a brief moment when I really believed I was going to get away. Then all hell broke loose.

Marked and unmarked police cars came flying from every direction. Flashing lights. Sirens. The whole show. Cops started jumping from the cars and aiming their weapons directly at me.

"Stop!"

"Police!"

"Put your hands in the air!"

I could see the look in their eyes. They wouldn't lose a second's sleep after blowing me away. I raised my hands into the air. One of the Hudson County's Task Force threw me against a car and pulled my hands behind my back.

"Robert Vidal, you are under arrest for conspiracy to distribute cocaine. You have the right to remain silent."

Just like on F—-ing television. Only one problem. This wasn't television. It was my life… going down the tubes.

I was taken to the station and isolated in the interrogation room where I was questioned for hours. These guys wanted information concerning three Colombians who were arrested at the same time I was. They were also looking for any information they could get regarding the coke trade in Newark.

"Come on, Vidal, spill it about the Colombians. Make your life easier."

"What?"

"Don't get cute with us, Vidal. Spill it. Tell us about your Colombian connection. And don't act like you don't know what we're talking about." "Huh?"

"Smart ass, huh? Keep it up and we're going to F—- you good, Vidal. We'll F—- you so good you'll never see the light of day again except for your five minutes in the exercise yard."

"I love you, too," I said in mock sweetness. Then my tone got serious. "Look, I'd help you guys if I could, but I don't know anything."
"Bullshit."

"I don't."

"Cooperate and maybe you'll get to go home tonight."

Needless to say, I never saw the inside of my home that night. Instead, I spent the day and night in the crowded Hudson County jail. Nice place to visit. Wouldn't want to live there. The place stunk of soiled lives and piss. The food they gave us was fit for capital punishment—to kill the prisoners, not to let them enjoy their last meal!

"What is this shit?" I asked when I got my first meal. My "meal" consisted of a hard-boiled egg the color of sick eggplant and a cup of water that looked like the swimming hole for dead cockroaches. So much for my normally healthy appetite.

I called my wife, who got in touch with Joe Ferrante, a reputable attorney. Once he came into the picture, it was only a few more hours before I was back out on the streets. I kept up the "wise guy" front the whole time I was in that jail. I was the tough guy to the cops, not giving an inch. But as soon as that fresh air brushed up against my face and I felt the street beneath my feet, I had some second thoughts about my current occupation. Losing your freedom can do that.

I thought back to the scene when I was arrested, to the many guns pointed at me and I realized that any small "accident" would have been the end of me and no one, except maybe my mother and my wife, would cry for me. Even my baby girl was too young to know me.

And then there was the indignity of the process. I'd never suffered that way. I'd never had to undergo such embarrassment. I had always been the master of my life. Not in that jail. There, I was no different than the bottom feeders of the world. I never wanted to go through that experience again. Never.

I told myself then and there that I would get out of the business. I had everything I needed. I had money. I was okay. I was out. Yeah, right.

A week hadn't gone by before I was back at the Royal Tavern, bragging about what a good lawyer and money could do. "Welcome to America, friends," I said, bragging about the influence of the all-powerful dollar. No, by the end of the week it wasn't that I had to get out of the business, just that I had to reassess how I was conducting business.

I stopped carrying guns on my person. That was just too risky. But I made sure that they were never far away. I distanced myself from the actual product. I was cleaning up my act.

Not for long. Within a few more days, I was back to my old ways. I was showing off large quantities of coke, carrying a gun, and flashing huge rolls of money. I was back to visiting all my favorite after-hours clubs. Hey, I was free and the money was rolling in! With each passing hour, my jail experience seemed more and more like just a bad dream.

I learned how the police got on to me. I had telephoned a Colombian contact in North Bergen County just a few days before the arrest. How could I have known that the Hudson Country Strike Force had a tap on his line? (I eventually was able to have the entire case against me dismissed. Beautiful justice system, huh?)

Zeizel wasn't pleased. Neither was her family or mine. My arrest was reported in the Jersey City paper. It was nothing to be proud of, I knew that, but I just tried to shrug it off as an occupational hazard. My mother thought it was more than that. The cops got lucky, that's all. I wouldn't happen again. Not to me.

It wouldn't take long for me to learn that this was only the beginning. On December 28th, I was being cuffed and having my rights read to me once again.

"When you going to get wise to this, Vidal?"

I just grunted.

It's amazing how fast things can turn sour. The day had started out pretty much like any other day. I was hanging out at the Tavern with my partner, Joe, and some of the guys. We were drinking and getting high. A pretty girl who went by the stage name of Wonder Woman was doing her thing for the crowd.

I was already tipsy when a drunk patron started heckling Wonder Woman.

"Shut the F—- up!" someone yelled at him.

He ignored the person and continued to heckle her. Then he started to make lewd gestures at Wonder Woman and the other girls on stage. For the most part, this was "business as usual" for the girls. They were used to getting a certain number of suggestions and proposals. Most of the time, the girls took it as casual flirting, which it mostly was. Contrary to the common view, most of the dancers were not whores, nymphos, or prostitutes. They were mostly just women trying to make a living or earn a little extra income.

Well, this guy was especially hard on Wonder Woman. "Why don't you come home with me and let me F—- your goddamned brains out?" he shouted to her. "I bet you like taking it in that big ass of yours, don't you?"

It was obvious that Wonder Woman had had enough of this guy. Some of the other patrons were mumbling about the guy and how he should shut up but they didn't want to get in the middle of something that could easily get violent.

When she couldn't ignore the guy anymore, Wonder Woman asked me to please do something about the guy. Joe, who was alongside me, heard her request and wisely took a few steps further away.

The drunk was still harassing her even when she was talking to me. So I looked at him and said, "Hey man, why don't you leave her alone? Can't you see she doesn't want anything to do with you?"

Joe was watching me with a wary eye. He knew how many drinks I'd already put away and lie wasn't sure about my judgment. He knew when I'd had too much to drink there was sure to be a fight if someone said the wrong thing or owed me something.

Well, this guy gave me a once-over and must have decided that he didn't have anything to worry about because he was bigger than me. That's the problem with big guys. They're usually stupid.

"Get out of the way," this drunk said to me, "before I F—- you up." Mistake.

Before he knew what happened, there were people pulling me off him and others trying to help him off the floor. It was a quick and violent exchange. He was trying to talk and I was trying to knock his

F——ing head off. All street fighters learn one lesson or they get their asses kicked. The lesson is simple: always land the first blow.

I had learned that lesson years before. I had delivered several hard hits to this idiot's head before he knew what was going on. He was in no shape to respond. My bodyguard was helping the guy to his feet and escorting him to the door.

Joe Belo came over. "Look, Vidal," he said softly, "why don't you go home to your wife and get some rest? You're jumpy tonight and you've had too much to drink. Why not go home now while the going's good?"

I nodded my head. He was right and I knew it. "Yeah, Joe, that's a good idea," I told him.

I asked Ralph to go start my Fleetwood. He came back a minute later. The battery was dead. That was a drag, but not a big problem. I had many friends in the bar so I looked for one who might have a credit card so I could rent a car. My eyes landed on Miguel.

"Miguel, you got a credit card, man?"

"Sure, Robert. What's up?"

I quickly explained my need for a rented car. He was more than happy to lend a hand. Little did he know what he was so enthusiastically getting into.

I got a few of the guys who were getting high with me to give us a ride to Newark Airport and the rental car area. Miguel got into the car. While he was waiting for everyone else to slide in, I had one of my friends pop open the trunk. As soon as it was opened, I stuffed a large, clear plastic bag filled with cocaine into a pair of jeans lying there. Then I grabbed my .380 automatic and got in the car.

"Let's go," I said.

As Flabio drove toward the highway, I leaned forward to Lazaro in the front passenger seat. "Here you go," I said, handing him some coke. "Excellent, Robert," he replied with a smile.

Meanwhile, Miguel was starting to look a little bit anxious. I think it was only starting to occur to him the mess he might have landed himself in the middle of Lazaro snorted some of the coke and then held a line in front of Flabio to snort while he drove. Then he fired up a thickly rolled joint packed with sinsemilla marijuana.

"Wow," I sighed, smelling the heavy aroma of the weed. I could tell from the aroma just how powerful the weed was. Lazaro and Flabio passed it back a forth a couple of times and then Lazaro passed it back to me. I drew in a couple of hits. I began to feel funny.

"Almost there," Flabio said as he turned into one of the entrances to the airport.

The car was filled with clouds of smoke. Miguel wasn't happy at all. "Come on, you guys, let me out here," he said.

I started to laugh. "Miguel, my man, we're in the middle of F—-ing nowhere. We can't leave you here."

"Sure you can. You guys are F—-ing crazy. Come on, let me out."

I couldn't stop laughing. The weed had gotten to me big time. My eyes felt like pinpricks and I couldn't stop laughing.

"Calm down," Flabio said to Miguel. "We're here."

He pulled into the National Car Rental area. He came to a stop alongside the curb and I got out, followed by Miguel. "Just be cool," I whispered to Miguel, trying to stop laughing.

"Yeah, I got it, Robert," he said, sounding annoyed.

It was eleven-thirty at night. No one else was in the reception area. Miguel went to the counter and started to take care of the paperwork. I got beeped and went to the pay phone to return the call.

Inside the small phone booth, I got a glimpse at my reflection in the chrome. Man, were my eyes bloodshot. That was some killer weed! I was still talking on the phone when I looked over at the counter. Both the manager and the receptionist were looking directly at me.

"What the...?" I wondered. And then I discovered what had caught their attention. When I placed my elbow on top of the phone, my jacket rode up and my .380 was exposed.

The manager and the receptionist whispered to one another, all the while stealing worried glances in my direction. A second later, Miguel came over to me.

"They saw your gun, man," he whispered urgently to me, confirming exactly what I feared.

"We have to get out of here," I told him.

"We're almost ready."

Miguel got the car keys and the contract. We headed outside where Lazaro and Flabio were still waiting.

"What took you guys so long?" Lazaro said, leaning out the window. "We've got trouble."

"What's up?"

"I heard a description of you coming over the intercom system. They said a man fitting your description was carrying a gun. They called the cops, Robert. We got to get out of here! Now!"

That was enough to bring me down from my high. "Come on, you guys," I said, trying to think rationally. "You're high and coked up. You're being paranoid. Just calm down."

Meanwhile, Miguel's eyes were wide like two flashlights, just glowing with fear.

"Miguel, you and me will go in the rental," I ordered. Then I looked down at Lazaro. "You guys go back to the bar. We'll meet you there."

Lazaro and Flabio started to drive away. Miguel and I started walking across the lot, looking for the car. As soon as we spotted the four-door Delta **88** we started for it. Just then, the manager came out of the building and called to us.

"I have another car for you guys," he called out.

"F—- you," I said under my breath. "No, thanks," I called back. "This one is just fine."

Miguel's hands were trembling as he started up the car. He pulled out of the stall and headed for the security guard's booth. The guard checked all the paperwork and then flashed us a smile. "Have a good night, you guys," he said as the steel gate opened.

"Thanks," Miguel said nervously.

The F—-ing guard even waved to us! Unbelievable!

Miguel pulled out of the lot and onto the roadway. As soon as he started to drive, he glanced over at me. "Vidal, why you getting me involved in this shit? You know I don't mess with drugs or do any of that illegal shit."

I looked at him. The son of a bitch looked like he was going to cry. I felt a little sorry for him. He was a nice guy who worked hard at his job. I'd known him since grammar school.

"Hey, don't worry about it, Miguel. Everything's gonna be just fine." I took a couple of hits of coke to settle myself down. But as we drove on the roadway exiting the airport, I started to get nervous, too. My thoughts were mostly on Lazaro and Flabio. I'd stuffed almost a kilo of coke in the trunk of Flabio's car. That was almost sixty thousand dollars' worth.

I watched for their car, but it didn't come by. I could feel that something was wrong.

"Look, Robert, just drop me off somewhere, okay?"

"Shut up, Miguel. You don't have nothing to worry about. Nothing's going to happen to you."

I guess the authoritative tone in my voice settled him down. Meanwhile, I had to start thinking rationally. I slowly took out my .380 and slid it into the air conditioning vent. Then I turned and headed back toward the airport.

As we came back near the National Car Rental area, I could see I spotted them with the trunk open and with two spares out on the road. As I drove closer, I could see that the two back tires were flat. The stupid F—-s must have backed into the steel pins of the security track in the parking lot. And they had all that cocaine in the trunk....

As I drove closer, a Port Authority police car pulled up behind them. I decided it was wise to stay back. But, after a minute, I knew I couldn't leave those guys alone. I parked the car. "You sit tight," I told Miguel.

"Where are you going?"

"I'll be right back," I told him. Then I got out and started to walk over toward Flabio and Lazaro.

Suddenly, from out of nowhere, uniformed Port Authority officers and cars came screeching up. Shotguns and revolvers were drawn. These guys weren't fooling around.

"The one with the gold chain! He's the one!"

"Hey," I said nervously, "what's going on?"

"Don't move!"

I didn't so much as breathe as the cops patted me down. They found seven .45 caliber bullets in the pocket of my leather jacket. Nothing else.

"Where's the gun that goes with these?" the cop demanded. "You a cop?"

I shook my head. "No." I knew to keep my answers real short and real simple. This wasn't a tea party.

I glanced over as some of the other cops got ready to search Flabio's trunk. I felt helpless. I had my hands cuffed behind me. There was nothing I could do. "Think, Robert," I told myself. "Dammit, think!" Suddenly, I came up with something. "Hey, I know what you're looking for. It's not in there!"

The cops turned and looked at me.

"The gun," I said. "I have the gun. I have it." Now I had their attention. "It's in the rental," I told them. "In the Delta."

I'm sure Miguel was shitting his pants when two officers went over and started to search the car. But they came back empty-handed.

"Where the F—- is it?" the sergeant demanded. "We'll strip both cars until we find it!"

I knew he was serious, too. I glanced over at Lazaro and Flabio. Their eyes were glittering like diamonds. I could tell from twenty yards away that they were high as kites. The cops surely knew. Damn.

The thing about coke that sets it apart from other drugs is the more you use it, the more you crave it. The high is so rapid and intense that it is like nothing else in the world. But when it wears off, it leaves you desperate and depressed. Most people will do anything to get high again. If they were about to crash, there was no telling what they'd do—or say—to be able to get high again.

"The air vent in the Delta," I called out as two cops started toward the Pontiac again. "The gun's there."

A few seconds later, a cop emerged from the front seat of the car, displaying the .380 like it was some damned prize fish or something. That stupid cop was grinning like a Cheshire cat.

The sergeant wasn't so impressed. "There's another one somewhere. He had .45 shells in his pocket. He sure as hell can't use those in that."

"Holy shit!" I thought. "They'll find the coke for sure now."

My knees were weak as the cops stayed around the four of us with their guns drawn and trained on us. I think Miguel was really ready to crap his pants. Lazaro and Flabio were edgy and anxious. The cops just needed one bad excuse to make a "mistake" and shoot.

Lazaro leaned toward me. "Hey, Vidal," he whispered, "is all the perico still in the back?"

I shot him a look. It was just my luck that one of the cops heard him. Not only that, he understood him. This cop went over to the lieutenant and told him what he heard.

"Let's check out that trunk again," the lieutenant said.

Bingo! Out come the rolled up jeans and the jackpot.

One of the cops started laughing. "Don't tell me you guys need all that just to support your own sorry habits."

I gave him one of those "I don't know what the F—- you're talking about" looks and kept my mouth shut.

The cop didn't let up, though. "You look surprised. Don't tell me that I put it there and you don't have any F—-in' idea where it came from."

The cop practically read my mind.

"Forget that shit," he said. "It's confession time. You're all going to jail, so you might as well make it easier on yourselves. Who's going to cough up some information? Come on, guys, don't everyone raise their hands at once."

Call it the power of suggestion, stupidity, or just plain old dumb luck, but Miguel, Flabio and Lazaro all looked directly at me. The F—-s had given me up without saying one damned word.

"Okay, guys, you know the drill. You have the right to remain silent...." It was television-land all over again. Miguel and I were placed in the back of the same squad car.

Chapter Twelve

"Hey, Vidal, they're going to let us go, right?"

I didn't answer for a minute or so. I was listening to the constant squawking on the police radio. I knew it wasn't fair that Miguel was in this situation. It wasn't his fault. Still, it was what it was. "Miguel, there was a lot of coke in that bag. But don't worry. I've got plenty of cash. I'll get you a good lawyer. I'll have you out in no time. Just keep your mouth shut, got it?"

"Yeah," he said with a mixture of sadness and worry. "But my mother is waiting for me. She always has my dinner waiting for me right about now. She's going to be worried sick."

I didn't think I could feel any worse for Miguel but I did. I felt like that proverbial piece of shit. Here I was, going to jail for something I'd done and I was dragging along an innocent friend who had only tried to help me out of a jam. Looking into Miguel's eyes while we were riding in the back of that squad car pretty much took care of any illusions of power and respect I might have felt. All I saw was my old friend's pain and uncertainty.

We were taken to the Third Precinct in Newark. The small prison cell felt all too familiar to me. Damn. Was my life worth this?

Within forty-eight hours, Zeizel and Sam had put together the $25,000 bail for each of us. Once again, I swore I'd never go through that again.

And once again, as the hours and days went by, the experience seemed to have happened to someone else. I was back to business as usual. I promised myself that I'd be more careful. Being locked up wasn't for me. It had been a mistake. I'd gotten unlucky. I'd just be more careful and everything would be fine.

This is what I told myself, but there was still a voice inside that told me I was talking bullshit. I was selling about ten kilos a month. I'd been busted for possession of a kilo. The cops aren't fools. They bust you once, they know to keep an eye on you. They knew I had to make up for the product they'd confiscated. They had my number. Now they were calling the shots, even if I didn't know it yet.

More than once in the course of the next few weeks, I was approached by undercover cops interested in making a buy.

"I don't touch that stuff," I said, not willing to take any chances with a stranger.

One time, a guy came up to me, a guy I'd never seen before. "Hey, man," he said, coming close, "you Vidal?"

I looked at him. "Who wants to know?"

He ignored my question. "I heard that you were the man to see if you wanted the best."

I narrowed my eyes and looked at him. "Yeah? And where did you hear that?"

He shrugged. "Word gets around. I heard it through the grapevine."

That struck a chord in my mind, and before I knew it, I was whispering the first few lines to the classic Marvin Gaye song of the same name. "Oooh, I bet you're wondering' how I knew, 'bout your plans to make me blue...."

This guy and his partner looked at one another and then back at me like I was losing it. "What?"

I shook my head. "Nothing, man."

"Look, Vidal," the guy's partner said, stepping up, "don't you remember selling me an ounce last Tuesday? That shit was good, man. The best. I just brought my friend along because I turned him on to some and he'd like to cop some, too." He leaned closer to me. "You probably don't remember me too good. You were pretty drunk at the time," he added, chuckling like him and me were best friends. Which we weren't.

Now it was my turn to look at him like he was losing his shit. I stared him straight in the eye and brought my face so close to his that the stink of the dying Tic-Tac on his breath filled my nostrils. "Look," I told him in a voice low and menacing, "I don't sell drugs. Period. I don't sell them. I don't want them. I don't do them. Don't force any shit on me." Then I leaned back. "I think you got me confused with someone else, Officer," I added.

/ 21

No matter how much alcohol I might drink, I always, always, remember my customers.

This pissed him off big time. He opened his mouth like he was going to say something a few times but each time he just closed it again with no words coming out. Finally, he just turned and walked out the door, his buddy tagging along after him.

I smiled as the door closed behind them. Then I chuckled to myself. "Didn't even say good-bye." I shook my head. "Some people just got no manners."

I'd sent them away that time, but I knew they'd be back. Them and a thousand more just like them.

Chapter Thirteen

One thing about the drug lifestyle—it involves a lot of partying. Every night is party night. And I was right in the middle of this lifestyle. For me, partying and business overlapped. I couldn't do one without the other—and I didn't want to. Call it a perk. What do you expect when nightclubs and bars filled with topless dancers are your place of business? The Rooftop. The Crisco Disco. The Swiss Corner. These were just some of my favorite after-hours clubs. There were other places, hundreds of them, twenty-four hour places. They didn't have names. They didn't have addresses. But drug people knew where to find them. Just follow the endless flow of money, drugs, and sex.

These places were "equal opportunity" clubs. Doctors, bankers, lawyers, sports stars, corporate honchos. They used to come to my turf after their operas, or their games, or their nights out in their fine restaurants. They used to come to my turf when they were bored with their perfect little lives. They'd drop their wives off at home, maybe wait for them to fall asleep, and then it was out to the all-night clubs. Out to the places filled with drugs, with cash, with jewelry, with drug dealers and their gorgeous women spilling out of their dresses, and fancy cars lined up outside.

And if one of my customers in banking saw one of my customers in law enforcement...each getting high...well, what of it? No one had to state the rules. They were understood. What you said in those places, what you did in those places, stayed in those places. Period.

No one needed to see their name in the *Post*. It was all about the party. In places like the Crisco Disco, my clothes, the money I flashed, the drugs I carried quickly made me a member in good standing at the VIP bar. There, at private tables, complimentary bottles of Dom Perignon were brought over. I would pour a large mound of powder on the glass tabletop and we would all go for it. I always came in with eight or ten ounces. There was never any need to be greedy. There was more than enough for everyone.

There was no selling at Crisco. It was all party. I gave out my beeper number to anyone who wanted to become a customer. But that was for outside. Inside, it was just the party.

At this time, I was abusing and punishing my body so much it was a wonder I could even get up the next day. Cocaine. Downers. Alcohol. All night, every night. And then the same thing the next day.

And then there were the girls. Hundreds of them. Girls and more girls. I wanted every one of them. Every beautiful go-go dancer. Every female bartender. The sex was as available as the drugs. Everyone was doing it.

Adultery? Sin? What did they have to do with me? I was on a free ride. Everyone was doing it, right? This was what my life was all about. Sex, drugs, power. I had made something of myself. I was a king.

Those days, I used to pay $45 an hour just to have a limo parked outside, waiting to take me wherever I wanted to go next. I might be in the club for hours. But I wanted that limo there. Waiting.

The limo was the least of it. It wasn't like I was teaching Romper Room or something. I also had protection with me all the time. I tended to cross paths with Gustavo and that was always dicey. And there were others.

Most of the time, I was heavily armed. Sometimes, I would pay someone to carry my weapons for me. There was always someone happy to do it. In fact, there were people who felt honored that I trusted them to watch my back and be my bodyguard. And it was a lucrative gig. $200-300 a night. Cash.

I depended on my bodyguard. There was no place I went, not one minute of the day, that I didn't have a confrontation with Gustavo on my mind. Even when I was clubbing for relaxation instead of business, Gustavo was there. Partying is no time to let down your guard— unless you have someone covering your back. Me, I had a small army.

They were like a wall around me and danger, allowing me to party on and on. I was out of control. I was a different creature than the man my parents had raised me to be. They had tried to instill in me values and morals; they tried to give me their sense of right and wrong. They tried to raise me to behave properly in the eyes of God.

But I was living on a wild roller coaster and I wasn't interested in any of that. At the time, I believed I didn't need God. I had drugs. I had power. I had sex. I hardly thought of my wife and daughter, who stayed at home worrying about me, the only ones who loved me. Zeizel cried herself to sleep at night, never knowing if I would come home or if someone would come to tell her I'd been gunned down. She never knew if gunshots would ring through her house again, threatening her and our daughter.

Those days, I always had five to ten ounces of coke on me just to party with. I'd buy drinks, hand out coke, be the big shot. Management didn't mind if I handed out the coke, but they frowned on selling.

Every club was the same. I had a table that was always mine. When I arrived, I led my entourage to the table. After we were seated, the people started to make their way over, like the faithful to the pope. They would come and gawk at the mountain of coke I'd put out on the table.

"Yo, Vidal, is that medallion around your neck real gold?"

"Hell, how you keep your head up with that heavy thing?"

It hadn't taken me long, but I had become Ruben. I had become a show-off. It wasn't enough that I had it all; I needed to make sure everyone knew that I had it all. I was king of the world...until I came home to my wife. Then I was like every other husband dragging his ass home after being out partying.

"You're never here with me and Erica!"

"You stink of alcohol!"

"I can smell cheap perfume on you!"

The worst was the bulletproof vest. Every time she saw me take off the vest, she started to cry. It was then I knew that all her anger at me really masked how much she worried about me and loved me. And it busted me up.

"Ain't nothing to worry about, Zeizel," I told her. "Lots of crazy people out there."

When I didn't think I could take her complaining any more, I decided to show her a good time. I bought her an expensive mink. The same evening I brought it home, we ate at New York's famous Tavern on the Green. Night after night, I took her to New York's and New Jersey's best restaurants.

Did it work?

No.

She could see beneath the mask. My beeper was like a jealous woman, never giving me a moment's peace. Even out with the woman I loved, that damned beeper made it clear that Zeizel might be my wife but I was married to my business. I had customers that needed to be serviced. And if they didn't get their coke from me, they'd go someplace else.

I couldn't afford to have the word go out that I wasn't reliable. The profits were too good. I was just like every other businessman. Strike while the iron's hot.

One guy who wasn't complaining at all was Paco. Our partnership was bringing him tons of money. He was making about $20,000 a kilo, smuggling the drug into Florida and then having his men deliver it to New Jersey.

I had to make up the money I'd lost when I was arrested. That little learning experience had cost me around $100,000, what with the cost of the coke, the bail money, and the lawyer. I was working as hard as I could to move the drug.

At the same time, I started to notice that Sam and Bobby were spending an awful lot of time at the bar. That wasn't like them. They generally came in and bought what they wanted, had a drink or two to be sociable, and then left. Now they seemed to be taking awfully close note of what I was doing.

"What's that son of a bitch up to?" I wondered, watching Sam watch me. "It's something. Dammit, I know it. But what?"

One evening at the Royal, I came outside and saw something that made me even more suspicious. Sam was taking down license plate numbers from some of the cars parked outside. "What the F——?" I couldn't figure what he was up to. I knew he wasn't a cop, so why would he be writing down license numbers?

I watched him take down the number of one of my Colombian connections. He wrote the number on a matchbook, folded it and then casually stuck it in his pocket as he walked away from the car.

"Son of a bitch," I muttered under my breath. "What the hell is he up to?"

Back inside the bar, I went over to my bodyguard and crew. "Keep a closer eye on Sam from now on. He's up to something."

"You got it, boss."

Like I didn't have enough to worry about already. Every day, I was adding more weapons to my little arsenal. Just in case. One thing was true: a dealer could never be too paranoid. Or, as my friend once told me, "Even paranoids have real enemies." That was no shit.

A short time after that, Vick, a customer of mine who had made silencers for guns, a man who knew of my interest in gathering a few good men together, came into the bar. It was known among a small circle that the time was coming when I would be ready to confront Gustavo. This customer was in that circle.

He walked in with a tall guy, about six-two, six-three. This guy must have weighed two-fifty or so. He had dark, black hair and a very serious look about him.

"Hey, Vidal," Vick said, leading the man over to me. "I want you to meet a friend of mine. Say hello to Wayne."

I nodded at this mountain of a man who was clearly not to be taken lightly. He grunted back at me.

"Wayne used to be a marine. He trained in Special Services." Then he leaned closer to me and whispered so low I could barely hear him. "He'll get rid of anybody for you as long as the price is worth his while."

I nodded again and glanced from Vick back toward Wayne. Looking at him, I had no doubt that what Vick said was true. I extended my hand to Wayne. "Let me get you a drink," I said. Then I ordered drinks for both of them. Vick also indicated that Wayne liked coke, so I gave him half an ounce. Gratis.

Within a couple of weeks, Vick, Wayne, and Sam were spending just about every evening in the Royal Tavern. They had connections in the Mafia and were well known in the Italian-American community. Hell, I'd walked into an Italian bar with them and the people just about fell over themselves to show these guys respect.

I was at one such bar when an old Italian friend of mine leaned over to me and put a bug in my ear. "Be careful," he said. "Sam's no good. No good at all."

I looked at him and he nodded his head.

"Don't believe me, but they tried to kill me in a Bloomfield Avenue restaurant not that long ago."

Now the old man had my attention. He went on to tell me that he and Bobby were both connected to the Campisi family. He ended by telling me to steer clear of garbage. "Get too close to garbage and you can't help but get the stink on you," he warned.

I understood his warning. I didn't trust anyone who killed for money. There was no allegiance there. If they'd kill for me for money, they'd kill me for money, too. Business. Nothing personal. But I needed people with me who were professional, who wouldn't blink when the shit hit the fan. I was going to need a very strong hand in my confrontation with my enemies.

These guys, along with my crew, would give me the edge I needed. Day by day, hour by hour, it became clear what I was doing. I was putting all the pieces in place. I was preparing for war, a war I wasn't interested in losing.

I was generating an awful lot of cash. No one wanted to see that cash cow destroyed. I had plenty of offers for back up.

I had an army willing to march with me through what I now call the Garden of the Wicked Ways. In that Garden, there was violence, murder, and moral decay. In those days, I felt right at home in that Garden. I will never forget the years of my life lost in that Garden, years that could only be reclaimed by faith in God. I had wounds that only God, through His Son, Jesus, had the power to heal.

But I wasn't ready to be healed. Not yet.

Chapter Fourteen

One night, at about three a.m., I told my chauffeur to park our stretch limo in front of the Swiss Corner on 36th Street, an after-hours spot patronized by Latin drug dealers. In the back of the limo, I was surrounded by Carlos Nortennos, Joe Santos, and Carlos the Cuban Marielito.

"What the F—-?" I muttered under my breath, spotting one of Gustavo's friends making his way to the limo. He leaned closer, trying unsuccessfully to look through the heavily tinted glass to see who was inside. I reached for the .380 strapped against my calf.

Did he know I was in the car? Did he have a gun?

I slowly raised the gun and slipped off the safety. I didn't take my eyes off him. I had already decided that I would shoot him dead at the slightest provocation. Around me, I could hear my guys drawing their guns and releasing the safeties. With my left hand, I slowly lowered the window.

His eyes widened and you could smell the fear on him as he found himself staring down the barrel of my gun. I let him stand there for a few seconds before I spoke. When I was sure that the reality of his situation had sunken in, I said, "You looking for me, paisano?" My voice was steady and low.

He couldn't find his voice to answer.

I slid over in the seat, never lowering the barrel of my gun. "Come on in. Have a seat," I said, patting the limo seat.

"What's the matter? Vidal, I have no problem with you." He kept repeating this in Spanish over and over, like he was reciting the rosary. "Come on, have a seat," I said softly, my gun never moving.

He finally realized he had no choice. A soft tremor ran through him and then he slid in next to me. I quickly patted him down for a gun. He was clean.

My guys started to put their guns away, but they still kept a close and wary eye on him.

"So," I said, taking a conversational tone, "what's going on?"

He knew what I wanted to hear and he was in no position to refuse. "Hey, Vidal...you and me, we got no problems, right?"

"Not yet," I told him.

His eyes widened in fear. "Gustavo's the one that's looking for you...ever since he made bail on a New Jersey arrest...."

He talked fast. He knew he was giving me some of what I wanted. He had the nerve to tell me he wanted me to front him half a kilo of cocaine so he could make some money. "I got customers waiting, Vidal," he said. "A half kilo would set me up good." He babbled on about how much he loved my jewelry and how I was tops.

In my mind, I gave him credit for balls. He was trying. But he wasn't going to get what he wanted. "Look," I told him, "here's my beeper number and an ounce. You get in touch with me when you see Gustavo." I looked him dead in the eye. "There'll be something in it for you if you do."

"You got it, Vidal. No problem. Absolutely."

I didn't trust him but I wasn't going to do anything else with him, so after letting him stew a few more minutes, we let him out of the car. "Now get the F—- out of here," I said as he scampered away.

"Scum," Joe muttered.

I shrugged. "Useful scum," I said thoughtfully. He'd given me some useful information on Gustavo's movements. Based on that information, a plan began to take shape. The next night, I was going to go looking for Gustavo.

I added Johnny Karate to my entourage. Johnny was 180 pounds of all muscle, a fourth-degree black belt in karate, and no one to F—- with.

At four in the morning, the place was well lit and packed. I was on edge. I didn't like being there but my focus was on Gustavo. He was the son of a bitch who had tried to kill me and my family. I had no forgiveness in my heart for him.

We sat at a round table that faced the front entrance. Outside, Carlos the Marielito waited with the chauffeur, watching. I went into the men's room and looked around. I wanted to be familiar with the place before all hell broke loose. I was familiar with a lot of people there and so I shook a lot of hands—mostly drug dealers and their girlfriends.

Looking back, we must have been quite a vision. Me and my guys were all wearing double-breasted designer suits and hats like Al Capone. One hour turned into two and then three. After a few hours and Gustavo not showing up, we started drinking and doing coke.

After a while, we left and went to another club, Felecia's, an after-hours club set above a body shop on 55th. Felecia's was packed with drug dealers and users. The lighting inside was bad. When we got inside, a friend told me that someone had been killed there a few days earlier.

"The body got dumped outside like plain trash," he said with distaste.

Death. It was everywhere. It was the background noise. If the person who died (was killed) was someone you knew, you considered revenge. Otherwise, the news was about as interesting as hearing that someone had come down with a cold.

That wasn't always the case with me. I remember the first time I dealt with death was when two of my high-school buddies, Orlandito and Frankenstein, were killed.

They'd gotten involved in drugs, but not for long. One night Orlandito was murdered outside a Brazilian bar while he was making a phone call. He never made it out of the booth. He was shot at least nine times. People in the area talked about how the pool of blood flowing from the phone booth reminded them of another killing, one that had taken place only the night before.

Morbid curiosity took me to that phone booth to see the place where my old friend had been murdered.

Frankenstein was beaten to death with a hammer, ripped off by prospective buyers.

But the death that tore me up the most was when they killed El Gallo. He had invested his drug money. He had vast land holdings. He had cars. Boats. A plane. His gambling junkets involved hundreds of thousands of dollars.

It went down that El Gallo's brother got in a jam out in Vegas. Something to do with some money he owed someone. When El Gallo heard about the situation, he went out West to straighten things out. Turned out the whole thing was a set-up. When El Gallo opened the door to his hotel room, a gunman was waiting for him. He was shot several times in the neck.

El Gallo had been responsible for a number of killings in New York and Florida. Live by the sword, die by the sword.

His murder stirred up a lot of resentment in his powerful Cuban organization. Vengeance was brought to bear on anyone having anything to do with El Gallo's murder. People turned up dead in Vegas. In Miami. Everywhere. Bodies were found stuffed in alleyway trash containers. In trunks of abandoned cars.

The lesson was obvious for everyone to see. Dealing and death go hand in hand. A sensible person would have learned something simple from that lesson—don't get involved in dealing. I got something else from it—don't ever be without a gun. My logic was simple. I'd rather be arrested and taken away by two cops than be carried to my grave by six.

I started going to the shooting range several times a month. I even thought it would be a good idea for Zeizel to be good with a gun, so I took her to the shooting range with me.

"Here," I said, handing her a .38. "Let's see what you can do."

From twenty-five feet, she hit the bull's eye five times out of six attempts. Five for six! I was impressed. I felt more comfortable with her handling the gun. But then I thought about what would happen if someday she caught me with another woman. Then I wouldn't be so happy about her shooting skills.

Zeizel's first day at the shooting range was also her last. No sense in taking unnecessary chances.

Chapter Fifteen

In the back of my mind, I was always trying to figure out that evening outside the bar when Sam was writing down Paco's plate numbers. In April 1983, I was going to finally start to figure it out.

I was sitting at the bar at the Royal Tavern, sipping a drink, when Sam came in. I didn't acknowledge his presence. I kept my attention on my drink. I hadn't seen him around for a few days. I was sure he'd been up to no good.

"Robert," he said, coming up to me, his voice filled with excitement, "I made a score!"

I turned and looked at him, trying to gauge something...some kind of sense of what I was about to hear. I could already feel in the pit of my stomach that something was very wrong. I was about to find out exactly how wrong. "What did you do, Robert?"

With that simple invitation, he began to tell a tale that would change the course of my life—and the lives of others—for a long time to come.

"I've been gathering some information," he said. I immediately remembered him writing down the license numbers. "I found out where one of your suppliers, the one named Paco, lives."

"Shit," I thought to myself as the muscles in my neck and jaw tightened. I had the incredible urge to strangle him now, before I heard another word. But I willed myself to remain calm and to listen.

"Me and Wayne went to this eight-story building in Elizabeth. Fifth floor. We went to the door and rang the bell." He chuckled to himself, feeling like he had figured it all out. "We had police badges, you know. People pay attention to police badges. So we rang the bell and a short Spanish guy opens the door as far as the chain goes and looks at us...."

The short, Spanish guy was jumpy and nervous to begin with. Seeing the police badges really frightened him. "What do you want?" he asked.

"We're police officers," Sam told him. "We have a warrant to search the premises."

The guy hesitated but then opened the door.

"Who are you?" Sam asked him. "And where's Paco?"

"I...I...speak not much English. I am Colombian. My brother Paco is not home. Que pasa?" He was sweating and shaking, scared to death by these two "cops" in his brother's apartment.

"Where are the drugs?" Sam demanded. "The cocaine. We know your brother is dealing!"

Not getting an answer, Sam and Wayne cuffed him and then ransacked the apartment, turning it upside down in their desire to find coke, money, and valuables. They dumped drawers. They flipped the mattresses on the beds. They turned plants upside down and dumped the soil on the carpet. But they couldn't find any drugs. Minute by minute, Sam and Wayne were getting more and more pissed.

"Come on, you little F—-," they said, grabbing Paco's brother and dragging him to the middle of the floor. "Now listen, we ain't cops, you hear? We're your worst nightmare. If you don't tell us where to find the shit, you're dead!" Then they drew their weapons and pointed them straight at the Colombian's face.

Paco's brother was terrified. No one had ever dared to come into his brother's house before, to disrespect him in such a way. He started to whimper and cry.

"Shut up!"

He couldn't stop.

"Dammit, shut up!" Sam shouted, slapping Paco's brother across the face. He fell over. He knew that these two Norte Americanos were serious and would do exactly as they said. "Don't kill me! Don't kill me! Please! I am a working man. I'll tell you. I swear. Don't hurt me. I'm just a harmless man. I'm a homosexual. Don't kill me, please!"

Sam looked down at Paco's brother with contempt. "No shit," he spat out. "Now get the drugs."

The Colombian moved away from them, shaking like a leaf. He went into the kitchen, keeping an eye on the two men who were keeping an eye on him. He brought a kilo and some cash back into the living room. It had been stashed in a secret compartment in the refrigerator. Now that they had their money and drugs, Paco's brother asked them to please leave. But Sam and Wayne had other ideas. They didn't want to leave anyone behind who could identify them. So they decided to whack him. They both screwed silencers on their .22's.

"No! No! Please, no!"

They slowly tightened their fingers on the triggers...suddenly, the doorbell rang.

"Shit!" Sam said, looking over at Wayne. Wayne shrugged. As Sam went to the door, Wayne gagged their hostage. Then he took his place on the other side of the doorway with Sam.

Outside, there were two young boys. They had come to visit the gay Colombian, to get some coke in exchange for allowing him to indulge his sexual appetites. Wayne took out a police badge and then opened the door. The smiles and giggles of the boys were quickly replaced by stunned and frightened silence.

"What do you want?" Wayne demanded.

Silence.

"Get the hell out of here before I lock you up, too! This is police business."

They were gone as quick as they could get their legs to move. After they had disappeared, Wayne stuck his head out into the hall and looked up and down. Satisfied that no one was there, he came back in and closed the door.

"Okay, let's finish this," he said to Sam.

"Forget about the faggot," Sam snapped. "Just get everything and let's get the F—- out of here."

"But he can identify us!"

"So can those two kids," Sam said. "Let's get out of here before they start shooting off their mouths."

As I listened to this story unfold, I felt my anger building. God, I wanted to kill Sam right there and then. Meanwhile, Sam thought he was the smartest F—-ing guy on earth. He was chuckling as he finished the story.

"So that's it, Vidal. I got a kilo and seventeen thousand in cash. And you know what, old buddy, I'm going to split it with you."

That was the last straw! I could hear the blood rushing through the veins in my head. "Are you F—-ing crazy?" I snapped. "Do you know what you've done? Those Colombians were my ticket to being a rich man! They would have made me a millionaire! You're out of your F—-ing mind!" I wanted to strangle him until his brains—what little there was of them—popped out through his ears and eyeballs. "These Colombians will kill you and your whole family! They're like F—-ing savages when it comes to revenge. "Why the F—- did you do this, Sam?"

Sam looked at me like I was the one who was crazy. "Vidal," he said in a calm tone, "don't worry. You have plenty of sources."

The F—-! I reached behind my back and pulled out my .45. I flicked the safety and chambered a round.

"Whoa. Take it easy, Vidal," Sam said. "If there had been twenty or forty kilos, you and me could have retired."

I shook my head and put the gun back. Not that I'd changed my mind about wanting to kill him. Just that this wasn't the time or the place. Once again, I tried to get him to understand the situation he and Wayne had gotten us all into, but it just wasn't sinking in.

"Sam, you and Wayne are nuts. We're making a lot of money. You didn't have to do this. Especially to a large and powerful supplier like Paco." I shook my head. "I had all the pure cocaine I needed. He's going to think I'm behind this. His brother will I.D. both of you and Paco will link you to me." I guess the look in my eye had finally brought Sam down from his high. "Get the F—- out of here, Sam. Beep me later on tonight. We may have the start of a drug war on our hands."

I watched Sam as he left. He got into a two-door I'd never seen before. Wayne was behind the wheel.

"F—-," I muttered as I motioned for the barmaid to come over. "Double shot of Sambuca," I told her. And I meant it. Sam and Wayne had created real problems this time. Like I didn't have enough to worry about, now my supplier was going to think I'd set him up. Shit. I had to think. This could easily become a war.

I looked around. Joe Belo wasn't around. I went to the phone and called my guys. I wanted my most reliable guys there with me—that was for sure. I got up and went to the office so I could check my gun in private. Everything was fine. I counted my bullets.

I expected trouble. I had no doubt it was coming. The only question was when. Even if Sam and Wayne didn't know it, I did. The Colombians weren't people to F—- with.

I started to consider the situation. I didn't like sticking around, knowing the trouble that was brewing on the horizon. But I had never been one to run from danger. Now wasn't the time to start.

It was all weighing on me. The pressure from Zeizel. The knowledge that Gustavo wanted me dead. And now this. The seconds ticked by slowly. Two hours crept by from when Sam left the bar. It had been over a half hour since I'd called my guys to get their asses to the bar. Okay, maybe things would work out. I could feel some of the tension easing from my limbs. The Sambuca was working its magic.

"How the F—- did Sam get Paco's address?" I wondered. "And where the hell did he get police badges?"

I remembered a time on Bloomfield Avenue when a squad car came by to pick him up. They took him somewhere to get some money and then brought him back. Could they have gotten him the badges? I didn't know. Maybe he'd had the plates checked by his contacts in the police department. I'd always been impressed by his contacts in law enforcement. But now, I realized that those connections could be as dangerous as they were helpful.

I was sitting there, trying to put two and two together when the door suddenly opened up and Paco walked in. The door closed behind him and he waited while his eyes adjusted to the light. He looked around, taking it all in. Then his eyes locked on mine. My heart was pounding so hard I thought it would break through my chest. I had to convince him I didn't know anything about what had gone down earlier that day.

He stood there for what seemed like an eternity...then his men walked in and formed a semi-circle around him. I didn't need to see any bulges in their tailored suits to know they were well armed.

"Shit," I thought to myself. "Where are all my guys?" They should have been there already. I had no choice but to play the situation as it lay. I waved Paco over to me. "Que pasa, Paco? Quiere un trago?"

No answer.

His men were also giving me baleful looks.

I let my voice grow angry. "Do I owe you money or something, man? What's with the looks?"

He narrowed his eyes at me. "Que huvo hermano! It wasn't nice what you did!" He pointed his finger at me. "Don't play with Colombians!"

"Don't beat around the bush," I said. "What the F—- are you talking about?"

He gave me a long, cold glare. Then he laid it out. "My problem is that your men did wrong and are going to die for it. Now I have to find out if you had anything to do with it, too. Because if you did, then you're going to die, too."

I knew I wasn't in the strongest position in the world but the fact was that I was getting pissed. I was innocent and I didn't appreciate his threats. "Don't disrespect me, Paco. What's wrong?"

I got up from my seat and started to walk toward him. Every one of him men moved his hand to his jacket. I knew I couldn't give any of them an excuse to use the guns I knew they were packing. As I walked toward him, I casually flicked the safety on my .45. As I took another step, about eight of my men walked in the door. Okay, now the odds were better.

"We have a problem, Vidal," Paco said. "Two of your men ripped me off for five kilos, $100,000 in jewelry, and over $17,000 in cash." He looked steadily at me. "That's almost half a million dollars."

While Paco was talking, some of my men approached me while the others fanned out around Paco and his men.

"Everyone just relax," I said. "Have some drinks. Paco and I have some business to discuss."

We both knew that between his men and mine, any sudden action would result in terrible bloodshed. So we had to play it cool. Standing close to him, I could feel the anger coming off his body like heat. "Vidal," he said to me, his eyes smoldering, "Sam and Wayne are F—-ing dead men."

He then told me what his brother had told him. Almost word for word, it agreed with the account that Sam had told me.

"Vidal," he said when he'd finished, "we don't play F—-ing games. Help us. Tell us where these guys are. Where they hang out. I want them chopped up in little pieces. Until this is done, you and I can't do business. Not until this is all straightened out."

I understood. I wasn't happy, but I understood.

"I have your beeper number," Paco said. "I'll keep in contact with you."

I nodded. Then I wrote down the address of Sam's bar. Paco took the piece of paper, looked at it, and then put it in his pocket. Without saying another word, he walked out from the bar.

The standoff ended without violence, but damage had been done. I was hurt that Paco could suspect me for what had happened. I thought he knew me better than that. I was now also without one of my main sources of cocaine. What was more, I still had to keep my eyes open. I knew that the Colombians' way of carrying out revenge was to spill a lot of blood. I didn't want it to be mine. The heat was going to be on everyone.

Another thing that pissed me off was one difference between Paco's story and Sam's.

Sam had lied to me, selling me cheap. He'd said one kilo. Paco said five. Paco also told me about the jewelry. They agreed only on the amount of cash.

Dammit. Sam couldn't be trusted. Something was going to have to be done about him... if Paco didn't get him.

It was several days later that I saw Sam. I had heard that he was using his North Newark bar, the Squire Inn, to sell the product he had stolen from Paco's brother. Word was he was doing well with it. He walked in and started up a conversation with me. We talked business, with the conversation finally settling on his cousin, Bobby. I'd given Bobby some coke on consignment and hadn't received my money. If there had been some problem, I would have understood if he'd spoken to me. Instead, he'd made himself scarce.

I had given him the coke on Sam's word. By not making good on his end of the deal, Bobby had rendered Sam's word undependable. "I'm going to kill him, Vidal," Sam said.

I looked Sam in the eye. "Sam, don't forget Paco is looking for you."

Sam's expression never changed. "And don't forget that I'm looking for him, too. I'm not afraid of Paco. Killing is my game." Then he let out a chilling and mirthless laugh. Sam wasn't anyone to fool with, but between him and Paco, my money was on Paco.

Later that evening, I met with Vick, who had also seen Sam.

"Sam wants to buy three kilos from me," Vick said. "He's got the cash to pay up front."

I saw Sam's game clearly. He knew that Paco was Vick's supplier. "Vick, Sam is looking to kill or kidnap Paco to take his money and coke. He's using you, man." I knew that Sam had already ripped off Paco's brother and that now he was moving in for a real score.

Vick heard me out, but I could see that everything I was saying went in one ear and out the other. His only concern was for his profit. He didn't consider that he was putting his own life in jeopardy.

The deal was to go down in the parking lot of the Queen Elizabeth Diner in Elizabeth, New Jersey. Vick would be the middleman. He would get the money from Sam, take it to Paco, and then return with the drugs.

Things didn't quite work out that way.

When Sam gave Vick the bag of money, Vick checked the bag and saw that some of the neatly wrapped stacks of twenty and fifty-dollar bills had nothing but paper in the middle of them. It was only then that he realized that everything I'd told him the day before was true. The fact that he was with Mark and Wayne and that the crazy Marine was wearing black gloves and had a gun on his side only reinforced Vick's growing sense of dread.

He knew that however the deal went down, he'd look like he was helping to set the loser up. In short, that he was F——-ed. He didn't have much time to work out a plan.

When they got to the diner, he told Mark and Wayne that the cocaine was in the diner and that he'd have to go in alone to make the transaction. "Okay, go ahead," Wayne said.

Five minutes after Vick closed the door to the diner, the place was surrounded by police cars.

Sam was furious. Only a small handful of people had known when the deal was going down. As he was being led away, he saw Vick being led away by another cop. "You F——-ing rat!" he shouted. "You called the cops on us! I saw you!"

Vick shook his head. "Not me, man. Can't you see I'm going to jail, too? Jesus, Sam. Think! Why would I call the cops on myself?"

This explanation seemed to calm Sam, but only a little. Sam always denied to me that he'd called the cops. But I knew it wasn't me who called. And Vick's bond was only five thousand dollars. Everyone else's was at least three times that much.

The next day, I was at the Classic Auto Body Shop when Sam walked in. He wasn't in the mood to chat. He had a message to deliver.

"I want to get Paco," he said simply, without anger. "I want to take all his cocaine and his money and then kill him." It was a statement of fact. There was no discussion. This wasn't something he wanted to do. It was something he was going to do. Period.

He was sure it was Vick who called the cops. "I saw him on the phone, Vidal. He's a dead man, Vidal. Dead."

Sam was serious. It showed on his face. Someone was going to pay.

As soon as he left, Manny Lopez, the owner of the shop came over to me. "Stay away from him, Robert," he said, his voice deep with concern.

In my heart, I knew that Manny was right. But I couldn't change things. Not then. I ignored my gut. "Manny, Sam is hanging on a string. His talk is bullshit. He's been talking about killing someone as long as I know him and no one's dead yet. He's just letting off steam."

Even I didn't know how wrong I was...or how soon I was going to find out just how cold-blooded Sam could be.

I had my own men on high alert. I could have killed Sam myself but that wasn't the way I wanted to be rid of him. I knew that, sooner or later, the Colombians would solve my problem for me. I didn't have any doubt about that.

So, I knew I only had to bide my time. The Colombians would take care of Sam and then things could get back to normal again.

Chapter Sixteen

I didn't know how to make a sanctuary for myself. How does a man make a sanctuary to save him from himself? Not even when my baby turned a year old. Zeizel made arrangements for a party at the North Bergen Holiday Inn. We invited about a hundred people, from her side of the family and from mine, plus a few of my business associates. I'd invited both Sam and Wayne a month earlier. They both showed. Sam even brought his wife.

It ate at me that some of my family wouldn't come. They'd heard rumors about my business dealings. They said I was hanging out with criminals. Others in my family refused to believe the gossip.

My mother, sisters, and brother were there. They weren't in denial. They believed what they were hearing. But they were there anyway. Not that they were happy with me.

My mother told me she was praying daily to the Father in the name of Jesus for me to mend my evil ways before it was too late. She looked at me with tears in her eyes. "I want you to be the son I worked so hard to raise," she said. "Come back to the Evangelist church." She wanted me back at the church where I'd first accepted Jesus Christ as my Savior in 1980.

But I wasn't ready. Not yet. I was the prodigal with no thought of finding a road home. I had to turn away from looking at her. I couldn't bear to see her love and concern. "No, Morn," I told her. "I've got things got to take care of. I can't afford to be soft." Satan himself couldn't have given a better answer.

Her beautiful eyes filled with tears. I had cut her deeply with my off-the-cuff remark. She tried not to show it but her pain was obvious.

I couldn't bring myself to say I was sorry. Inside, I couldn't answer why I was always hurting this fine woman. She had done nothing in her life but love me and yet all I did was repay her love with pain. She was my guardian angel, and yet here I was talking to her without any respect.

The D.J. I had hired began to play loud disco music. D.J. Animal from New York knew how to put some life in a party. The beat drove thoughts of my family from my mind. I was once again thinking about my life of money and partying. Outside, I could see a long line of stretch limos and luxury cars. This is what life was all about. My business associates were enjoying the music or getting high in the men's room.

But my mother wouldn't let up. She looked at me in that disapproving way mothers have. She wasn't impressed by the heavy gold jewelry my friends and their women were wearing. She knew how that jewelry was paid for.

Even Zeizel was on my case. I was sitting at a table, watching the festivities, when she came up to me and whispered in my ear, "Robert, why do your friends mean more to you than family? Everything is your friends. You give them drugs. You give them money. You go out of your way for them. But you don't do what you need to do for your family."

I couldn't argue with her. I knew she was right. I tried to change the subject. "Come on, baby, can't we just celebrate Erica's birthday? Give me a break. Oh, by the way, we're going to continue the party at the condo in Secaucus."

She sighed and rolled her eyes. "Whatever you say...."

I looked at her suspiciously. I knew my wife. She was a strong woman and she'd given in way too easily. There was more coming. I could feel it.

"Whatever, fill my house with coke addicts and criminals...." "Shut up, Zeizel!"

But she didn't shut up. "I should have known you'd pull something like this."

"Zeizel!"

I couldn't win. She was right. I was being an asshole.

Later, Sam gave me two ounces of coke as a party gift. He said he knew I liked to give stuff away so he wanted me to have some of Paco's stuff. He followed that with his mirthless laugh. Then he and Wayne left.

As I'd promised, the party continued at our condo. Coke and liquor. Loud music. All the while, my baby slept peacefully in her room.

Little by little, I had allowed myself to be seduced by cocaine and money. I had let them take the place of God in my life. My mother had been right to cry.

Chapter Seventeen

Things started to spiral out of control. Sam told me how he'd tried to kill Bobby over the debt he owed me. "He F—-in' double crossed me," he growled at me when I asked him if he was sure he wanted to go that far. "He's buying coke from another source with your money. That reflects on me. I vouched for that piece of shit and look what he does...."

More and more, I knew that Sam was bad news for me. I didn't realize just how much until the day after he'd come to me with the news he'd tried to kill Bobby. I was at the Costa Brava Bar with Jackie Fresco, who I'd been seeing for several months. She and I had a good relationship. I liked her a lot and I trusted her. We were talking when her friend from school, Cheryl, came over.

"I gotta head out," Jackie said. "I'll see you two later." She gave me a kiss and then left the bar. Cheryl and I continued a conversation, one that quickly became very interesting. Cheryl had spent a lot of time with Sam and Bobby. In fact, she was seeing Bobby.

"He treating' you good?"

She shrugged. "Good as I can expect, I guess." She paused. "Bobby's not the problem. It's Sam...."

Something in her voice got my interest big time. "What do you mean?"

She leaned closer to me. "Sam's working out a plan with the Bureau of Narcotics to have you busted," she said.

"You're crazy," I said.

"You think? With you out of the way, he'd step in and take all your customers...."

I was more shocked than I was willing to let on. I had known Cheryl a long time. She sure didn't have a reason to make up a story like that. It made sense in my gut. I studied her face. She was a pretty girl. A good girl. It bothered me that Sam and Bobby had convinced her to get into prostitution. It wasn't right that a nice girl like her had to sell her body for drugs. But now I had bigger concerns. Would Sam really try to set me up? If he did, he was F—-ing with the wrong guy!

I may not have wanted to listen much to my mother when she talked about God, but I sure believed her when it came to the Golden Rule of the street: Do unto others before they do unto you!

"Don't tell anyone please what I told you, okay?" Cheryl asked me. "Yeah, no problem," I told her.

"I...I just thought you should know."

I told her I wouldn't tell, but there was no way I could keep this information to myself. My guys had to know, too. If I was being set up, they were sure to get caught up in the trap. From the time that Cheryl told me, the information kept boiling up inside me.

So, the next time I ran into Sam, which happened to be at the Classic Auto Body Shop, I was armed and ready to do some damage.

"Sam," I said, coming up to him, "I've always treated you with respect, right?"

"Yeah, Vidal. Why?" he asked, looking at me, puzzled. I could see he was already working angles, trying to figure out why I'd come at him with such a question.

"And I've always given you and Bobby all the cocaine you've asked for, without any money up front, right?"

"Yeah," he said, his voice wary now.

Chapter Seventeen

"And my guys, they've always treated you with respect, right?"

"Yeah," he said. "Vidal, what the F—-'s this all about?"

"If I always treated you so good, why the F—- are you looking to set me up with the Essex County Narcotics Bureau?" I asked angrily. Just like that, boom, he knew what was what. I knew. There was absolute surprise in his eyes. There was no way I should have been able to find out about that.

"Who...who...who the F—- told you that? That's bullshit. I...I want to know who's telling you shit like that," he demanded. Then his voice softened. "Shit, Vidal, I'm your friend. You know that. Someone's trying to F—- with our friendship. Tell me who it is, Vidal, and I'll skin them, I swear it."

"The person who told me didn't lie," I said simply.

"Tell me who it was," he said, his voice menacing. "I won't rest until I know who this rat is."

I decided to play it different. I now knew all I needed to know—and Sam knew that I knew it. "Don't sweat it, Sam. I know. That's all that matters."

But he kept wanting to know my source. That's all he really cared about. He wasn't so concerned anymore with the information itself—that damage was done. What he cared about was revenge. We kept arguing back and forth and, in the heat of the argument, I said that Cheryl would never lie about something like that.

Sam's eyes blazed with anger. In a single motion, he drew a switchblade and flicked it open. "She's F—-ing dead, Vidal," he said simply. "I'll kill that bitch."

As soon as I saw the knife, I stepped back and reached for my gun. I could tell by the look in his eyes that he was serious. Dead serious. I'd seen him worked up before, but never like this.

"Take it easy, Sam. Just take it easy. We'll forget this, okay?"

After a couple more minutes, Sam abruptly turned and walked out. Manny and I exchanged nervous glances. Neither of us gave voice to the simple truth we both knew—Sam wasn't about to forget any of it.

I remember April 24, 1983, as a warm and beautiful spring day, the kind of day that makes you forget that your whole life is tied in with violence, sin, and death. The flowers were starting to bloom and the air was fresh. Me and a bunch of guys were at the body shop around two-thirty in the afternoon, drinking and getting high. Carlos Vidriero, Ralph, Carlos El Marielito, High One Buck, Jr., Manny. Guys I knew and trusted. Guys who'd been with me a long time. We were all in a good mood. It was springtime. Right?

Suddenly, the doorknob turned. We all tensed. Everyone who was supposed to be there was already there. Every hand reached for a weapon. I got up from my seat and moved quietly to a window. Parting the curtain a fraction of an inch, I saw Sam standing outside the door. I mouthed his name to my crew. High One drew his .25 caliber and chambered a round.

Sam knocked on the door. I looked at everyone. They nodded. They were ready for anything.

Sam burst in as soon as I opened the door. "Well, Vidal, we did it," he boasted as he came in, not looking around to see who all was there. "We got Bobby last night."

I heard what he said but I didn't believe him. I didn't want to.

"Day like today, the bodies should be stinking by now," he observed casually. Then he looked dead at me. "Cheryl got hit, too. And another girl. We hit Bobby first. I did that. Killed him slow. Yeah, he died real slow."

He still hadn't noticed anyone else in the room. Suddenly, he stopped and looked around, seeing he had a crowd of listeners, all giving him their undivided attention. He motioned to me to step aside. "Come outside with me," he said.

I shrugged. But as soon as his back was turned, I whispered to High One to cover my back. As we stepped outside, High One came to the door and watched us. High One and I had been friends since we were eleven. He wasn't going to let anything happen to me.

"Nothing to worry about," I told High One. "We're just having a little conversation." That was for Sam's benefit. High One was watching and getting ready to act against the worst.

As we walked on the gravel outside the shop, Sam continued his gruesome tale. The girls had been executed while giving blowjobs to his men. They'd wrapped their guns in towels and then just shot them. Bang. Like that. I could feel my stomach turning. But there was no emotion in Sam's voice at all. No remorse. It was like he was describing a scene in a movie.

"Here's my problem, Vidal," he went on. "We dumped the guns in the river and now we need to get some more. Can you get us some guns?" He put his hand on my shoulder. "Do that for me, okay?"

There was some discussion among my men about whether they'd really killed them or if Sam was bullshitting. But then, when we were driving around, a bulletin came over the radio. The bodies of two females and a male had been found in an apartment. Blood was everywhere. It seemed to be an execution-style killing.

"F—-," I said under my breath. I couldn't believe it. Now there was no doubt in my mind the kind of person Sam was. He'd killed two innocent women and his own cousin. I was convinced that he would stop at nothing.

"What should we do?" High One wondered. We all knew that the heat would be on everyone until the murders were solved. These were too grisly for the cops not to pursue them. High One looked at me. "This guy was going to dime you to the Bureau," he reminded me. "Not to mention ripping off Paco."

I nodded my head. Sam was a danger to everyone, not just me. He had to be stopped. My guys and I went back and forth about what to do. After all, business was going to suffer until the crime was solved. After a great deal of soul searching and debate, during which we discussed High One's brother, an investigator for the Essex County Prosecutor's office, we came up with a plan. Once the decision was made, we pulled over to an all-night diner in Newark, a place called Caruso's.

"Call the cops," one of the guys said.

"That's risky," I said. "Sam's got contacts in the police department."

"Then let's call the state police. Those guys are clean. They'll arrest their own F—-ing grandmothers." That was true. So, that's what we would do. We called and told the operator that the man responsible for the triple murders on South Orange Avenue that day had been arrested several days earlier at the Queen Elizabeth Diner with guns and drugs. We told the operator the caliber of the guns used in the killings, giving credibility to the call.

"This is not a hoax," we told the operator.

"What's your name?" the officer wanted to know. "What's your name?"

"Tony," my guy said. Then he hung up before the call could be traced.

After that, we got our weapons together. We switched to a car Sam wouldn't recognize and then we went to a Portuguese bar. We didn't know what the next few hours would bring, if we would live or die.

I wondered if High One would speak with his brother or not. I didn't ask. As we sat at the bar, we were all tense. There was nothing more to do, not now. We could only wait to see what would happen next. If Sam learned that someone leaked information to the police about his involvement in the murders, he'd come at that person with all the rage of Hell. He wouldn't be satisfied until that person was carved up into little bits and fed to the dogs.

Me, I wasn't interested in becoming dog meat. Not one bit.

Chapter Eighteen

The next time I saw Sam was an afternoon a few days later at the Costa Brava Bar. I was having a few drinks with High One and some of the guys when Sam and Wayne came in. I was shocked to see him. I thought they were in jail. As soon as I saw Sam, I reached for the .38 snub nose I carried in my ankle holster. As I did, I felt High One's hand on my wrist.

"Relax," he said when I looked at him. "I've got my .25 and I'm ready."

Sam spotted me and walked over. He had the newspaper folded over his hand. I got more and more tense the closer he got.

"Look, Vidal," he said when he got close, "the F—-ing *Star Ledger* belongs to me. Front page." He leaned closer as he tossed the paper to me. "Someone dimed me out to the cops. They arrested me but had to let me go. Insufficient evidence. They wanted me to take a polygraph. F—- them. I said no way."

I was quiet, watching him. He kept looking at me with a hard, unwavering glare.

"You know what this means, Vidal."

"No, what?"

"One of your guys ratted me out with a phone call to the cops." I wondered how he knew it was a phone call.

"You know who it was, Vidal? I swear I'll kill the bastard. You know I will."

I knew it. "Sam," I said steadily, "the guys on my crew don't squeal. Period."

Then I turned away, trying to ease the tension in the air. "By the way," I added as an afterthought, "you look pretty good in that picture. Younger than you do in real life."

"F—- you."

I shrugged. "You guys want a drink?"

They both refused. No one spoke for about thirty seconds and then Sam said he had something for me outside. A gift. I felt my heart drop. Maybe this was it. Walking outside with them, I was sure it was my last walk, even with High One trailing behind and the .38 in my waist.

Turned out, the gift was a large caliber handgun. Sam wanted me to get him and Wayne some smaller caliber guns.

He and Wayne drove off, leaving me standing with a bag in the parking lot. Holding a gun. High One came over. We stared at one another in disbelief. There we were, holding a bag containing what we were sure was the weapon used in the triple murders.

"I'm gonna dump this gun down the sewer hole," I said, breaking the silence.

High One had another idea. "Let's take it to my brother." He looked in the direction Sam's van drove off. "He's trying to set you up, right?" I thought about it for a minute. "Okay. Go get your car."

I'd known both High One and his brother since I was a kid. That was a good thing. I needed the faith that a history gives you to deal with this situation. I don't know that I would have talked to anyone else. Within an hour of arriving at his brother's house, I'd laid out the whole story to him.

"I'll see what I can do," High One's brother promised.

I felt more relaxed than I had in a long, long time. I really believed that things would be taken care of now.

Yeah, right.

Chapter Nineteen

The next evening, around eight o'clock, I was at Carlos the Portuguese's apartment with him, High One, Ralph, and Carlos the Cuban when my beeper went off. I looked down at the display and I saw 99999. Emergency.

I dialed the Tavern. Chico picked up the phone. He was short of breath when he picked up the phone.

"What's going on?" I asked anxiously.

"Sam and some other guy are in the parking lot. They're looking for you, Vidal. And they don't look too happy."

"Okay, thanks, Chico. Take care of yourself."

I'd been hoping I wouldn't have to worry about Sam, but that seemed to have been wishful thinking. Still, as I've said a hundred times, it helped in this business to be a little paranoid. I'd had all my distributors keep an eye out for him. This time, it probably saved my life.

Less than ten minutes later, I got another beep. This one was a Union County number followed by 22. That was a code I'd worked out with Sam, one that indicated he was in Union County—at least twenty minutes away.

Rather than call Sam right back, High One and I decided to call his brother's office and let him know the situation. Lt. Flamingo of the Newark Homicide Division answered the phone. After explaining the circumstances, he asked how many people were with me and where I was calling from. I told him.

"Does Sam know of that address?"

"No."

"Okay, then sit tight and wait for me."

The authorities were now aware that Sam and his thugs were armed and after us. Now, there is an unwritten code that going to the law in any situation is taboo. After the call, I had second thoughts about what I'd done. After all, if Sam came after us and we ended up on top, it would have been justifiable homicide, right?

I worried about what my guys must have been thinking. But the fact was, what was done was done. Now we had to clean up the apartment for whatever might happen next.

I hid all the handguns in the sofa bed in the living room. We stashed the triple-beam scales and money in other spots throughout the apartment. We gave the place a once over and then another once over. The last thing we needed was for the police to see something to give them probable cause and allow them to search the place.

There was no contraband visible. Carlos went to the fridge and took out Buds for everyone. Less than fifteen minutes after the call, there was a knock at the door.

"That cop must have driven like a lunatic," I said, glancing at my watch. I started to prepare myself for the inevitable questions as I headed toward the door. Suddenly, Ralph called to me.

"Don't open the door, Vidal! It's Sam. He's got a sawed-off shotgun!"

Shit. I knew I had to remain in control, but this was a terrible situation. We were all young and inexperienced in this kind of situation. If my crew saw me panicking, it would be all over.

Meanwhile, my heart was pounding and the adrenaline was coursing through my veins. In about two seconds, I'd already fished the guns from the sofa bed, passing out a .38, a 9mm, a .380 automatic, and a .25 automatic. I kept the 30-30 Luger for myself. The Luger only held six shots but the gun was originally designed to hunt buffalo. Six shots should be more than enough.

"Open up, Bobby, it's me," Sam called as he twisted the doorknob. Sam was one of the few people who still called me Bobby.

Whispering, I motioned Carlos the Cuban to take the 9mm and position himself in the bathroom. I sent Carlos to the bedroom overlooking the front door. No one hesitated. We all knew that Sam had committed murder only a few days before. He wouldn't think twice about doing it again.

High One, Ralph, and I headed out back to the cement yard and up the ladder to the roof of the adjoining apartment. Once in place, I looked down at Sam still at the front door, trying to coax us out of the apartment. I aimed my pistol. Just then, Ralph started to panic. I turned to calm Ralph down and Sam took the first shot, which echoed loudly between the two buildings.

"Shit!" I leaned over the edge, took aim and let go two rounds. The first was so loud I never even heard the second.

Sam realized that he was not in the best position to play cowboy so he made a break for cover. I pumped two more rounds in his direction and he ran toward his car.

He jumped in. A second later, it sounded like a gunfight in Vietnam. We all pumped shot after shot into the car. Holes tore into it three at a time.

We continued firing until Sam screeched down the street and his taillights disappeared. All that we were left with was an eerie silence and a lot of questions. Did we hit him? Where the F—- was that lieutenant? And what did we do now?

The last question was the first I tried to answer. It was self-evident. Get the F—- out of there!

Even in the middle of chaos, things can be strangely calm. As we were leaving the building, we passed an elderly lady who looked at us and said, "You boys better stop playing with those firecrackers."

It was almost funny. Here was a lady who, confronted with all the evidence that something terrible was going on, saw the harmless instead. She wasn't like me, who tended to see the harmful in everything.

We all climbed into a silver and burgundy Seville and took off. We passed the police, who were on their way in as we were on our way out. We knew the car stuck out like a sore thumb so we abandoned it and walked towards Tony's Pizzeria. We'd only just put the guns in a bag and placed the bag in a trash can when a friend positioned on the coner warned us about a slow-moving car coming our way.

"Undercover cops," I said knowingly.

Sure enough, within minutes we were being transported for questioning. I didn't mind the questions the cops were asking so much. It was the questions in my mind that were bothering me the most.

Why didn't Lieutenant Flamingo make it to the apartment? How had Sam dialed a Union County number from only two blocks away?

I figured that someone could have dialed the number for Sam, but then that meant that someone was helping Sam set me up for death. Who the hell was that?

Chapter Twenty

The shit had hit the proverbial fan. I had to assume that now Sam, Mark, and Wayne knew that it was my crew that had rolled on them. What that meant was that, in addition to Paco and Gustavo, I now had Sam's Mafia assassins after me as well.

I didn't feel guilty about what happened to Sam. F—- him. Sam had tried to set me up with the Bureau of Narcotics. Bottom line, he was just getting a taste of his own medicine. Now, what bothered me was that innocent people could now be hurt or killed for no reason other than being friends of mine.

The police said not to worry, that they would provide protection. That wasn't convincing to me. They couldn't be around twenty-four/seven. My enemies could.

No sooner had we left the police station than we began to cover our tracks. The plan was to disappear until we could figure out how to get out of the predicament we were in. We found an apartment on 68 Rome Street. I got my hands on a small arsenal and as much ammunition as possible. I had to explain to Zeizel that I couldn't stay with her and the baby.

"You gotta stay with your mother until all this blows over," I told her.

Tears streamed down her face.

"Zeizel, I promise, when this is over, I'll be a real husband to you and a real father to our baby."

Once again, my crew turned to liquor and cocaine. But it was at this time that a new enemy broke our tight circle, an enemy from within. This enemy took the form of a rock. Freebasing became a daily ritual for some of the crew.

One hit, that's all it took. The cloud of euphoria was unbelievable. There was nothing I'd ever experienced like freebasing. If Satan took physical form, it would have been in the form of this rock. It could turn God-fearing women into street whores in a day. It could turn brother against brother. It could make a mother steal from her starving children.

Members of my crew began to blow hundreds of thousands of dollars of profit by using instead of distributing. As a supplier, I was hit hardest of all because I seldom got paid for the drugs they were using.

I now wore my bulletproof vest everywhere I went. Everyone I saw was a potential assassin. One night, as I walked home from the nearby grocery store, a cat knocked over a trash can. My gun was drawn before I could even think and an innocent cat came awfully close to meeting its Maker.

The rock made you paranoid. It made you crazy. It was happening to Buck, Jr. High One and Carlos were now living just to stay high. They weren't thinking of anything else.

Buck was so paranoid that he was convinced that there were two hit men following him around, wanting to kill him. It got so bad that he actually pulled over his car and walked into the downneck Market Street Third Precinct and told the cops they were going to kill him. The cops. Asked him where he was staying, he told them 68 Rome St, by The Spanish Sangria restaurant. So several Newark detectives came to the apartment....who once inside started to scanned the area with their eyes. Then suddenly "Nobody move" they noticed the AR-15 leaning against the bedroom wall. That led to a search, which in turn led to the discovery of several hand guns, shotguns, and rifles along with plenty of bullets. Not to mention more than a half a kilo of cocaine. Everyone was arrested and wearing metal bracelets on their wrists and in the cop cars on their way to Police Headquarters, 22 Franklyn St Newark NJ. For a family portrait and fingerprints. For hours my calls to their beepers were not answered I feared the worse, "Did Sam's people get to them?

After approximately 10 hours. The crew started to make bail and I got all the details.

But Now I lost about eight guns and my enemies were well armed. One guy will be happy one of my main gun suppliers Billy Shears who was an associate and gun supplier to the Mafia. The Mob was not happy when they found out he was supplying me with guns a known cocaine dealer.Not to long after that- Billy was found dead in a trunk of a car....maybe? It was mafia mathematics: I could turn on Billy under pressure and Billy turns on them.

Chapter Twenty-One

It was during the summer of 1983 that I learned that the cops are not always the "enemy." It's a strange thing about cops and criminals. They occupy the same streets, but supposedly on opposite sides of some "line." But the truth is, the "line" is more of a gray area. And criminals often stray to one side, when they help the cops, and cops just as often stray to the other side.

I knew the heat was on after the shoot-out. I was going to have to cool off or retire from the drug trade. That summer, I kept sales to a minimum, selling only to those who bought in large quantities. My profit margin would be greatest and, at the same time, I'd be able to keep a lower profile.

About this time, two local cops began to spend time at Costa Brava during working hours. I'd known both of these guys, Peter Gomez and Predest Davis, for a while. I went to high school with Peter's two brothers. It was a strange feeling, chatting it up with these guys at the bar with their police car parked right in front. But they were cool, and never made it seem like they were on official business. Which, as it turned out, they weren't.

After checking in almost every day for several weeks, Peter asked me for some coke for his brothers.

I looked at him funny. I couldn't tell if he was setting me up, if he was serious, or what. "Peter," I said, "what gives? You looking to set me up? You know my background, but you're a cop for chrissakes."

Peter shook his head. "Don't worry. It's for my brothers and some girls."

I still wasn't sure what to make of it. I looked over at Predest who just smiled and said, "Don't worry, Vidal. It's cool."

Fine, then. I wouldn't sell to them, though. I gave them a gram at a time. From that day, we had a bond of trust. I guess on some level, we'd all crossed a line and we had to watch one another's backs.

I started feeling more secure, having Peter and Predest coming by in their cruiser to check up on me. After a few months of our arrangement, I gave them my beeper number and assigned them their own I.D.s. I gave Predest "13" and Peter "17." It was after I'd given them my beeper number that they finally admitted to me that they were both users.

Through them, I met and became friendly with a number of Newark police officers. As far as I ever knew, these other cops never used drugs. With them, I was very careful never to do anything that might arouse their suspicion. I was always clear on who was the "good guy" and who was the "bad guy." These guys gave me several Fraternal Order of Police shield stickers and some Newark police shirts. How could I have known when I received these simple gifts that they would play such a prominent role in what was to come?

Ralph Cicalese, another cop, lived right around the corner from the Costa Brava. He was a friendly guy. Not so well known for making drug busts, despite working for the narcotics task force. He used to drive by the bar with his wife in the car and wave.

"Hey, Vidal, how're you doing?" I'd wave back, and the glimmer of the sun would reflect off the heavy gold hanging around my neck and wrists.

I'd known Ralph since we were kids. I used to pass his parent's house on my way to play basketball on Oliver Street.

I never really gave much thought to the cops around. They were friends or a necessary evil. It didn't matter. They were there. But then, one night Roger, along with three of my closest friends, Carlos Vidriero, Joe Santos, and High One, told me that they'd gotten wind of some information.

"A trap's being laid for Lytwin and Leone," Roger said. Lytwin and Leone were two members of the narcotics squad and the FBI was looking to take them down for stealing money taken in drug raids. "Keep quiet about this, okay?" he added.

Not too long after this, Joe Santos and I were pulled over by an unmarked car. I wasn't troubled, we were both clean. It was just one of the annoyances of life. Joe got out of the car and told me to stay put. "I'll take care of this." He spoke to a couple of officers for a minute and then they all walked toward the shadows of an underpass. That seemed odd to me. Why the hell would they be going to a dark, deserted place? But lie was going peacefully, so I didn't think much of it.

I looked over at the unmarked car and spotted another guy there. It was Ralph Cicalese. I thought about what Roger had told me. Then I thought about how Ralph had once given High One a break when he'd caught him with a pocket full of Quaaludes. I decided I'd warn him about the FBI trap so he could steer clear of it.

I went over to the car and shook his hand. "I got some information you might want to know about," I said to him. He listened to what I had to say and then he shook his head.

"They're on the wrong track," he said, softly. He didn't say anything else. A moment later, Joe returned with the other cops and then we got back in the car.

"You know those guys, Joe?"

He shook his head. "They're just faces. They wanted to talk about us. They know you're dealing a lot of coke in Newark."

"So?"

"They want us to throw some names their way. They could make a few busts, clear away some of our competition."

"What? Are you crazy?"

"Don't get excited, Robert. They'll stay off our case."

"But if we give up dealers in the area, we'll ruin our business! Don't forget we deal to most of them!"

Joe just shrugged. "Whatever. Here's their card. Think about it."

Now I knew things were going to get hot. If we refused to give up information, then the cops would lean on someone else to give us up. Meanwhile, my coke sales were going down. Paco and I had become sworn enemies. I had to worry about him sending his Colombian assassins to gun me down at any time. And if not them, then Sam's guys. My bulletproof vest became my best friend in those days. Even though Sam was now in the Essex County Jail, he had managed to put out a contract on me and members of my crew.

I knew it was smart to lay low. But I didn't. I didn't want to give up the partying lifestyle I'd come to love so much. I wouldn't—or couldn't—stop abusing. Still, I knew things had to change. I moved my wife and little girl from the condo in Secaucus to a six-room apartment on 70th in North Bergen. The move was hurried and stressful. Zeizel was a nervous wreck from beginning to end.

"Is this what you want? Is this how you want to live?" she kept demanding.

I didn't have an answer for her. No, I didn't want to live like that. I didn't like putting her and my baby girl through the stress and fear, but I didn't see any way out. I had to protect them from danger. I knew how to take care of myself, but I felt vulnerable in a horrible way when it came to my family. I had no way of knowing who, when, or how they would come at me.

While my energy was devoted to this concern, life was going on. My baby was learning to walk and speak her first words. But was I the doting father she deserved?

No. I kept stumbling home at three or four in the morning, stinking of liquor and another woman. I entered our apartment with a pistol in my hand and another in my waistband.

Zeizel was always ready to let me have it. "What kind of man are you?" she'd demand. "I need you here! Erica needs you. And where are you? Out with your criminal friends to all hours of the day and night, drinking, doing drugs, hanging out with whores! What kind of life is this?"

"Baby," I would say, knowing that I could always sweet-talk her. I just needed to calm her down. But one night, there was no calming her down. From the moment I walked in, she insisted I was sleeping on the sofa.

"I'm tired of it," she said. "You put me and Erica last and I'm tired of it."

There was something in her voice, something beyond anger, something beyond bitterness, that cut me. I knew she was right. I couldn't even look her in the eye. That night, after checking out all the doors and windows, I lay down on the sofa and tossed and turned in a troubled sleep. My nightmares were vivid and horrible! I heard steps in the hallway to the bedrooms "I saw Sam's face and the wooden floor cracking sound. I said to myself as I awoke and jumped out of the sofa like a Cobra snake with my 9 MM, in my right hand and finger in the trigger and pointed it down the hallway! I was petrified I had the gun inches from my beautiful wife's face. Zeizell was hysterical and started to cry."Robert it was not the gun it was your eyes-they looked demonic something strange is in you I not only seen it I felt it Robert you are not the same man I married .Zeizel kept crying. I kept trying to explain to Zeizel but she couldn't hear me.

In the coming days, Zeizel moved her clothes out. She had finally had enough.

"Don't do this, baby," I told her.

She closed her eyes and a tear squeezed out.

On the day the movers came, the phone rang. She was close to the phone but I was closer. "Yeah?"

There was a man's voice on the other end. "Is Zeizel there?" "Who's this?"

"Glenn," the man said.

I hung up the phone and looked at Zeizel, who was starting to pace nervously.

"You bitch," I spat out. Zeizel was a beautiful woman who always attracted attention. But I'd never thought...I narrowed my eyes. I'd never thought about her at all.

"What do you care?" she wanted to know.

I couldn't find the words to answer her. I could feel the only good thing in my life falling away and I couldn't think of what to do about it. Later, she told me she'd already contacted a lawyer and was filing for divorce.

Now there would be nothing tethering me to something good and pure. I moved into the Liberty Motel on 69 St and Tonnelle Ave in North Bergen NJ, a dive run by Indian immigrants and used mostly for drug deals and cheap prostitutes. There wouldn't be any more coming home to a nice condo for me, to look at my wife and baby sleeping peacefully. Now, it was a filthy hole paid for at a daily rate.

I could still see Erica whenever I wanted and I would still see Zeizel on occasions in different places, but I knew I was adrift. It scared me and depressed me. There were advantages to living from hotel room to hotel room, though. It hampered anyone's ability to track me—enemies or authorities.

With my wife filing for divorce and finding comfort in another man's arms, I started spending more and more time with Jackie Fresco. As our relationship grew, we became close. How could she have known what she was really getting herself into?

Chapter Twenty-Two

Around September, I moved from the Liberty Motel to the Holiday Inn in Newark. It was cleaner, more comfortable, and only minutes from the local bars in the Down Neck area of Newark. Not that the move was entirely my choice. The North Bergen police were putting a lot of heat on the Liberty, what with the prostitution and drugs. In the process, they asked a lot of questions about me. After all, what was a guy driving the kinds of cars I was driving doing renting several rooms at a time in a dive like the Liberty?

My inside information at the police department kept me aware of the interest in me. I was always careful to register under different names at the hotel. I was careful only to allow my most trusted distributors and loyal friends to visit me at the Holiday Inn.

My drug sales were still down. I was trying to be careful. But some things didn't change. I still spent money freely, and I still partied at all the discos and bars. "Low profile" is a very relative term. I was in my room on the morning of September 3, waiting for a couple of dealers to bring me money they owed me, money I wanted to have for the Labor Day weekend.

Oscar and Roli brought me my cash right on time. When I told them I was leaving for a little fun in the sun, Roli asked if he could brings some girls to the room for some fun of his own.

I shrugged. "Sure. Just don't drink all my liquor and don't F—- with the pistols in the top drawer."

"No problem, Vidal. Thanks," he added as I tossed him the key.

Everyone gathered close to me when I got to the clubs. There I was, pockets full of money and coke, gold glittering around my neck and my wrists: I was the generous drug dealer, handing it out for free.

Zeizel used to say that I was too generous. "You lend out your cars, your money, your clothes, your drugs. About the only thing you don't loan out is me."

The weekend was fun. I had needed to get away. What I hadn't needed to do was to come back. I gave a friend of mine a ride back to Newark. The traffic made me crazy.

Stuck for hours, Luis and I kept doing coke. I still had four ounces in rock form in my pocket when we finally made it back to the hotel. At the front desk, I paid for another day. It was then that I was hit with a hundred-dollar phone bill for the previous two days.

"What?" I couldn't believe how Roli had abused my generosity.

Luis just shrugged his shoulders and told me not to sweat it. "He's an asshole," he said off-handedly.

When we got back up to my room, I tried the key but it didn't work. "What the F—-?" I started to get a sinking feeling. I called the front desk from the phone in the hallway to complain. The assistant manager came up and tried his keys, but none of them worked.

"Let me go down and get some others," he said.

As soon as he left, I felt panic growing in me. I quickly hid my remaining four ounces of coke under the large, black ashtray in the hallway. "You clean, Luis?" I asked him.

He nodded. "Yeah."

A minute later, Newark cops were coming at us from both sides of the hallway.

"F—-," I whispered under my breath.

I knew I was in trouble for the guns they'd find in the dresser, but I was surprised to hear a cop say, "Here it is," even before a single damned drawer was opened. I looked over toward this cop and there he was, holding the Newark police shirt. After that, they did find the guns.

"You have a permit for these?" they demanded.

"What? Where did those come from?" I asked, feigning shock. "Yeah, right."

These cops weren't about to miss a thing. They were ripping the lining out of my five-hundred-dollar suits. They did get several grams from Luis—I guess that was what he meant when he said he was clean.

When they'd finished trashing my room, both me and Luis were transported to the Third Precinct. They also confiscated my little red Corvette, along with my other cars that displayed the police shields in the window. It was then that I felt like the wind was knocked out of me—I was getting an inkling of just what these guys were gunning for.

It was only later that I learned how all this had played out. There had been a complaint from the hotel about a "police officer" getting drunk and harassing guests. Roli had gotten hold of my shirt and decided to have a little fun. I decided that I was going to give him a beating for the inconvenience he had created with his stupidity. This was a bad scene.

Peter and Predest were feeling the heat from internal affairs. "Vidal," they said when they visited me, "don't say anything."

"Take it easy. I'm not going to say anything. Just stay calm."

Even making bail, I knew things had to change. You know what they say—the world keeps going on and on, no matter what's happening in your life. Well, my own problems with the law hadn't slowed down any of my enemies' interest in having me killed. In November, a customer of mine, John Vetella, a NJ Mafia associate called me and told me that a guy he studied karate with had been hired to kill me.

"What? Are you kidding me?"

"Vidal, you know I don't play like that," he said. "But this guy is for real. This is what he does for a living."

"Thanks for the heads-up," I told him.

"The guy's name is Tarzan," he went on. "I want to bring him to meet you."

I wasn't sure how I wanted to play this. "You're not setting me up, are you, John?"

"If I was setting you up, I wouldn't be this stupid," lie pointed out.

Maybe not, but even so, I wasn't taking any chances. For our meeting the following night at the Costa Brava, I was pulling out all the stops. I brought out my best guys. If someone wanted me taken down, they'd have to take down my best with me.

My guys were all in position. I was drinking Scotch and Amaretto like water. Frank Sinatra was crooning in the background of the bar, singing about how "revenge is sweet." One of my guys came running in. John had parked his car over by Tony's Pizzeria. He and another big guy in a kun Fu outfit were coming.

"Okay," I said. "Get back in position and be ready." I checked my guns. I was ready when they walked in.

This Tarzan guy dwarfed John, who stood six-two and 190 pounds. The owner of the bar came over to me.

"Robert, please, no shooting in the bar."

"Don't worry," I told him. "We're only here to talk."

John led Tarzan over and introduced him as the guy Paco had paid to kill me.

"Nice to meet you," I said, looking directly into his black, deep eyes. Then I drew my gun and pointed it directly at his chest. With my movement, my guys all reacted and drew their guns.

Tarzan didn't even blink.

"Come on, Vidal," John was saying. "Put them away."

"What's the matter, Tarzan?" I asked, stunned by his calm. "Didn't the guy who hired you tell you I had all these toys?"

From the corner of my eye, I could see that Carlito from the Mariel Boat lift was itching for the order to shoot. "Carlito, guarda la pistola," I said, easing the tension in the bar.

After that, Tarzan shook my hand and told me that Paco had paid him five thousand dollars to kill me.

"That's it?" I asked, trying act insulted. "Well, how about thinking about working for me?" I pulled out a bag of nearly seven ounces of coke. I could see that Tarzan was interested. He was a user and dealer. My generosity immediately paid off.

By the end of the night, I'd given away more than fourteen thousand dollars of coke. But I was alive.

Once he was high, Tarzan became a big talker. I remained a little leery of him. It's not a bad rule of thumb to move cautiously with anyone who kills for money. But, over time, Tarzan and I became partners. He eventually became my right-hand man and bodyguard, along with his brother, Angel—a.k.a. Green Eyes.

Through them, I came to know some of the top Black and Puerto Rican drug dealers in Newark. Tarzan and Angel were part of a broad network of drug dealers of all races. It turned out that there was no more equal-opportunity employer than drugs.

During that time, Tarzan and I looked for Paco but we couldn't find hide nor hair of him. Word was that he fled back to Colombia when he learned Tarzan and I had joined together.

"F—- him," I thought to myself. In the years to follow, Tarzan and I would do fine together. We'd also become very popular with the Newark Police Department.

Chapter Twenty-Three

Things started happening faster and faster. Late in September, 1 had gone to the Newark Police Department to file a complaint with internal affairs over my arrest at the Holiday Inn. I had never recovered my personal property, which, with all the suits, boots, and other things, amounted to nearly ten thousand dollars in value.

"Hey, Prince of the City," Officer Barry Calicelli called out when I came in. I ignored him.

Officer O'Connor questioned me about my missing property. After a couple of minutes, he tried to strike up a casual conversation about drug abuse in the police department.

"Who's using in the P.D., Vidal?" he asked.

I shrugged my shoulders. "How would I know?"

He started tossing around some names, names I knew. He mentioned Peter and Predest's names, along with Ruben Cabreras's. This guy was right on the money. While I was denying knowing anything, two undercover detectives approached me. One of them was Ralph Cicalese. They started questioning me about drug dealers, too.

"I wish I could help you guys," I told them, "but I don't know."

They asked questions about the police shirt that had been found at the Holiday Inn. O'Connor was very interested in the shirt but I just kept claiming ignorance. At one point, I glanced over at Ralph and he winked at me.

It was getting to the point where I couldn't go more than a few days without being hauled into the police station. I was brought in to the Essex County Prosecutor's Office in November to be questioned about the triple murders. I didn't have much patience with the whole process. It was a lot of "hurry up and wait." They dragged me down there and then left me to pace on the third-floor balcony, waiting to be called in to the office. I wasn't the only one hanging around. I recognized one of the detectives in the hall, a well-dressed guy who looked to be in his late thirties, despite having a head full of silver hair.

"Vidal," he said, motioning me over to him. When I came closer, he introduced himself as Tommy Gilson. "I had a chat the other day with your friend High One...," he said. He then went on to say that High One had implicated me in the murder of Ruben Perrone in North Bergen. He must have seen the disbelief on my face because he quickly added that getting that information had required them to slap High One around.

I couldn't believe what I was hearing. High One was like a brother to me. But I couldn't take the chance that he actually had ratted me out. "High One's nothing but a junkie," I said with a shrug. "He must have been high on dope."

There was something about Tommy that made him comfortable to talk to. As I would soon learn, we would become a lot closer in the near future. After a few more minutes, Tommy asked me to keep the information to myself.

I couldn't believe that High One would have said that stuff. Maybe it was my quick wealth after Ruben's death. High One must not have known just how much I looked up to Ruben.

Despite my promise to Tommy, I couldn't very well keep that information to myself. When I ran into High One several days later at the Costa Brava, I stepped up to him and got right in his face. "What's this shit I'm hearing about you ratting me about Ruben's death?" I demanded.

His face froze in pure panic. He opened his mouth and the words poured out. "No, Vidal, no. How can you think that? I wouldn't... it's not true. That detective's lying. F——-ing liar..." He told me that he did get slapped around but all the detectives wanted to know about was my drug business and that he didn't tell them anything.

Because, in truth, I had nothing to do with Ruben's death, I let it go. Still, something didn't feel right to me with High One after that. I couldn't trust him the same way I always had. I continued to use him in my drug business but I was more careful around him.

I should have been even more careful. If I would have stopped and asked myself how the prosecutor's office always seemed to know so much about what I was doing then, I might have really distanced myself from High One. But I didn't have a crystal ball to gaze in. Probably just as well, on some level.

Along with Joe Santos, I was arrested again on November 29. Attorney Joe Ferranti got me out again, but when we went out to eat afterwards, he warned me to steer clear of Newark.

"They've got a hard-on for you and you're too hot. Cool down."

I knew to take his advice seriously. He was connected and had a number of reliable sources. So when he told me to stay clear of Newark, I planned on doing exactly what he said. That night, I gathered some of my guys and announced to them that I was going to Miami for a while. I was going to meet with some of my Cuban connections there, among them Roger and Rene.

Chapter Twenty-Four

We were dressed to kill when we arrived in Miami, all white and gray double-breasted designer suits and Italian shoes. Not only did we look like a million bucks, but the twenty thousand dollars I was carrying made me feel like a millionaire. When I left Newark, I left behind my stress and worries. In Miami, I was neither predator nor prey. I wasn't packing and I wasn't looking over my shoulder and around every corner.

The warm sun on my face didn't hurt either. November in Newark can be harsh. Here, the balmy breeze was like a beautiful woman's touch on my skin.

We took a double room at the Ritz, one facing the ocean. We spent the next day trying to get some color into our sorry white asses. The nights were spent in the discos.

High One and I were quickly identified as high rollers. We flashed cash and were immediately accepted by others who were known to indulge in the benefits of fast money.

Good weather, good parties, good music, and beautiful women. I liked Miami just fine. Truth was, though, even when I was with these women, I often found my thoughts drifting to Jackie. I missed her. I wished she was with me.

We'd been in Miami a few days when I met up with the Azulejo Brothers. Their Cuban ancestry gave them a very stable connection. Although they were well known as drug smugglers, they kept a low profile. No flashy jewelry or cars. They dressed in sports jackets.

"You look like F—-ing insurance salesmen," I joked.

They laughed. "Maybe, but I'd rather look like an insurance salesman than a prisoner."

Point well taken.

We couldn't agree on a price for a kilo of coke. The price they gave me was no better than what I could have gotten in New York without the danger or hassle of trying to bring it in. I ended up buying half a kilo from a Colombian. It wouldn't satisfy the demand, but I wasn't about to risk being busted carrying drugs on an airplane.

"This is the life, isn't it, Vidal?" High One asked.

"Yeah, Miami's nice," I agreed. "But we got to start heading back to Newark."

High One frowned. I understood his feeling. Miami was great. But we were just visiting. Newark, good or bad, was our home. I was a New Jersey boy through and through. I called one of my crew that evening to tell him we'd be heading home.

"Better come soon, Vidal," he told me. It seemed that a new dealer in town was stepping on my turf.

We left that night. High One made a reservation for a first-class seat. I called an hour or two later to reserve a seat in coach. This was to ensure that if one of us was busted, the other could call an attorney and get the bond.

We boarded the plane about ten minutes apart. While we were both wearing suits, High One was wearing a pair of cowboy boots with two bags of coke tucked into each boot. He quickly settled into his first-class seat, put on his headphones, reclined, and closed his eyes.

I glanced over at him as I passed through on my way to coach. It seemed that the shots of Sambuca and the beers he'd had before boarding the flight had helped him relax. I was more or less the decoy on the flight, dressed in my flashy clothes and bedecked with gold jewelry. If they were going to finger someone as a coke dealer, I would be the one. I sure as hell looked the part. But I was clean. High One was the one who could face fifteen to twenty for possession. Not that we didn't have faith in our high-priced attorneys.

Everything went off without a hitch. High One stepped off the plane and, not having to wait on any luggage, went directly outside, hailed a cab, and went to the Newark Airport Motel. The ex-maintenance man there had already received his ounce of coke and we had already received a master key to all the rooms. High One would hide the coke in one of the empty rooms where I use to hide some of my guns and money.

I picked up the luggage and took a taxi to the Howard Johnson's on Rouet 1-9. Within an hour, I'd been in touch with several members of my crew. A short time later, Jackie returned a call to my beeper. Seeing her number show up made me realize just how much I'd missed her.

Chapter Twenty-Five

"**S**o, who the hell is this guy?" I asked my crew, wanting to hear about the new guy in town. I looked at their faces. It was good to see Tarzan there. He and I had gotten real tight in the past couple of months. He was the best at what he did. And I appreciated it.

There were a lot of shrugs and mumbles of "Don't know, Robert." There was one thing everyone agreed on. This guy had a scar on his face. Other than that, no one seemed to know much about the guy, so I gave some of my men instructions to hang out in the Latin bars over in the Ironbound section.

"Let me know when you find him," I told them.

A few hours later, my beeper went off. Ralph. When I called him back, he told me that a tall, black Cuban was flashing a lot of gold and money at the Night Light, a bar on Ferry Street.

"Set up a meeting between me and this guy," I told him. "Set it for the Costa Brava tomorrow evening."

The following evening, I was already in a familiar booth when the Cuban arrived. He stood nearly five-ten, about 165. He was dressed very well and wore several heavy gold chains around his neck. He looked around and spotted me and came over.

He extended his hand to me. I took it and then we introduced ourselves. As a gesture, I ordered drinks for the whole bar. Then me and Culebra, whose name meant "snake," had a little talk. At first, we talked business. Supply and quantity of product.

"I hear the name 'Vidal' everyplace I go," Culebra said. "The word on the street is that you're the main distributor of product around here and that you've got a lot of men working for you. They also say your crew are feared and very violent."

I laughed. "Violence is part of the game," I said with a shrug. "I've got a lot of street-level dealers who try to avoid paying their debts."

"I don't have that problem," Culebra said. "I deal only in cash. From everyone."

I narrowed my eyes. Who did this boat-lift refugee think he was talking to? Coming to my bar and bad-mouthing how I do business? But I didn't say anything. I had to play it cool. As it was, he couldn't seem to take his eyes off the hundred thousand dollars' worth of jewelry I was wearing. I knew that he'd taken note of my white '83 convertible Buick Riviera outside, with the license plate reading VIDAL. Let the bastard know that I wasn't a nickel-and-dime coke dealer.

Later, as I cruised around with Tarzan and High One, I thanked High One for carrying back the product from Miami. I knew it wasn't enough to satisfy my clientele. There were more and more users. As a result, there were more and more dealers. For some, their habit drew them into the business. For others, it was the dream of big money.

Despite the growing criminal activity, Newark was a beautiful city. There were new businesses opening everywhere. From where I was sitting, the future of the city was bright, no matter about increased drug crime and trafficking.

In the coming weeks, I heard a lot about Culebra. Seems he'd been bragging that he was supplying me with product. He kept telling people that he was the man. You can imagine what I thought about this bullshit. The man had a big mouth and I didn't like it.

The more I learned about him, the less I cared for him. He'd killed a man in Miami. I figured this was how he'd obtained his coke. I wanted to see this guy again face to face and see if he would insult my organization then.

One night, my beeper went off. It was Ralph with news that Culebra was in the El Pais bar.

"I'm on my way. Keep an eye on him," I said. I was anxious to meet "The Mouth" again.

The bar was crowded, and it was only Ralph and I coming to meet this guy. Ralph was powerfully built and was packing, but we wouldn't be much of a real match if things turned nasty.

When the Cuban spotted me, he smiled. I motioned for him to come over to where I was sitting and he did. I could feel my blood boiling as he came over.

"Hey, Vidal..."

"Don't you F—-ing 'Hey, Vidal' me," I said. "Let's go outside where we can talk."

I wasn't interested in getting into it with him inside the bar. But as soon as we were outside, I let him know what I thought. "You've got a F—-ing big mouth, you know that?"

"I hope you're ready to get the shit kicked out of you," he said calmly.

I shrugged. "Let's go then," I replied.

We started out boxing. He was fast, but I had twenty pounds on him and 1 knew that when I came in on his body, I'd hurt him. As we jabbed at one another, people started gathering around to watch. Having people watching only fueled my hatred for this Cuban. Boom, boom, boom. I landed three straight punches to his head, which I followed with a knee to his groin. I knew a knee to the groin was hardly fair in boxing, but I didn't see any referee around so I figured, F—- him.

I could see the pain register on his face. Then I swept his feet and he went down hard. I grabbed his belt behind his back and then ran his head into the nearby fire hydrant.

"Bastard," he spat out. Despite the wide gash in his head and the loss of blood, he was still fighting mad. He managed to clamber to his feet and land a few solid punches.

Our fight had moved from the parking area to the sidewalk to the street.

"That's enough, Robert," Ralph was saying. "You're blocking traffic, man."

I didn't pay any attention to him. Instead, I lifted the Cuban up and body-slammed him to the street. I knew he was hurt, but he kept trying to fight back. It was only then that I heard the air filling with the sounds of sirens. I looked at my hands, which were covered in blood. So was my face.

I turned and looked in time to see Ralph disappearing into the crowd. The police cruiser was there before I could even decide to run. Shit. I knew I was in trouble.

Suddenly, the doors to the cruiser opened and two cops jumped out. "Vidal, what's going on here? Who is this guy?"

I felt relief flood through me. It was Peter and Predest You want us to put a gun on this guy?"

I shook my head. "Take him to the mall parking lot up the street."

The crowd that had gathered for the fight was now registering surprise. They couldn't figure out why the police were asking me for my advice on what to do next. And then, when they handcuffed the Cuban and pushed him into the police car, they didn't know what to make of it.

I followed after the police car to the parking lot by the Pathmark store. As I drove, I knew just how lucky I'd been. If any other cops had shown up, I'd be under arrest already. Instead, I was being asked how they could cooperate with me. Sometimes the world just worked in funny ways.

Once in the parking lot, I stood and talked with Peter and Predest while the Cuban stared at us in disbelief.

"So what do you want us to do with him?" Peter asked me.

"Take him for a ride and then let him go," I said. "He needs to learn a lesson. But he's harmless."

Culebra called over to me in Spanish, asking me what was going to happen to him.

198

I told him nothing was going on. "Just don't forget this," I said to him. "This is my neighborhood. You got a big mouth and you talk too much. You better find someplace else to do business, got it?"

He looked from me to the police officers and back to me. Then he nodded his head.

Later that night, Peter and Predest joined me and my guys at the Casa Storia when they'd finished their shift. We sat around, snorting coke and drinking Dom Perignon.

From that night on, my bond with these two police officers was strengthened. I trusted them. When they called my beeper, I always returned the call right away. I gave them coke and cash whenever they needed it. I thought of them like I thought of any other member of my crew.

There was only one problem with this relationship. Word spread fast on the street that I was paying off the police. It didn't help that I was very high profile in my relationship with them, taking them to discos and bars in stretch limousines.

Chapter Twenty-Six

My dad was always on me to leave my life of crime and constantly looking over my shoulder. I'd been giving him money and letting him stay with me for a while. He'd see me coming in night after night, my clothes ripped, covered in the blood of some lowlife, dead-beat drug dealer I had to beat up to collect my money from.

"Get a real job son and leave this dangerous life," he told me. "Buscate un verdadero trabajo hijo y déjà esta peligrosa vida"

I couldn't get him to understand that as soon as I got a "real" job, my enemies would come for me and kill me. Besides, I liked the life I was living. I was the man. I had other men willing to put their lives in jeopardy for me.

Of course, my lifestyle didn't help him much. He was still hanging out in bars and drinking, trying to dull the pain of a painful life.

About this time, Tommy Gilsen approached me and alerted me that there was an active warrant for my arrest in Harrison.

"What the F—- do they want to arrest me in Harrison for?" "Sale of a stolen vehicle."

"Dammit," I snapped. A drug dealer had given me a Corvette as payment for a deal. I knew the car was stolen but he'd sworn to me that the bill of sale was legal. All I could think about was how I was going to make that scumbag pay for this. "Thanks for the heads-up," I told Tommy as I turned and started to walk away.

"No problem," he said. "Listen," he went on, getting me to stop. "if you want, I can arrange for you to turn yourself in and make bond."

I looked at him. As I considered his offer, I wondered why he was making it. After all, we were pretty much on opposite sides of things. Still, the offer was a good one and it made me think more positively about Tommy. "I'd appreciate that," I told him.

On March 22, I turned myself in and was escorted to the Harrison Police Station by one of Tommy's comrades, Detective Green. Even handcuffed, I felt like I was in charge as I went into the building, went through the procedure of being photographed and fingerprinted, and was then let out on a one-hundred-dollar bond. I was back on the street less than an hour after being brought in. What a rush!

When the initial rush wore off, I started wondering about Tommy's motivation again. Tommy was good friends with my new lawyer, Tony Fusco. I was figuring that Tommy wanted me to testify against Sam in the triple-murder trial.

On June 10, I was notified that Jack Murray and Tommy wanted to see me. I had been subpoenaed to answer some questions. I didn't want to but they assured me that everything was going to be fine. Hell, what could I do?

I was taken to a motel for protection. I wasn't even allowed to make a phone call. The next day, I was taken back to my motel to get some fresh clothes. Then, back at the motel, we met up with Maria and Mike, who were also scheduled to testify.

Maria was one beautiful woman. She had incredible features and a body any man would drool over. She also had reason to hate Sam and Bobby. They had forced her into a life of prostitution and kept her in check with coke and pills. Mike, too, had been burned by Sam and Bobby.

"Hey, Robert, you got any money I can borrow?"

I shrugged. "Sure," I said and took out some twenties, counted out three and gave them to him. As I did this, the officers' eyes widened in shock.

The next day, Tommy asked me why I'd given Mike that money. "He needed it," I said.

"And you gave it to him just like that?"

"Why not?"

The following day, I was brought into court. I'd been arrested. I'd been to jail. I'd been questioned. But I'd never been in open court before. I didn't like it. I was nervous. My throat was dry. It seemed like everyone on the jury could see right through me. I was called to the stand and Al Constant, the prosecutor, started by asking me about my criminal record.

Possession, guns, more guns, more cocaine. Stolen car sale. Hardly a job description of a choirboy.

"Tell me, Mr. Vidal, about the conversation you had at the Classic Auto Body trailer on April 24, 1983."

I told him what Sam had said, how he'd "gotten Bobby and Cheryl" and if the weather stayed like it was "the bodies will start stinking."

The prosecutor thanked me and then the defense attorney began his grilling.

Dale Jones and Cathy Waldo. They weren't pulling any punches. "Mr. Vidal, how much money do you make as the drug kingpin of Newark, New Jersey?"

The question did more than piss me off; it got me so infuriated I couldn't think straight. I was thinking that I wasn't the bad guy here. I wasn't the one on trial for murder. I hadn't done anything wrong this time.

I looked over at Sam. Without his hairpiece, he looked ten years older. That bastard had tried to murder me ten months earlier and now I was looking at him, thinking how old he looked. Damn. What right did these assholes have to make me seem like the bad guy here? This guy tried to kill me and now they're trying to shift guilt to me? F—- them!

"About a million dollars a year," I said. The words were out of my mouth before I'd had a chance to think about the damage I was doing. Dammit. I knew I'd just blown it big time.

Now the defense had me where they wanted me. They insinuated that one of my hit men had done the killings on my orders. Wayne D.

Batlista had been there during the killings and now he'd worked out a deal with the prosecutors to become a key witness.

Now the defense was trying to clear Sam by suggesting that it was Wayne who'd committed the murders...on my orders!

When court was adjourned for the day, I left knowing just how badly I'd F—-ed up.

The next day, I was headline news. The papers couldn't get enough of my remark about making a million dollars a year. They just ate up the possibility that I'd been behind the crime.

Sam was eventually convicted for the crime. He didn't get the death sentence. The conviction cleared me of any allegation that I'd ordered the killings, but my time on the stand had given my drug operations too much exposure, way too much exposure. I knew I'd be feeling the heat of my arrogance and hot-headedness for a long time to come. I would have to cool off. Possibly even retire.

Yeah, I'd come out of it pretty bad, but Sam came out worse. It was revealed that he'd been playing both sides of the fence, working for the mob and providing information to the authorities. To me, justice had been served. He'd had no business killing those girls.

Now that he had been convicted, I knew that Sam was really dangerous to me. He would send hit men to try to kill me. He sure did! .Not too long after entering the Trenton NJ State.Penitentiary. Sam contracted a soon to be Parolee to kill me and cut me in pieces and sent some of my body meat to him in prison as beef burgers. This plan was uncovered by the Essex County Prosecutors office; when the hire hit man made a deal with them not to go back to prison on a parole violation.

I thought the authorities were sure to be trying to bring me down for bragging about making a million dollars a year on the witness stand. Instead Tommy informs me of Sam's getting new charges for putting a hit on me from prison. Is this luck or my mother's prayers are reaching God's throne of grace?

I didn't think things could get worse. Then Jackie told me she was pregnant.

Chapter Twenty-Six

"Jesus," I thought, "that's all I need, one more mobster looking to kill me."

Actually, Jackie's father was more understanding after I'd gone to him and explained that I loved his daughter and hoped to marry her from that time on Jimmy Fresco and I developed a strong friendship. After that, Jackie and I, along with Tarzan and a few friends, headed off for a little rest and relaxation on the beaches of Miami Fla. Spending tens of thousands of dollars with my crew... This was paradise to me no violence and no guns, just none stop partying showing off the hundreds and the bottles of champagnes..My spending and great tipping open doors every club we went into. We all knew we needed a vacation.

It was great therapy the ocean breeze free from those hours, weeks. And months of stress and guns everywhere.

Chapter Twenty-Seven

Miami was nice but the truth is that there's no vacation from the Devil. When you dance with him, you don't get much respite. We'd no sooner gotten back than Tarzan and I ran across a couple of guys I knew who associated with some guys who had beaten me up bad one night at 101, a local bar. I was drunk and I'd been jumped by two or three people who busted my head with beer bottles. I ended up losing several teeth and had my eyes swollen shut.

"Sons of bitches," I whispered.

Tarzan and I beat the crap out of them. They both required hospitalization. Just my luck, one of their fathers was a Newark police sergeant. So much for dumb luck.

Maybe it was that or the fact I was driving in a car with Florida plates, but Tarzan and I had just pulled into a service station when a Newark police cruiser came skidding to a stop about ten feet behind us. Both doors of the cruiser flew open and two cops jumped out.

"Put your hands on top of the car! It's all over!"

Not knowing what was all over, I looked over at the cops and was surprised to see that one of them was Ruben Cabrera, a cop I knew who happened to have a fondness for coke. I also knew that he sold stolen auto parts to a friend of mine on Thomas St. Dance with the Devil...

I also knew I had a .38 snub-nose on me and that Tarzan was carrying a fourteen-inch knife in his leg strap.

Ruben's hands were shaking as he pointed his pistol at the back of my head. Patting me down with his other hand, he found my pistol. Sliding it out, he called out, "Bingo!" Then he looked at me. "What the hell is this?"

Son of a b— enjoyed trying to cut my hands off with his handcuffs. As he pushed me down into the back of the cruiser, I looked at him and asked him if his urine was clean.

His face colored blood red. He tried to ignore me but it was clear that I'd caught him off guard. He knew what I knew. And he didn't like it. From the police headquarters, I called Tony Fusco and explained the entire situation to him. The next morning, Tarzan and I were released.

I felt like I was on top of the world. I'd been arrested over and over, but each time, I had the smarts and the connections to get out. But my confidence was false. Soon after I was released, I got a message that my mother wanted to see me.

"What does she want?" I muttered, looking at the number on my beeper. "Probably wants to try and convince me to turn to the Lord." I thought about not bothering, but I did go to her apartment on Adams St., in Elizabeth NJ.

"You carry a gun, Robert," she said, her voice strained with emotion. "I have to carry a gun, Mom," I explained. "I have to protect myself from all the people who want me dead." "Yes I hear it from others Felipe and is killing me inside, if it was not for the Spirit of Jesus in me and my faith in God I would had died of a heart attack worrying about you"

"A gun can't save you, Robert," she said. "Only the LORD Jehovah can save you. I pray for your life night and day" "Hijo por favor lee el Salmo 23" (Son please read Psalm 23 Jehovah is my Shepherd"

"Come on, Mom. Give it up. I've heard it all many times from her before."

"Your heart is so cold and hard. How did it get that way? You used to be such a good boy." Little did she know I no longer had the Spanish bible she had given me many years ago? I was like many people I had a Religious label but never read the Bible went to church or prayed.

I heard her words but their meaning didn't register with me. "Mom, I love you. I'll see you again soon. Okay?" once again her tears slowly appeared running down her pleading facial expression.

She promised to keep praying for me, praying for her lost son, the very same son who used to accompany the family to the Evangelist church. I knew she'd keep her promise, too. A mother's love is eternal. My mom is proof of that.

Today I clearly see and understand God's Word and Spirit gave her strength, her faith was unshakeable. She believed and told me many times. I pray you will be saved and that Jehovah's Angels protect you from your enemies and grant you a day of repentance and to serve Him. Her words will ever live in my mind despite me trying to erase them from my memory during those years in the garden of the wicked ways.

Chapter Twenty-Eight

People who live their lives in normal ways come to believe in the justice system provided by the police and the courts. Those of us who walk on the dark side of the law come to understand that street justice is often truer and more just.

During the summer of 1984, Puggy and Mustacho, two guys affiliated with the New Jersey mob, crossed my path. They were well known as violent thieves with a specialty of ripping off drug dealers. Despite their reputation, I dealt with them frequently. Before long, they owed me thousands of dollars. I wasn't surprised. It was common knowledge that they were hooked on the pipe. Like everyone else who experimented with freebasing cocaine, they soon found their lives reduced to being servants of the drug.

"No more," I told my distributors. "Until they're paid off, no more coke for them."

It wasn't long before I was hearing stories of them sticking guns in the faces of dealers. I ignored their many calls. For about two weeks, I refused to think about them.

Then High One told me that he'd run into them and they'd threatened to pump him full of bullets.

"Bastards," I seethed. "What did you do?"

He shrugged. "I gave them a couple of ounces. Hell, Robert, I had to. They'd kill me if I didn't."

High One's actions pissed me off. I understood High One's behavior, but his acting out of fear sent a message about me that I didn't need to have out on the street. Who did these two think they were F—-ing with? Didn't they know who I was? I had my own reputation for anger and violence.

Well, if these two weren't aware of who I was, I was going to make them good and aware...and soon. I instructed my guys to watch for them. As soon as they were spotted, I wanted to be beeped. Then I went to get Tarzan.

My beeper went off within a couple of hours. Mustacho was in the Costa Brava. "He's a dead man," I thought to myself as I began speeding in the direction of the bar.

We circled around the block several times, making sure there were no police around, and then we parked down the road. "You go inside," I said to Tarzan. "I want you there when I get there."

I waited another ten minutes or so and then I followed after him, tucking my .380 snug in my waistband as I got out of the car.

Once my eyes adjusted to the dim lighting in the bar, I spotted Mustacho at the back of the bar, all the way in the back. Just as I began moving toward him, he called out to me, "Where the F—- you been, man?"

His comment only pissed me off more, if that was possible. I was watching his hands, not his eyes. If he was going to go for a gun, I was going for mine first. As soon as I was a couple of feet from him, I shouted at him, "Who the F—- do you think you're talking to, asshole?" As his eyes widened, I demanded to know if he had a gun. "Yeah, you got a gun. You don't have the balls to yell at me like that without a F—-ing gun."

I reached down and patted his waist. As I did, I positioned my head several inches from his nose, ready to splatter it if he made one move. He didn't. He never flinched as I removed his .45. I pulled the hammer back and stuck the barrel in his crotch. "You want me to blow your balls off?" I asked him.

I had his attention now. He was scared. "Come on, Vidal, there's a bullet in the F—-ing chamber. Cut it out. I got no beef with you...."

"No? Then why the F—- you threatening my men? You think you don't bleed, Mustacho? Well, if you do, you're wrong. I'll show you that you bleed like every other stuffed pig in the world."

"Vidal, come on. Hey, let's talk. Relax, relax Come on...." I calmed down a little, hearing the pleading in his voice. The more he pleaded, the harder it was to maintain the kind of hate I needed to blow him away. Basically, I respect people and I expect them to respect me back.

Listen to a junkie long enough and you're going to feel sorry for them. They'll say and do anything to get you to help their addiction. They are the world's greatest salesmen. I ended up giving him his gun back. By the end of the night, I'd given this guy a sack of cocaine. Unbelievable. I'd come to the bar determined to kill or maim him, and here I was, giving him dope.

And, as it always is with junkies, I was wrong to feed his addiction.

Later that summer, I was paged by Carlos the Marielito Cuban. When I called him back, he was talking so fast I could hardly understand him. Miguel had been killed, that much I understood. I didn't get the whole story until later, from David Napoly, a Newark fireman who had been drinking at the Casa Storia when the whole thing went down.

An argument had broken out over someone stealing a fifty-dollar bill off Miguel's table when he went to the men's room. Then Mustacho stabbed him in the chest. After that, Puggy shot him.

I couldn't believe what I was hearing about these two. Miguel wasn't a drug dealer. He was just a hard-working truck driver who happened to stop in to have a drink with his friends. Now who the hell was going to tell his four kids that their father was dead?

"It was horrible, Robert," David said. "He was fighting so hard to live. He was in a pool of blood from the wounds and those bastards were still kicking him in the face...."

My own blood boiled, hearing this account. I could have hired people to kill these pieces of trash, but I wanted to do it myself. This was personal. I called Tarzan, along with his brothers, Green Eyes and

Duran. Then I sent some of my other guys out looking for Mustacho and Puggy. I also got one of my guys to get me an unregistered car with unregistered tags.

Then I got down to coming up with a plan.

At about eleven-thirty, I was paged. I looked down at the number. "It's F—-ing Mustacho," I said. The atmosphere in the bar was thick. "Where are they?"

I looked at the first three digits of the number. "North Newark," I said. They were less than fifteen minutes away. I called the number. After several rings, Puggy answered.

"Hey, Vidal, how the F—- are things over there?" he asked. "Did you hear what happened to us?"

"I heard," I told him in a voice as cold as ice.

"Well, shit happens," Puggy said, his words slurred. It was no surprise that he was high. "Can we see you, man? We need something for the night."

"You guys are behind on the last package," I told him.

He started laying it on thick with his con about how he'd take care of everything as soon as his clientele settled with him.

"I'll tell you what," I told him. "Meet me at the Frelinhansen Avenue Diner, over by the Department of Motor Vehicles."

"Okay, thanks, Vidal. Don't forget the stuff, okay? Just don't forget the stuff."

As I hung up the phone, I was thinking, "Yeah, don't worry. I won't forget anything."

I took Tarzan with me and told everyone else at the bar that it was okay, that the two of us would handle it.

"Robert, let us come and help...."

I raised my hand. "We'll take care of it."

Tarzan and I slugged down a couple of shots of Sambuca and then checked our weapons. I had my .38. He had a .45, even though he didn't like guns.

We only had about twenty minutes to come up with a plan. We knew that Mustacho and Puggy would have to drive down McCarter Highway 21 South to get to the diner. We headed in that general direction. In our unregistered car, I was hoping to have the element of surprise on them and catch them.

We had been waiting in the parking lot of a tire repair center when their light green Ford LTD went by. "There they go!" I said to Tarzan as I zipped out after them, keeping our lights off until I was on the highway, a couple hundred yards behind them.

I caught up with them gradually, not wanting them to get suspicious. As we came closer, I told Tarzan to roll the window down. "And duck down unless you want your F—-ing head blown off." I raised my .38. Just then, headlights in my rear-view mirror caught my attention. "Dammit," I muttered as a yellow Nova pulled up alongside me.

I glanced over at the driver. He seemed preoccupied. He passed by us and I noted the small antenna on his trunk. My heart started pounding. This guy was a cop. I'd come this close to having a cop witness me trying to blow Mustacho and Puggy away. Wouldn't that have been my luck?

I worried that he'd seen me raise my gun and had already called in for back up. All this was racing through my mind as we pulled up to a red light. Almost as if he was answering my questions, the Nova pulled past Mustacho, ran the light and headed south down the highway.

The light turned green. I hung about fifteen, twenty yards behind the LTD.

"What the F—-?"

"What's the matter?" Tarzan asked. He was still crouched down on the floor, unable to see anything.

"They passed the turn-off where we were supposed to meet." I'd no sooner said this than the driver realized his mistake and hung a u-turn over the divider in the middle of the road and pulled onto Frelinhansen Avenue.

Now what was I supposed to do? If I followed him, he'd know he was being tailed. What choice did I have? I had to cross over. We'd lose the element of surprise and have to deal with the situation head-on. As I sped up, I could see them looking back at me. They knew they were in trouble now. They might not have known it was me, but they knew something was going sour.

I pulled up closer to the car and raised my pistol. They screeched to a stop. The doors opened as they began firing at us. I took aim and pumped four rounds into the front of the car. The windows exploded. As we passed them, I pumped two more rounds into the front seat.

"I'm hit! I'm hit!"

"Good," I thought to myself, hearing someone screaming into the night. Just then, the back windshield exploded as it was hit by a bullet. I pressed down on the accelerator. I glanced down at Tarzan. "Why the F—- didn't you shoot? We could have been killed!"

"I told you, I don't like guns. I use my hands and my feet."

A bus on the opposite side of the road had witnessed our little gunplay, which meant we had to dump the car in case someone could identify it. The blown-out windows were more than enough probable cause to get us arrested anyway.

We dumped the car and then caught a cab to the Airport Motel in Newark. Once we were there, we started to relax a little. That is, until two hours later, when the numbers 666 showed up on my beeper. Mustacho and Fuggy. I didn't call back. A short time later, the number showed up again. Damn. They were still alive.

That's just what I needed, two more sworn enemies.

After that, I kept a sawed-off shotgun near me all the time. I had to be ready. To let down my guard would be to put my life in danger. But it isn't easy to always be "on."

After about two weeks, during which time the streets were buzzing with word of Miguel's murder and the shooting, I started to let my guard down a little.

Tarzan and a few others came with me to the Night Light bar. I had Tarzan and Angel stay close to the front door. I didn't want Mustacho or Puggy sneaking in on me. I had my shotgun nearby. But there wasn't any real chance of either of them sneaking in. They were on the pipe hard and that meant that they didn't care about how they looked. They would stick out like sore thumbs. No, my major concern was them rushing in and slinging lead before we had a chance to respond.

By ten-thirty, I was feeling no pain. I was relaxing at a table close to the back when a gentleman walked up to me and poked me in the chest with his finger. I was annoyed that some drunk was coming up and bothering me. As I looked at his face, he looked vaguely familiar.

"I could have killed you if I wanted to, Vidal."

It was Mustacho...but dressed in a nice suit, with his hair cut and clean-shaven. "You tried to kill us, Vidal. I know it was you. You're the only one with the balls to try."

"You're crazy, Mustacho," I said. "Why would I want to kill you?" I was talking almost as fast as I was thinking. He could have killed me if he'd wanted to, stabbed me in the heart with an ice pick before anyone could have moved. That taught me a very important lesson—never, never let your guard down. Not if you want to wake up to smell the coffee the next day.

Puggy and Mustacho stopped coming around for a few months. Mustacho was indicted and appeared as a witness in a homicide case in Newark. He was defended by my attorney, Tony Fusco. He beat the charges. It didn't hurt that none of the witnesses would testify.

It wasn't long after that that Mustacho was found dead, his head riddled with shotgun blasts. I guess it's true what they say: "Live by the sword, die by the sword."

Chapter Twenty-Nine

Maybe to be a really good cop, you have to think like a criminal. The problem with thinking like a criminal is that, unless you're very careful, you start to act like one, too. There were plenty of cops I didn't want to cross in Newark. But there were more than a handful happy to make my life easier—a kind of "you scratch my back, I'll scratch yours" arrangement. Whether they wanted or needed drugs, money, or a bit more party than their lives were giving them, these cops inhabited a netherworld of corruption. At the time, I used to think it was fine that they wanted to hang with me.

Now? Now I have trouble looking back on them with any respect. Sympathy, yes. Forgiveness, yes. Respect, no.

I had cop friends in the Essex prosecutor's office. I had cop friends on the beat. 1 had cop friends everywhere. One needed money for his kid's medical expenses. Another needed coke for his wife's habit.

Tommy Gilsen was a good contact in the police department. Chick was another one, but I had to figure it wasn't just his wife using. Through Chick, I met another narcotics detective, Dennis. I'd known Dennis from the neighborhood when I was growing up. I was pretty sure Dennis was using. The fact that Chick introduced us only reinforced my suspicion.

My relationship with Chick grew so that he was asking me to package the coke for him so he could sell it to other officers on the force. "There's a lot of cops using these days," he told me.

I told him I'd get back to him and tried to stall. After all, it was hard enough to collect from drug dealers. How the hell was I ever going to collect from a cop?

I now knew a number of Newark police officers and detectives who used. There were a bunch of others who enjoyed the easy money that came from having an easy-going relationship with me. But these guys were the minority. Most of the Newark police wanted to bust my ass so bad they could taste it.

This small handful of "rotten apples" was protecting me from the others who only wanted to serve their duty to protect the law-abiding people of Newark. They wouldn't be successful for much longer.

About this time, a good friend of mine who had grown up in the same neighborhood as I had made a fast entry into the drug trade. He went by the name "Milkman" and that's how everyone referred to him.

One time around March 1985, Milkman approached me in the Casa Stoia with his two Cuban Marielito bodyguards flanking him on either side.

"Hey, Milkman," I said, not bothering to glance at his two friends.
"Vidal, how are you, man?"

"I'm okay," I said, not interesting in making small talk with him. I hadn't seen him in a while and people didn't just show up and start talking you up for no reason at all. Not in my business they didn't. They wanted something or they needed something.

Milkman needed coke. He wanted ten kilos of it. "I'm good for the cash," he added.

I let out a soft chuckle. The newspapers were still hot with my stupid boast during Sam's murder trial. As a result, I had been playing it very cool. Ten kilos was hardly what I had just sitting around. "I can get it though," I told him. "Touch base with me again in the next few days." I let him know that I'd only be the middleman. It wasn't my stuff so he wouldn't be paying me. "Cash up front," I said.

"No problem, Vidal. No problem."

I spoke with one of El Gallo's right-hand men, a Puerto Rican named El Gran Joe, or as he was known on the street, The Great Joe. I set up the deal, knowing that I'd make a nice bit of change doing nothing but being the go-between.

A week went by with no word from Milkman. I began to think maybe he'd gone to someone else to set up the deal when I got an emergency call from one of the Azulejo Brothers in Miami. Roger told me that the Milkman had ripped them off.

"He F—-ed me up good, Robert," Roger complained. He told of how the Milkman had slipped him a Mickey and then, when he was passed out, had made off with three kilos of coke and two of heroin.

"I'm dead, Robert," Roger said in a panic. "If I can't come up with the $425,000 to cover my suppliers, they'll take it out of me bit by bit until I'm dead."

I knew he wasn't kidding.

"Robert, please, you and Tarzan have to help me. Find these guys. If I don't come up with something soon, they'll cut me up in pieces and put me in the trash."

"Okay, calm down," I said. "I'll watch out for the Milkman. Call me back in about twelve."

Another week went by and I still hadn't heard from Roger. I was beginning to think that he'd been killed. I couldn't shake the feeling that I could've been the one in Roger's shoes. After all, the Milkman had come to me first.

After another week, I ran into Roger. God, I couldn't believe it was him. "You had me F—-ing scared, man!" I told him, hugging him tight. "I'm so happy to see you alive!"

His suppliers had given him thirty days to come up with the money—or the bodies of the two men who F—-ed him over. But after a month, Roger still didn't have the situation under control. If I'd had the money, I would have tried to help. But I didn't have it. Now Roger and his whole family were in trouble. That's how the Colombians worked. It wouldn't have done Roger any good to go into hiding.

They'd have killed one member of his family at a time until he was flushed out.

Usually, they'd be waiting at the funeral. Then they'd gun down their target during the funeral service. They didn't care. It was business. And the Colombians didn't F—- around when it came to business.

On June 13, Rene, Roger's brother, made a down payment on Roger's debt. He paid more than money. He was gunned down in the El Palacio Bar in Newark. It was a cruel murder. Rene was nothing but a good guy. He had gone straight long before. He'd bought a tractor-trailer and settled down to an honest life. He had a beautiful Brazilian woman who had given him a son. Now his son would grow up without a father.

I went to Rene's funeral. As I looked down at him lying in that coffin, I couldn't stop the tears from streaming down my face. He was only thirty years old! It wasn't right. It just wasn't right.

Another one of my friends, dead. And for what? Drugs. Greed. Power. Money. As the tears ran down my face, I couldn't make sense of it. We were all living our lives in fear. We carried guns all the time. And still there was no safety or sanctuary. How was I ever going to find safety again?

If I didn't get shot down like Rene, I could be turned in to the police. At any moment, everything I believed was important to me could be taken away. And I felt powerless to do anything about it. It was worse than a dog-eat-dog world. It was something more cruel and heartless.

A few days after the funeral, I went to meet Chick at his mother's house. After I handed him the package of coke, I mentioned my feelings about Roger, and how he was still in trouble. "He's got a price on his head."

Chick must have misunderstood me. He lowered the police radio in his hand and looked me dead in the eye. Then, in a voice barely above a whisper, he said, "Vidal, for a kilo, I'll bring you his head in a shoe box."

I looked at him, unable to believe what I was hearing.

"You tell them that," he went on. "In a shoebox."

I was stunned by what I heard. But I didn't doubt that Chick was serious. He had a look in his eyes, a hunger that I recognized from my years on the streets, a hunger that said he'd do anything at all to get what he wanted.

"No," I told him, "Roger's my friend. He's in danger. I want to help him."

Chick shrugged. "Oh," he said.

I remained shaken by his initial reaction. I knew I wasn't the only criminal Chick hung out with. He was tight with a hit man for the New Jersey mob. I'd seen him with this guy a number of times. But I'd never thought that they'd be involved in joint ventures. I mean, whatever else I might have thought, Chick was still a cop. Maybe he strayed into a gray area now and again, but he was still a cop.

A few weeks later, Roger opened the door to his apartment and was greeted by the business end of a gun. Two blasts into his stomach. Left for dead, Roger was in a pool of his own blood when one of my bodyguards happened to come by. He rushed Roger to the hospital in time to save his life. Appropriately enough, this bodyguard's name was Angel.

In the following weeks and months, rumors of Milkman's whereabouts and antics would reach me. Word was that he was bragging about his big house in Beverly Hills. That he was flashing big money and gold all over, money and gold that had come from the sale of his stolen merchandise.

The thing is that with street justice, you always have to pay the piper. Milkman was talking up a big life, about his house and his Mercedes and all that. But none of that stopped him from being escorted out of a bar by a couple of Latin men who, by all accounts, did not look amused.

Milkman and his two Cuban bodyguards were shot and then cut up into pieces. The pieces were put into garbage bags and dropped off all around New Jersey. They never got to enjoy the "fruits "of his stolen labors. The house remained unfurnished. The mileage on the Benz remained low. You always have to pay the piper. Trouble was, the piper was fixing to play for me.

Ripping off drug dealers was popular in the drug trade in the 80's. It was better than robbing banks for many. This is one of the main reasons drug dealers carry guns to protect their goods and themselves. Even though when large amounts of money or drugs are involved most likely all witnesses are killed.

This led to many killings and perpetrators were intensively haunted along with innocent family members in vengeance for their unforgiving betrayals. For example here is a case during my time in the streets.

In Miami Fla. Where Miami Police officers Ripped off a big shipment of 1000 kilos of cocaine. The defendants-including Ricardo Aleman,27, Rodolfo Arias,30, Osvaldo Coello, 26,Arturo De La Vega,27, and Armando Garcia,24, - were charged with running a multi-million-dollar rip-off ring stealing from drug dealers and their customers.

Two drug smugglers Armando Un Roque 50, Two drug smugglers, Armando Un Roque, 50, and Pedro Ramos, 38, were key witnesses against the River Cops. Prosecutors Sullivan, Trudy Novicki and Russell Killinger pointed out the conspicuous spending of the five Miami patrolmen and two ex-cops. Some bought new homes, furniture and expensive cars with cash. They took island vacations and treated themselves to sophisticated electronic equipment. The River Cops saga began on July 29, 1985, when the bodies of three drowned smugglers were discovered in the Miami River. A group of men dressed in police uniforms raided the Mary C at Jones Boat Yard as a cocaine shipment was being unloaded. Six smugglers leaped into the water; three drowned. A few days later, the body of cocaine dealer Luis Rodriguez turned up in a crate in West Dade. The investigation of his death led police to Un and Ramos, who had done drug deals with the dead man.

Gradually, a case was built. Prosecutors said the cops were in cahoots with drug dealers who frequented the neighborhoods they patrolled. They used their badges and police powers to steal cocaine and cash, betraying their Oath to public trust to protect and Serve. 1 Timothy 6: [10] For the love of money is a root of all *kinds of* evil, for which some have strayed from the faith in their greediness, and pierced themselves through with many sorrows.

Chapter Thirty

Like the birth pangs of a mother about to give birth, the signs were increasing that my life on the streets was coming to a close. On July 4th, 1985, I was pulling away from my new favorite bar, El Molino Rojo, on 44 St and Hudson St in Union City NJ. When I heard like firecrackers go off. "Damn kids," I thought to myself.

Later, I heard on the radio that three people had been killed and three others had been critically wounded in a shoot-out at the El Molino Rojo. Realizing how close I'd come to being in the middle of this violent incident, I visited my friend Jesus to find out what happened.

"Some Cubans from Miami. They started shooting the place up. I jumped behind the bar and grabbed my .45...." He averted his eyes as he told me about the screaming and the river of blood as the victims, most of them innocent patrons of the bar, were shot.

Juanito died that day. One of the innocents. He'd just gone into the bar to get a drink and avoid the hot July heat.

For a while, the crowd at El Molino Rojo was smaller than usual. No one was anxious to visit the scene of a mass murder. But, as the days went by, the people started coming back. It wasn't long before I was back in my spot, playing the familiar role of generous high roller.

I bought rounds for the bar. People repaid me with rounds. I drank a few shots but that was it. I had business later in the evening and I couldn't afford to be in a drunken stupor.

Two young Cubans came in. Not very well dressed. They were putting the money together to get drinks. They called the barmaid over and told her to set me up with another round. I was touched by their gesture. I'd seen them putting their last wrinkled dollar bills together.

"Thank you anyway," I told them. "I have had too many drinks already. Besides, I have to leave in a few minutes."

Their attitude immediately changed, taking my polite refusal as a personal affront. One of the Cubans came behind me. The other moved closer to my side.

"What's the matter, amigo, we're not good enough to buy you a drink?"

I tried to explain the situation to them again but they weren't interested.

Meanwhile, I couldn't tell what the Cuban behind me was up to, if he was getting ready to attack me or what. "Who's this guy behind me?" I asked the Cuban in front of me. "He's making me uncomfortable." He was, too. I wasn't packing and I was nowhere near clear of their intentions. If push came to shove, I would have to rely on my martial arts skills. But, in a dance between lead and flesh, the smart money is always on lead.

The Cuban came from behind me and tried to smash a glass in my face. I blocked him and broke his nose with my other hand. In quick succession, I brought them both to the floor with quick kicks to their groins.

As they crawled up from the floor, they considered their next move. Pride gave way to pain and they stumbled out the door. Unfortunately, because of the earlier shootings, the police were always near the bar. The Cubans pointed me out as their assailant and I was once more placed under arrest.

"Come on, guys," I complained, "it was self-defense."

"Tell it to the judge."

Chapter Thirty

I didn't have to. My attorney got me released on bond and the charges were eventually dismissed. But it was just one more incident, one more scream that blended in to the background noise of my life. I couldn't shake the feeling that something was wrong. But I didn't know what and I didn't know what to do about it.

Within weeks of this incident, I was contacted by the Caponegros, two brothers from the neighborhood who told me they had a deal for me that was too good to be true. Trouble with deals that are too good to be true is that they usually are—and so they're usually set-ups for something. I was suspicious but I had always trusted the Caponegros and they told me that they had known the contact for years. Still, someone willing to pay almost twenty-five percent above the going rate...

I wasn't really interested in meeting new faces but, against my better judgment, I gave Tarzan the okay to set up a meeting with this guy. The next evening, I observed Tarzan deliver half an ounce to the guy as a sample. No doors blew open with cops so maybe, just maybe, this deal was on the up and up.

Less than a week later, I heard from one of my friends at the Bureau of Narcotics that the Caponegros had set me up. "You sold to an undercover cop," I was told.

No way. I refused to believe it. I'd known those bastards since grade school. Why would they sell me out? We were friends.

My contact shrugged. "Okay by me. If you think they're your friends..."

The next time I ran across one of them, I broke his arm. I might have done more but I somehow respected what we'd once been to one another. 1 couldn't give up the feelings of brotherhood I'd had for both of them so easily.

But the truth was dawning on me. I could no longer even trust the ones who were closest to me. That was the reality I was stuck with. My best friend would set me up one day. If not for drugs, then for money, and if not for money, then to stay out of jail. It was a house of cards and it couldn't help but come down sooner or later.

As a result of this added pressure, I became more and more violent. One night, Tarzan, Angel, and I got into a fight at the Oceanic

Bar. It was payback for some guys who'd beaten up a friend of mine, a guy named Pupo. The fight started inside and continued outside. I was pistol-whipping one of the guys when the gun went off and blew a hole in his arm.

"Let's get out of here," I said.

Things were getting too hot. They had reached a boiling point when, the next day, I was paged with the number 1-9999. I no longer allowed people to page me with phone numbers, only codes. This was a code for Chick's mother's house. The 9999 told me it was an emergency. Rather than call her, I immediately drove out to her house.

I found Chick there. He told me to follow him down to the basement where Dennis was waiting for me.

"It's bad, Vidal," Dennis began. He then went on to tell me there was a warrant out for Tarzan, Angel, and me.

"What for?"

"Come on, Vidal, everyone knows you shot the guy at the Oceanic." Then he shrugged. "I'm one of the detectives supposed to deliver the warrant," he said. "But I threw it in the garbage."

"I appreciate that, you know that."

"Yeah, I know."

I handed him five grams of coke, and gave another five grams to Chick. I wanted them to know how appreciative I was. As I left the house, I noticed their undercover car down the road. Since they were both on duty, I could only conclude that both Chick and Dennis were using themselves...and that someone knew about it.

Only July 26th, things went from bad to worse. Fast.

When we arrived at the Newark Motel, Tarzan and I headed toward the lobby. As we came closer, we could hear a loud argument taking place. A tall, black-haired man was cursing out my friend Billy Shears. Now, Billy had always watched out for me. He warned me of anyone suspicious hanging around in the Motel or parking lot and he was also my gun supplier. He was also associated with the NY and NJ Italian mob and he was not someone to whom anyone should have been disrespectful too. What was worse, I quickly recognized the tall black-haired man as a thief and small time drug dealer, whom I had given free coke to in the past to stay on his good side so he wouldn't try to rob my room.

Now, I just wanted to bring down the tension. "Hey, let's tone it down," I said.

The words had no sooner left my mouth then the guy sucker-punched me in my face. I replied with several quick blows to his head. He moved in and wrapped me in a bear hug, he was like 60 lbs ,heavier than me; so I gave him a head butt to the nose. The gun I had in my back fell to the floor as he released me. He spotted the gun and lunged toward it but I moved quicker, kicking him in the face.

I reached down and picked up the pistol as drops of blood from my face hit the tile floor. The dope and alcohol in my system was making up a witches' brew of evil. I didn't seem to care that several people had gathered at the sound of the argument and that now there were people standing around watching. I checked the gun as the guy started crawling for the door. When I looked up, he was out the door. I began to chase him. When I was within fifty feet of him, I squeezed off two rounds. I hit him with the second.

As I came closer, I calmly pointed my gun at him and then shot him twice more in the head.

That's when reality began to settle in. I turned and saw all the people watching. Damn.

"What the F—- did you do that for, Robert?" Angel wanted to know. "This is crazy," Pupo added.

Their comments only fueled my anger. "You wouldn't be saying that if he'd picked up the gun instead of me' would you?" I was angry and frustrated. I knew what a mess I was in. "Come on, we've got shit to do!" I began barking orders at everyone. Tarzan and Angel helped me load the body in the back of one of my Cadillac's. I told the limo drivers who were lined up along the parking lot that they hadn't seen a thing. We found the shell casings and then we got ready to leave.

As I climbed into the car, I looked back and saw Billy Shears cleaning the blood with a wet mop. The girls were also watching in shock! they had come along with us to the motel for some fun. I couldn't even describe the looks on their faces. I guess they'd never seen their date kill a man before.

Tarzan and Angel were the only one who didn't seem bothered at all. To them, it was all as natural as a bloody fight in a Newark bar.

I headed north on 1-9. As we approached the Pulaski Skyway, I decided to dump the body into the Hudson River. I thought to do it on the Hudson County side, to take some of the heat off me in Newark.

In the middle of the bridge, we stopped, put on the flashers, and then, when the traffic was clear, took the body out of the car. I shot one more time into his head and then we dumped him over. We all watched in silence as the body fell down to the river.

As I turned back toward the car, 1 saw the blood dripping from the bumper. I wiped the bumper down with a motel towel. Then we got in the car and drove away. As we drove, I kept my eyes out for a place to dump the gun. When I spotted a good place, I wiped it of finger-prints and then threw it out. I threw the clip and the shells at different spots along the river.

Meanwhile, I was starting to get nervous. What the F—- had I done? Who was that guy who had murdered a man in cold blood? Was it really me? I had gone over the final line now. There was no going back. No undoing history.

When we got back to the motel, I saw a pregnant woman get-ting into her car. I recognized her from seeing her in the past with the guy I'd killed. Now I had the added burden of realizing I'd made some unborn kid a bastard by killing his father.

I told my crew that we could never talk about the murder. Not ever. My Italian friends who were at the motel the night of the murder cleaned up the blood and tried to cover my tracks. They also put the fear in everyone there to keep them quiet. It looked like I was going to get away with this terrible crime. At least, that's what it looked like for a short time.

Things were only going to get more intense. I began dealing with a Cuban named Oreste Rodriguez. Not only did he own a large auto parts store and several junkyards, but he was also selling coke. Oreste had been good friends with my father in Cuba and so, when he asked me to front him coke on credit, I was willing to do so.

But week after week, I was fronting him coke and getting no money. Then I heard from a friend of mine that Oreste had been asking a lot of questions about my operation, especially about my contacts in the police department.

The combination of his debt to me and this news made me very suspicious of Oreste, especially when I heard he wanted to meet with me. I brought Tarzan along with me, which Oreste wasn't crazy about. Still, when we met with him, he said, "Well, I got some good news and some bad news."

With that, he brought out a large bag with something like four pounds of coke. Then he opened another drawer and brought out some more. As Tarzan and I looked at the fish scales of the rock, Oreste told me he'd been looking into my organization.

"I only took coke from you to find out what kind of operation you were running," he said. "Now, I got all the coke you want." He eyed me closely. "I was a little hesitant, you know, what with all the cops on your payroll. But my investigations showed you to run a good organization."

At that point, he gave me a package for the money he owed me and then he told me he would give me a kilo for twenty-five thousand. That was fantastic news because kilos were going for up to thirty-four thousand. That meant I would be making a much greater profit.

"But, Vidal, you've got to chill out on the violence and the bar fighting," he said. "You call too much attention to yourself."

Before I left, Oreste had given me four pounds of coke to sell. I was back in business big time. Once again, it seemed that my life was perfect. I had a direct supply to all the coke I wanted. Oreste loved the stacks of money I was delivering to him. He and I got closer. After a time, he let me in on his secret—Manolo and Padrino were smuggling in the cocaine paste and they were cooking the cocaine themselves with chemicals and ether.

I let out a low whistle. I could see the potential of such an operation. Millions and millions. I could see myself retiring to my own beach house in one of the Caribbean islands. Jackie, me and my four-month-old, Robert, would live happily ever after, with no guns.

Can you imagine, my mother was still trying to convince me to give up my life and go back to working a forty-hour week at GM in Linden NJ. She always preached to me when I saw her. As a result, our visits were shorter and shorter, and they came further and further apart.

Even my father tried reasoning with me. "Look at your brother," he'd say, pointing out my brother as an example of the benefits of living the straight and narrow life. (My brother wanted to be a Law enforcement officer.) He also had tried along with my sister to give me good advice to stop using cocaine and leave the criminal lifestyle.

But I didn't have the patience to listen and how little they knew, how deep I was, and the many enemies that wanted to kill me. I was back on top and this time I intended to stay there.

Detective Tommy Gilsen was visiting me often then. He started to warn me of a DEA investigation into the Delancey Street district of Newark. My father-in-law owned a. trucking company out that way so I called him and warned him.

Tommy was a great source and contact. He and I got closer during this time. I bought him a car. One Time he carried Cocaine for me in his undercover official Police vehicle.

Everything seemed to be going fine. None of the cops on my payroll bothered to let me know that I was a target of a homicide investigation. This led me to think I was in the clear. Adding to my false sense of security was the fact that another friend from high school had joined the sheriff's office in Essex. Now I had a few friends there.

I was glad they were there. After all, I knew for a fact one was a user. That gave me an easy way to influence my contacts.

Yes, I was king of the world. The problem with being king of the world is that you don't see the seams starting to come apart until it's too late. And for me, it had been too late for a long time.

After learning Oreste's secret and access to large quantities of kilos of cocaine. I told Tommy that I knew of a way to make millions in easy money. "I'll help you make some fast money, my friend. Count on it."

Chapter Thirty

Then we talked about the ways he could launder the money so he could use it. I kept taking care of all my contacts in the police department—Peter, Predest, Chick, Dennis, and Tommy. Of course, this was becoming more and more of a burden to me. Not one of them contributed a penny to their habit. They were costing me big bucks.

With the money rolling in, I purchased a new stretch limousine and a Coupe de Ville. I was there. I finally had my own limo. I couldn't have been happier. High One was my personal chauffeur. I was like that guy in the Monopoly game. All money. All class.

One day, I was approached by two men who wanted me to put them on my payroll as hit men. I'd heard my crew who knew them speak highly of them and their ability to get the job done. One was a white military Vietnam Veteran. The other an hispanic with a killer reputation. But I wasn't really interested in dealing with people who killed for money. So I called the Hispanic, the littler of the two over and told him that I wasn't interested in his services right then but if he ever needed some good coke at a great price, he should come and see me.

"I'll get back to you on that," he said. Then he introduced himself, telling me his name was Flaco.

Not long after, Flaco wanted to do a deal with me, but he played dirty. So I had Tarzan bring him to where I was in the bar. When he did, I walked over to him. As I did, I was sliding my knife from my sleeve.

"Why're you playing with me?" I demanded. "Tarzan watched your room, Flaco. No one came."

"You calling me a liar?" Flaco demanded.

"Hey, let's just relax," I said, trying to calm him down. "You don't know me, Flaco. You don't know anything about me." With that, I pulled out my knife and slit his face about six inches down his cheek. Tarzan moved to the door to make sure no one came in.

Flaco didn't so much as blink. He just watched me, ignoring the blood gushing down his cheek. I guest he was trying to intimidate me, which only made me mad. I took my knife again and slid open his entire left arm from shoulder to wrist as the blood poured out, this happened in about 15 seconds. Just then, his friend made a move to defend him.

I punched them both in the face. Tarzan jumped into the fray. I finished off the long-haired veteran while Tarzan beat the shit out of Flaco, breaking his hands, his fingers, and one of his legs. If I would not have told Tarzan "Stop that is enough' He would have killed both of them like a hungry jungle lion. The witnesses that night in the bar were terrified I was told the bar bought them several shots of liquor and they left .

Whatever wisdom Oreste had offered in warning me about bar fights had gone in one ear and out the other. Another fight the following week resulted in two more guys getting admitted to the hospital. One for stitches in his jaw where I had pistol-whipped him and the other for a gunshot wound to the head.

These two swore out warrants for our arrest. Carlos picked us up to avoid our capture. He was off duty and he used his personal car to drive us to Jackie's. Chick called me there to tell me that there was a warrant out on me and that I should surrender myself.

I never got the chance. The police arrived the next morning.

I made bail the next day but the short time I'd spent in jail was plenty of time for me to start putting two and two together. Chick was sounding

More and more strung out. I believe he gave the info to his Police friends. He knew I stood in my girlfriends Jackie's basement apartment at times. 'that was a good lesson." I was going to have to watch my own back from now on with Ralph Cicalese.

But that was only going to get harder and harder. The noose was tightening. I was involved in another fight at El Baturro Bar, with a guy who turned out to be watching me; he was one of the narcotics division's best informants, and I stabbed him thinking he was there to kill me. That day as Tarzan, Angel green eyes, Duran;Tarzan's brothers and myself exit the bar. The Newark Police Narcotic squad had the place surrounded."Don't move put your hands up" shouted the undercover cop as he pointed his gun at my chest. He could have shot me I had the shiny knife in my hand and I was trying to dump it. I was known to be an armed and dangerous drug dealer. He would have gotten an award for shooting me.

But…again God's grace intervenes.

What was worse, a girl that was dealing for Jackie had rolled over and was providing information about our drug activity. Johnny Viera and his brother, Fidel, were crowing, too. I'd never felt the heat like this before.

A few weeks later, Tommy called to tell me that a close friend of mine was providing information to the DEA concerning my organization. "There's taps on your phones, Robert they are watching you daily."

"Who's doing this?" I wanted to know. "Who's selling me out?" When he told me, I felt sick to my stomach. He named High One as the informant.

"No," I said. "Not High One. He's like a brother to me."

"Suit yourself," he said.

Several days later, Tarzan was arrested and my limo was impounded. The court wouldn't set bail for Tarzan. And none of my contacts would step in to help. Things had gotten too hot. Chick let me know that the FBI had gotten involved. They wanted to know about my contacts with corrupt police officers.

"They're everywhere," he said. "They're watching you F—-ing Everywhere," he said, struggling to keep the hysteria from his voice. "Don't worry," I said, trying to hold down the panic in my own voice. "Dennis thinks you might roll him out."

I shook my head. "Tell him not to worry. Everything's going to be just fine." So now I had the DEA and the FBI on my case. My cop friends were scared that I was going to roll them out and my other good friends were still being gunned down in the street.

What the F—- was my future going to be? A satin-lined coffin or a cold jail cell? It sure as hell didn't seem like it was going to be a tropical island.

The pressure was getting to me big time. By Christmas 1985, I was drinking way too much. I was abusing Valiums. I was so close to rock bottom I could scrape it with my fingernails. One time I felt an oppressive voice order me to end it, end it! The thoughts were instructing me to shoot myself in the head.

I was crossing over the Pulaski Skyway Bridge when something came over me. I don't know what it was. Maybe the sky broke clear and the stars shone different. Something! Maybe it was driving over the same spot Where I'd dumped a man's body. All I knew was that my stomach tightened in the kind of soul searching I hadn't done in years and years. I punched the buttons on the radio, not searching for music but for the sound of a voice that could give me some insight, some guidance. I stopped when I landed on a AM-Christian radio station.

"Deliver yourself to the Lord. The Son of God Jesus Christ! Today is the day of salvation! He is waiting for you! He loves you! He forgives you...."There is someone out there today listening on the Radio really hurting and full of anger and depression. REPENT of your sins.

The words of the Baptist preacher cut through the callousness of my soul. He seemed to be speaking just to me. Suddenly, I raised my eyes to the heavens and cried out for help. Tears sprang to my eyes as I repeated the words that the preacher invited me to say, "Jesus Christ SAVE ME!.On my own I started to repeat the name of JESUS, JESUS, JESUS, please help me!"My head moved from left to right and I couldn't stop weeping. I felt something leave me. I felt peace, joy .As I clearly remember I had a blue silk long sleeve shirt and my neck was full of gold chains and diamonds. But my tears had drench my chains and chest. I believe I was set free from what the Bible reveals and calls demons.

It was all coming together. Oreste was holding back on the amount of coke he felt he could trust me with. Word that I had killed someone was out on the streets. My Italian friends were trying to get me to kill a couple of people for them. But I couldn't. I couldn't kill anymore. My Cuban friends said I should take out Oreste because he was putting pressure on their organization.

It seemed like everyone wanted someone dead. The life was wearing me down, beyond down. I didn't have the resources to get Tarzan out of jail. I could only hope that he didn't say anything to implicate me while he was there.

The money, the glamour, and the thrill of dealing now were like the taste of ash in my mouth. And yet...and yet...I still couldn't give it up. I could cry out for Jesus' help, but I wasn't ready to let him into my heart and serve Him.

Tommy from the Essex County Prosecutors office met me at the Sheraton and he wasn't holding back. "You got to get out of town, Robert. I'm not shifting you. You're being named in a Federal indictment, along with almost everyone you run with."

"What do they want from me, Tommy?"

"The Feds are mostly interested in the corrupt cops," he said.

"Well, don't worry about me rolling you or Chick," I told him. "That ain't going to happen never."

"I know," he said.

I gave him a hug when he left and I thanked him. He'd saved my ass big time. I couldn't believe how close I'd become with him.

The warning had convinced me to lay low. I wouldn't receive coke and I relocated the heavy guns we'd been keeping around. I stayed in and spent much more quality time with my son and with Jackie. We threw him a big first birthday party at the Holiday Inn in Newark. It wasn't as festive as I would have liked. Hiring Wells Fargo security guards to screen invitations put a damper on the atmosphere.

I did hang on to a few guns. My thinking was simple. I'd rather be arrested with a gun by the cops than be caught without one by my enemies. If I had to go out, I wanted to go out with two, rather than six—meaning with two cops rather than six pallbearers.

Along the way, I came up with a strategy. I was going to tell the Feds I'd been an informer, and that was why I spent so much time with the cops. It was a losing strategy, though. There was no record of me leading anyone toward any arrests.

The noose was getting so tight now I could almost feel it chafing around my neck.

On March 16, 1986, Jackie and I spent the night together. The following day, I was to appear in front of a grand jury to help clear my friend, Al Stoia, the owner of the Casa Stoia. He had been held responsible for the shooting outside his bar.

That night, I couldn't settle down. I was pacing back and forth, knowing that it I was only a matter of time before I was arrested. I didn't know who I could trust. I hired a retired state police officer, Richard Childs, to stay with me until I was away from the grand jury. Even Tommy and Chick could turn on me. After all, if I was gone, I couldn't turn on them.

All during the breaks in my grand-jury testimony, I saw strangers watching me, looking out from behind newspapers, looking up from the drinking fountains. I was either paranoid or a dead man. I couldn't tell which.

Coming out of the court, High One and I were walking to our car when all of a sudden cops came out of nowhere. "Stop! DEA, don't move!"

In the Newark Federal Building, I was questioned by the assistant U.S. attorney, Edward Belinkas. He wasn't pulling any punches. "Robert, we know you've been paying off cops and giving them drugs. We've got it on tape. We've got pictures." With that, he tossed over some photographs of me with Chick, Tommy, Predest, and Peter.

They had it all.

"I'm an informer," I told them, sticking to my strategy.

"You're a horse's ass," Belinkas said before he instructed the officers to put me in a cell.

From the holding cell, I could hear my beeper go off. An agent looked at it and said, "It's his girlfriend calling from their house."

"Lock her up," Belinkas said. Then he came over to the cell and spoke to me in a low voice. "It doesn't have to be this way, Robert. She doesn't have to go to jail."

But I wasn't listening. I knew they just wanted me to set myself up. Soon, High One was tossed into the cell with me. He told me that he was asked over and over about Chick and Tommy.

"They said I'd get fifteen years if I didn't roll on them," he said. I laughed. "They told me I wouldn't get less than sixty."

"What the F—- are we gonna do?"

"Stick with the story," I said firmly. "I'm a user, not a dealer. Everything's going to be all right."

But this time, the authorities weren't about to fold. They brought Jackie in. We had both made sales to undercover DEA officers. They had the goods on us. A couple of days later, they arrested seventeen more of my "co-conspirators," including my father, my father-in-law, my mother-in-law, my sister-in-law, Pupo, and even Anthony Ruffin, a Newark cop who had served nineteen years on the force.

The media had a field day.

On visiting day, my family came. My mother was crying. But her tears weren't from sadness. She seemed strangely calm. "Robert, I had a vision of you with gray hair...."

"That's good," I said. "That means I'm going to live through this."

"You were preaching in a pulpit, Robert," she went on. "You'd found the Lord. I know it's hard for you, but this is the best thing that could have happened."

She found comfort in the fact that I'd been reading the Bible since being arrested. I was inching closer but I wasn't there yet.

High One made bond and I told him to keep everyone quiet. "Maybe this will all blow over."

I wasn't allowed to make bond. Every day, I read the Bible more and more. One evening, I called a Christian radio program and confessed that Jesus Christ was the Son of God, my Lord and personal Savior. I prayed with the man over the telephone, and as I did, I felt a terrible burden lifted from me and I was filled with great peace.

I had no doubts about the punishment that lay before me, but on a deeper level, my most serious problems had been taken care of. The prison chaplain, William H. Lothrop, helped me with my Bible studies.

Day by day, my faith grew. And not long after giving myself over to the Lord, I felt a calling in my heart to witness to others.

On July 24, I was found guilty on every count and faced life plus forty-six years. I never claimed innocence and knew that I would have to cooperate or face the full term. I didn't know what to do, so I decided to place myself in God's hands and let Him decide my fate.

On September 11, 1986, I stood before the Honorable Mary Ann Trump Barry for sentencing. The prosecution demanded that I serve the maximum sentence with no possibility of parole. After hearing them, she turned to me and asked me if I had anything to say.

With that opportunity, I took responsibility for my crimes. I told her about my commitment to my Christian faith. "If I could undo the things I've done, I would," I swore to her. "I am truly repentant."

I believe it was God's mercy even more than the judge's that she sentenced me to twenty years. Jimmy Fresco got four and Anthony Ruffin the Newark Police officer got twelve years. In October, Jackie was sentenced to four years because of her refusal to cooperate. Her sentence hurt me more than anything. Our son had neither parent with him.

The separation nearly killed Jackie. She missed her boy like oxygen.

In December, I was brought up on the murder charge, police corruption, and other drug charges. Tarzan had been arrested and was cooperating with the FBI. Pupo, too. I was in real trouble, but bless to be alive I had been wrestling with dreams and a feeling. That because I knew too much about Police corruption. That detective Ralph Cicalese or Tommy, were going to try to get me off guard and kill me.

Jackie tried to convince me to cooperate and answer questions before the grand jury. "Baby," she said, "they're going to try and get the death penalty on you almost everybody is cooperating with the FBI.

I didn't answer her. I couldn't. She looked small and skinny. She was suffering so badly from being apart from her son. Then she looked me in the eye and she said, "My attorney said it might even help on my sentence, too."

That hit me hard. After a bit more persuasion, I hired another attorney Robert Goodman and agreed to go in front of the grand jury. In March ,1990. Thomas Gilsenan and Ralph Cicalese Detectives from the Essex County Prosecutors office were convicted at trial and sentence; T.Gilsenan 15 years and R.Cicalese 12 years

Still, when it came time for my sentencing, once again before the Honorable Mary Ann Trump Barry, I didn't know what to think.

She gazed at me and confessed that I presented her with one of the toughest decisions she'd ever had to make. "The crimes of which you've been convicted were extremely violent," she noted. "Before imposing sentence, would you like to speak?"

I stood up. As I did, I looked around the courthouse. It was nearly empty. There was only a single reporter taking notes. There were none of the people I used to call friends and brothers, none of the people who loved to be around me when I was handing out money, liquor, and cocaine. The only people who had come were my new friends, my Christian friends. They were the ones who believed in who I had become and who believed in the transformation the Lord can make in a man. They were there with me. People of faith.

As I stood to speak, I felt the Lord's presence come upon me and I put my faith fully in Him. Putting myself at the mercy of the court, I spoke of my sincere repentance.

"I am growing in my life as a new man in the eyes of the Lord," I said. "I am truly sorry for the hurt I've brought to so many others. If I am given the chance one day, I hope to preach the Word of the Lord to schoolchildren, to save them from the life that I have lived. I hope to warn them of the dangers of drugs."

That day, the Honorable Mary Ann Trump Barry heard more than the voice of a man who had done wrong for so long. She heard the voice of a man who had met the Lord. And she heard the sincerity in my voice. She sentenced me to a twenty-year sentence to run concurrently with my previous sentence.

God had heard my mother's prayers. God had answered her and my prayers it was a miracle, the judge could have given me a life sentence.

Throughout my years in prison, my faith only grew stronger. I saw what God could do in a man's life. I saw how love and forgiveness redeem a man's soul while anger and hate only destroy it.

I was one of the blessed ones. For eighteen of my friends, violent death stole from them the opportunity to know the love and faith that I now know.

There are those who look down at "jailhouse conversions." There are those who are cynical and believe that criminals "get religion" just to minimize their punishment. They are wrong. I am living witness to how wrong they are. Even today, at the dawn of a new century, I am committed to living my life with Jesus. I am a free man, fulfilling the promises I'd made long ago in that courtroom.

Prison is behind me. The life that I had once held so dear is behind me. Ahead of me is the life that God wants me to live.

I am not the King of the World or the Drug Kingpin of Newark, New Jersey. I am only Robert Vidal, servant of the Lord. Thank God I am.

For some, prison is a cauldron of deep destruction. Despite the constant presence of guards, correctional officers, cameras, and steel, the anger and hate that drove so many to a life of crime continues to fester. Prison can claim a man's body, but his soul continues to be free.

If that anger and hate continue, then the time...the seemingly endless minutes in a day...becomes an evil ally. Creative skills are turned to destruction. The simplest things become weapons of death and destruction. Fiberglass shards are twisted into blades. Vegetable oil is boiled to scar a man's face for life, or to blind him. A mop ringer can crush a man's skull. A broomstick can be sharpened to become a spear, capable of puncturing the heart or lungs.

How can a man turn around in such an environment? How can an angry and sinful soul find redemption?

My answer is simple. A man turns from evil and towards good in prison as he does outside of prison, by the grace of God. The choice is always ours. Every moment. Every day.

A prisoner chooses to use the time in prison for good or for evil, for vocational training or to slide deeper into a world of violence and hate. Every man must choose between fellowship with God or fellowship with gangs, drugs, and gambling. A choice.

I have learned that when you make the right choice, Jesus meets you more than halfway. My life was not turned around all at once. It was turned around in steps, one at a time. Day by day. I only had to open my eyes a little and God was there, showing me His love and His blessings.

In prison, I learned the first honest trade I'd ever known. I learned to cut hair, to be a barber. Then I was made a barber instructor.

Jackie Fresco remarried and had another son. My son with her Robert Vidal Jr; is a gift from God graduated College and has his own business, he is 24 years old. My ex wife Zeizel remarried and my daughter Erica Vidal 28, graduate college and went to Harvard and became an attorney. My mother 84 stills pray's for us daily and thanks God for saving me and transforming me through Jesus Christ. Angel Aka green eyes was shot many times and murdered in Newark by one of our enemies while Tarzan and I were serving out our Federal Prison sentences. Tarzan got marry and has a family of eight and has not returned to crime..His other brother Duran got in trouble again with violence and has done like 19 years in prison.

I have dreamed and prayed to become a good, successful person and my dreams and prayers have all come true. Like all good things, my successes have not come easy. God made sure to test me. When I was first released from prison to Kintock a Federal halfway house in Newark NJ, I knew the struggles of an ex-con. I applied for work I had (7) days to find a job or I would be returned to Prison.

But it wasn't easy to find a job. All my prospective employers wanted to know was what my work experience was. And what was I going to tell them? Many employers did not hire me because my past criminal record and on parole. But I kept my FAITH in God to open doors for me and one of my cousins Eddie Calixto a correction officer got me my first job in Jenny's Barbershop in Elizabeth Ave, in Elizabeth NJ. Then I went to Alfredo's barbershop.

So, I worked long hours on my feet, gaining more experience. I saved each and every dollar I made. Each dollar was a victory for me, each was more than I'd made in the twelve years I spent in prison. For twelve years, I worked making eleven cents an hour. Now, I had money in my pocket once again. Clean earned money. God was with me. So it was in September 1998, six months after my release from prison, that I opened my very first barbershop, The Gifted Cutters Barbershop.

It seems like someone else who lived to party in those clubs. The money I'd made then was the reward of evil. But now, my success is hard earned and worthy. The Gifted Cutters Barbershop was so successful that I was able to open more shop's 2, 3, 4; 5. I own a beautiful car, a new Mercedes. Once again, I wear elegant clothing and jewelry, but now, my rewards are honest and my wealth is much greater than any car or piece of jewelry.

My faith is stronger and stronger every day. I know that God will continue to bless me. I have sold my five shops and opened a new one in Cranford NJ. As a new vision has surface with my calling in Christ as an Evangelist. My dream is to help built Christian Churches in poor countries and continue to preach the gospel of salvation in Jesus Christ and God will help me raise the money. To God YHWH be the glory through Christ.

As a drug counselor, I am always sharing the message that anything is possible. "Look at me," I tell young people. "If God cares about me, He cares about you."

2 Peter 3: 9

The Lord is not slack concerning His promise, as some count slackness, but is longsuffering toward us, not willing that any should perish but that all should come to repentance.

Criminal activity never made me a success. My faith in God has. I see the pride and love in the eyes of my mother and my brother and sister. There was a time in my life when I couldn't look them in the eye because I couldn't reciprocate that genuine love. I was too lost in evil. But now, I let that love wash over me and I am grateful for their patience and their love, support and prayers.

I don't know why I was allowed to survive those criminal years when so many others were not. All I know is that I am grateful, eternally grateful. And you know, sometimes when I try and think about why God has been so good to me, I think back to that homeless man on the bridge in Portland Oregon, the one I helped so long ago, when I was going to commit suicide, was he an ANGEL? or the empty milk container that hit the floor when Ruben's killers came to kill me and my family.

Hebrews 13: 1

Let brotherly love continue. [2]

Do not forget to entertain strangers, for by so *doing* some have unwittingly entertained angels. And I wonder if that was my moment of grace, the one that allowed me to live while so many of my friends died, the moment when the Lord truly touched me and began to prepare me for the glory that would follow. I wonder if it was at that moment when I first learned that the Lord really is always there, waiting for us.

I just want to close this book with this truthful final episode of my last days in the streets before my arrest. The man Flaco the Latin hit man whose face and arm I cut in October, 1985. at El Baturro Bar. He spread his word in Newark that he will kill me and cut me in pieces for what Tarzan and I did to him and his partner for cheating me out of $30,000. One of my men Angel spotted him in a local Newark bar looking for me with a couple of guys he was determine to kill me.

Another big enemy of mine was Vicente "El Cubano" who two of my men-Angel and Python ripped off for $160,000 worth of cocaine in Newark; he called me on my beeper from Miami Fla .And when I called him back, he in a rage cursed me out in Spanish and said to me "You made a big mistake for beating me down and letting me live! I will kill you! And be your worst nightmare! I was very upset at his angry threats and I responded "You have joined the back of the list of the people that want to kill me," "but you! I could kill you with my hands and teeth" –Veremos "We will see! He said". I do not want to detail precise locations or graphically describe more violence, but I do believe that my mother's constant thanksgiving and prayer to Jehovah in Jesus name allowed these events to end this way instead of murder;

As God's great mercy spare my life and put fear in me not to continue to pay evil for evil. I remember my mother writing in big letters bible scriptures and sticking them on the kitchen table and Refrigerator.

Philippians 4: 6

Be anxious for nothing, but in everything by prayer and supplication, with thanksgiving, let your requests be made known to God; [7] *and the peace of God, which surpasses all understanding, will guard your hearts and minds through Christ Jesus.*

A couple of my men and I went looking for Flaco, we had a good tip of where he frequently visit and surprised him and one of his men who were eating in a restaurant, as Flaco was about to put his fork in his mouth my cold Colt 45 was resting behind his ear and my two unfriendly looking friends had moved very close to their table armed, as I spoke these words to him "Today is a good day for you because a voice within me is telling me! Not to do this", I'm going to give you another chance instead of blowing your brains out!.. "But - I do not want to see you ever again and stop telling other's you are going to kill me!" For some reason Flaco was a light skin mulato, but that day his face changed color to a pale white: I don't know? If it was what he was eating that gave him bad indigestion, or the cold gun on his ear, or my words of warnings? He couldn't speak as he tried too, he just bowed his head. As I heard a whisper ok 'Oh'Oh'h, okk;

Then Vicente from Miami was not so lucky Tarzan and I got him in a hotel room where he came up to NJ to kill me. He made one mistake he was spotted by one of my crew; this was another appearance of God's grace and mom's prayers again. I discovered my enemies plot before I felt into their traps.

Psalm 124: 2

"If it had not been the LORD who was on our side, When men rose up against us, [3]

Then they would have swallowed us alive. That evening in a Hotel room, I had gotten a duplicate key from the manager who we knew. Tarzan and I caught him sleeping, he was unexpectedly shocked "I woke Vicente up with my colt 45, in his nose. We had a one on one fight, were he got a real bad beating by me and I knew then; that God's power had touched me months back.The evening in the Pulaski skyway when I was stressing and desperately seeking God's HELP, searching and listening to the AM, Christian Radio, I felt an evil presence in me depart from me, it was gone. I felt peace "Was it demons? I was now filled with mix feelings of anger and compassion; but mercy was now ruling my thought's in these urgent decisions on these evil men lives " I will not kill again" even though Vicente had come to NJ to kill me…I use the same words I told Flaco but in Spanish "I'm going to give you a break Vicente, I don't want to ever see you again!" {Te voy a dar un chance-no quiero verte denuevo!.) I can't give myself any credit for not killing these men; it was God's power in Christ that stopped me. I will always thank God and praise him for not allowing me to let my anger take vengeance on them. At that time I did not understand clearly what was taking place within me; but I know now it was God's grace.

Romans 12:20

" If your enemy is hungry, feed him;If he is thirsty, give him a drink; For in so doing you will heap coals of fire on his head Psalm 23: You prepare a table before me in the presence of my enemies. "To God be the Glory"

The federal DEA, the NJ State Police and a Newark special Narcotic Police force arrested me and most of my crew weeks after these events. My message to all "the time is near for the Rapture of the Church and to enter into the great tribulation; If you are not saved REPENT and accept the Son of God Jesus Christ right NOW as your savior and be baptize in water and ask God to fill you with the Holy spirit. Hallelujah!

2 Corinthians 5: 17

Therefore, if anyone is in Christ, he is a new creation; old things have passed away; behold, all things have become new. [18]

Now all things *are* of God, who has reconciled us to Himself through Jesus Christ, and has given us the ministry of reconciliation, [19] that is, that God was in Christ reconciling the world to Himself, not imputing their trespasses to them, and has committed to us the word of reconciliation. [20] Now then, we are ambassadors for Christ, as though God were pleading through us: we implore *you* on Christ's behalf, be reconciled to God. [21] For He made Him who knew no sin *to be* sin for us, that we might become the righteousness of God in Him.

By the blood of the lamb of God His Son Yashua Messiah "I'm FORGIVEN"

John 1:29

The next day John saw Jesus coming toward him, and said, "Behold! The Lamb of God who takes away the sin of the world!

It is my prayer to the father in His son Jesus Christ name; that this true story "Prayer in the shadow of death" will lead you to God's loving grace in Jesus Christ.

John 3: 16

For God so loved the world that He gave His only begotten Son, that whoever believes in Him should not perish but have everlasting life. [17]

For God did not send His Son into the world to condemn the world, but that the world through Him might be saved. [18] "He who believes in Him is not condemned; but he who does not believe is condemned already, because he has not believed in the name of the only begotten Son of God.

Dear brothers and sisters God is good and His mercy is GREAT for the sinner. As why me? I could relate to this scripture. 1

Corinthians 1: 26

For you see your calling, brethren, that not many wise according to the flesh, not many mighty, not many noble, are called. [27]

But God has chosen the foolish things of the world to put to shame the wise, and God has chosen the weak things of the world to put to shame the things which are mighty; [28] and the base things of the world and the things which are despised God has chosen, and the things which are not, to bring to nothing the things that are, [29] that no flesh should glory in His presence. [30] But of Him you are in Christ Jesus, who became for us wisdom from God—and righteous-ness and sanctification and redemption— [31] that, as it is written, *"He who glories, let him glory in the LORD." {Watch the movie by Girls Gotta eat entertainment} To God be the Glory..Amen Evangelist Robert F Vidal*

Figure 1 Celebrating my Brother John 2nd birthday in Havana Cuba, Robert 3 years, John 2, sister Hilda 5

Figure 2 The Ironbound Newark NJ. I love going back to the great Spanish and Portuguese Restaurants in the area.

Figure 3 The USS Mars AFS 1 The ship I was assigned to and my US Navy picture 1978

Figure 4 Where everything started "The job" with Ruben April 1982. His white Cadillac was parked most of the time where the white van is, Garden & Pacific St. Newark NJ (Say no to drugs)

Figure 5 Minutes after murdering Ruben Perrone the three Cubans came to my basement Apt in 1508 79th St North Bergen to kill me and my family. Thank you mother for your prayers. John 3:16,18

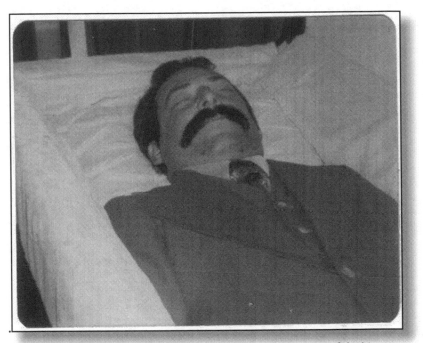

Figure 6 The Cuban drug Kingpin El Gallo "The Rooster "One of the biggest suppliers of Cocaine and marijuana of the 70's and early 80's.He and his brothers were responsible for a least 30 murders,mostly people who did not pay their bills.(Live by the sword-die by

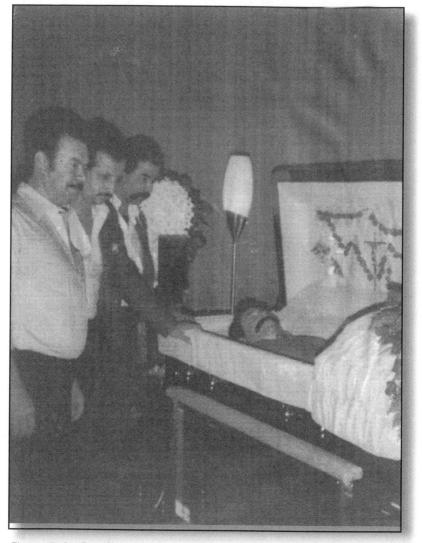

Figure 7 La Familial Alberto and Roger and Rene at El Gallos Funeral. Those responsible for his murder were all killed. Say NO to drugs "Death or Prison"

Figure 8 Over 500 grams of 18k gold. My first gold chain and medal I paid
$18,000 (No future in the drug lifestyle-Say NO to drugs - Death or Prison

Figure 9 One of Ruben's luxury apts. Here was where he showed me 8 kilos
of cocaine and gave me $5000 for clothing. North Broad St Elizabeth NJ.
Say NO to drugs.

Figure 10 *The Royal Tavern, go-go girl bar. Pulaski St and Chestnut St. Downeck Newark NJ. Were I spend a lot of time and was introduced to Sam. And where Paco and his men came to get me.*

Figure 11 *Were Sam came to kill us "The shootout" 168 Malvern St. Nwk NJ. We were in the basement Apt. Then made it to the roof of the brick building on left.*

Figure 12 My favorite Cadillac Limousine to the big NJ & NY clubs 1983, 84, 85. In 1985 I purchased my own Limo. Say NO to drugs.

Drug revenge claimed in triple-slay trial of kin

By DONNA LEUSNER

A Bloomfield man killed a cousin and two witnesses a year ago because the cousin was shortchanging him in a cocaine business, a prosecutor charged yesterday.

However, the defense contended defendant Sebastian Montouri, 53, is a "fall guy" for two other men so the cocaine distribution ring could continue operating.

Montouri, who could face the death penalty if convicted of murder by his own conduct, went on trial before Superior Court Judge Edwin Stern in Newark yesterday for the April 25, 1983, slayings of his cousin, Robert Foselli, 33, and Cheryl Pinkus, 22, both of Newark; and Maryann Wihnyk, 28, of Miramar, Fla.

"This murderer is a drug dealer," Essex County Assistant Prosecutor Alfred Constants 3d told the jury as he pointed to Montouri, saying at about 10 p.m. the defendant and two "muscle men" entered the second-floor Vailsburg apartment at 1122 South Orange Ave. to "teach a lesson" to Montouri's cousin and partner in the drug business.

The apartment where the bodies were found was raided in July 1982 by the Newark and State Police as an illegal "casino" allegedly operated by the Campisi crime family.

Four family members and four other men, indicted on the casino charges, are scheduled to stand trial today before Superior Court Judge Michael Degnan in Newark.

One of the "muscle men" in the 1983 triple slaying, 30-year-old Wayne DiBattista of Fanwood, is the state's key witness. Constants told the jury the eyewitness will detail the "brutal and vicious killing" of Foselli and the "cold-blooded unmerciful execution of two young, defenseless women."

Constants told the jury his office "made a deal out of necessity" with DiBattista. In exchange for his testimony, DiBattista had the murder charges against him dropped and pleaded guilty on charges of conspiracy to rob and to cover up a robbery.

Defense lawyer Dale Jones told the jury his client is the "fall guy" for Robert Vidal—who Jones said ordered Foselli's execution—and DiBattista, who Jones said was hired by Vidal to carry out the slaying.

Figure 13 The 1984 Triple murder trial Essex County Court Newark NJ.

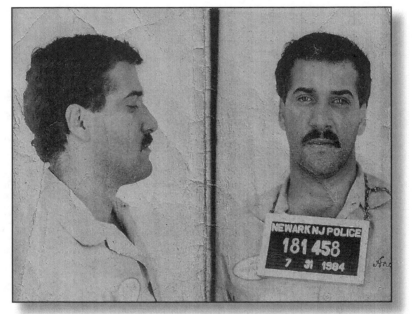

Figure 14 One of my arrest pictures July,1984.

Figure 15   First floor on right 7015 Grand Ave. North Bergen NJ
"Unforgetable night of the nightmare where I woke up and almost shot my
own wife "Dreaming Sam was in the house" Thank God nothing happened
and my wife and daughter left me for good the next day.

Figure 16 Location of shootout with the Mafia men who killed Miguel. Another miracle of survival. Thank you heavenly Father in Jesus name.

Figure 17 Manolo Vigoa and I together in 1988 @El Reno Ok. Federal Prison. Manolo was arrested by the FBI,DEA in Oreste Rodrigues junk yard in Ave P. in Newark NJ with 705 Kilos of Cocaine in a container $25 million worth. SAY NO 2 DRUGS.

Figure 18 In God's strength in Christ I continue with the promise to the Honorable Federal Judge Mary-Ann Trump Barry to help others SAY NO TO DRUGS.

Figure 19 Say NO to drugs and criminal lifestyles.

Figure 20 My praying Christian mother Georgina 84 and still praying daily, morning, afternoon. Night. We are on a mission for God - helping others hear the gospel. NJ July7 - 2011

Figure 21 Pulaski skyway were body was dropped and where I was touched by the Spirit of Christ when listening to AM Christian Radio, seeking God's HELP! Psalms 50:15 Call upon Me in the day of trouble; I will deliver you, and you shall glorify Me."

33217212R00159

Made in the USA
Middletown, DE
05 July 2016